Post-Conviction Relief: Advancing Your Claim

Kelly Patrick Riggs

Freebird Publishers
www.FreebirdPublishers.com

Freebird Publishers

Box 541, North Dighton, MA 02764
Info@FreebirdPublishers.com
www.FreebirdPublishers.com

Copyright © 2018
Post-Conviction Relief: Advancing Your Claim
By Kelly Patrick Riggs

All Freebird Publishers titles, imprints, and distributed lines are available at special quantity discounts for bulk purchases for sales promotions, premiums, fundraising, educational, or institutional use.

ISBN-13: 978-0-9996602-3-2
ISBN-10: 0-9996602-3-3

Printed in the United States of America

LEGAL NOTICE

FOREWORD

I was new to the Federal criminal justice system and did what I thought was the right thing: I hired legal counsel. Surely he would advance a sound, thoughtful, legal defense on my behalf ...

When the dust settled after sentencing, I realized that due to a number of mistakes made during the proceeding, my ultimate sentence was far greater than the lawyer's original guarantees.

After listening to other inmates speak about their own situations and having conversations with several "jail-house" lawyers, I decided to seek relief. The main problem, being new to this whole experience, was figuring out where to start. I wish this book had been available at the beginning of my journey seeking to reduce my sentence; it would have greatly reduced my learning curve.

At the end of the day, whatever course is taken, it will be you that lives or dies – no one else. Therefore it is extremely important that you educate yourself. If you knew back then what you know today, would things have been different ... a different plea, for example? By first educating yourself through this book before taking your next action, you insure that as you look back a year from now, you won't be kicking yourself yet again. This book was developed – written in plan and concise, easy to understand language – to educate you and provide you with a solid course to exercise your rights and obtain relief.

Dennis Bolze

SCOPE AND PURPOSE

Once again, I write in hopes of providing assistance that prisoners and their families need to be reunited. What's different about this book is my expectation in you. I trust you've mastered my first two books, for beginners.

Now, let's take things to the next level; let's start writing with additional purpose.

When trained lawyers file their motions, they are clear and crisp in their meaning. The only thing to do then is decide. When unlearned movants file, however, the court's personnel must first figure out what you're saying you want, which often is no clearer than a message from Apollo.

My purpose here is to make you a better thinker and writer by providing the necessary tools. If we want better results, we must file better work. I hope to affect those of you in the system by setting the standard by which all pro se litigants approach the court.

INTRODUCTION

This book is the third in a series of post-conviction handbooks, written to touch the lives of prisoners. If you have read my first book, "Post-Conviction Relief: Secrets Exposed," you will recall that I encourage everyone to continue the learning process. The interpretation of law and/or the practice thereof is constantly evolving every day. Think back about how many people you know who were waiting, expectantly, on *Beckles v. United States*. If you look back even further, to November of 2014, to Amendment 782, you discover another decision people waited for. The fact is, the legal landscape is constantly changing and with that so must your minds, if you want to be an effective advocate.

This book is a bit different from the first two. Rather than give you the answers, this one is going to teach you how to think, how to analyze what you read. As tempting as it may be to you, copying anything out of this book is a clear sign that you have failed to grasp its concept. Ladies and gentlemen, it's time you learn how to fish.

TABLE OF CONTENTS

CHAPTER ONE

COGNIZABLE CLAIM

You want to slow an Olympic swimmer down? Tie a fire hydrant to his ankle. That's right, fire hydrants have nothing to do with swimming and tying one to a swimmer will cause his failure. Likewise, if you include mindless nonsense in your §2255 claim, you're sure to drown.

If you're thinking about your own §2255 claims right this second, don't feel bad. I also, in my own arrogance, slowed my §2255 court because my claims were over-inclusive. So, let's take this one step at a time. What is a claim? A ground? A fact?

Example:

Claim – my conviction and/or sentence is unlawful, I have a right to be released.

Ground – My attorney provided constitutionally ineffective assistance of counsel.

Supporting Facts – My attorney suffered a debilitating conflict of interest, etc.

With the previous example in mind, I want you to consider the guidance of 28 U.S.C. §2255, "… claiming the right to be released upon the ground …," now let's apply some critical thinking.

The field of law is controlled by the text of statutes. Statutes are memorialized with a combination of written words. I believe that there exists no issue more critical than word usage and definition. Take for example, the word "claim" as used in 28 U.S.C. §2255. Now, we all know what claim means, right? Maybe!

The word "claim" has 6 different definitions in Miriam Webster's Dictionary, not counting the sub-descriptions. Each has the potential to change a person's thinking depending on the word's application. Because of this, the application in §2255, that implies a singular definition is controlling. In this statute, the word "claiming" refers to, and only to, "the right to be released." Nothing else nor any other definition matters.

In making this simple, realize that if you have filled out a §2255 motion you are claiming a "right to be released," from what is a different matter entirely.

Now that you know you're "claiming the right to be released," let's move on to "upon the ground." Back to my favorite point, what does "ground" mean?

How is it defined? As most, you're probably searching for your dictionary. Well, you can stop. In this effort, to advance your thinking, it's time for your thinking to mature a bit. Our laws are written in English, so what's the problem? It's our application. The courts don't speak a different language than you and I. But, the law they speak of and apply is limited by a statutory understanding. Take for example, an exercise I recently witnessed in a legal research class, what does the word "strike" mean? Well, that depends on its application; bowling, baseball, court, etc.

With all this in mind, Congress stated what each critical word means within each application to reduce confusion. These people who practice law don't speak a foreign language nor do they change definitions to confuse you. The problem is: you're now in a very precise environment, so your loose understanding of English won't apply.

Now then, what does "ground" mean? If you want to know – and you must if you want to succeed – go to the statute. You have selected 28 U.S.C. §2255 as a vehicle for relief, so before you fill out the motion, go find out how to operate it. All words that have a restricted use in the statute are particularized in the statute. Filing under a statute you have a poor understanding of … is equivalent to a 15-year old trying to fly a fighter jet with a learner's permit.

In 28 U.S.C. §2255, you find the word "ground" applies to four different and very precise circumstances:

(A) "… the sentence was imposed in violation of the Constitution or laws of the United States …"

(B) "… that the court was without jurisdiction to impose such a sentence …"

(C) "… the sentence was in excess of the maximum allowed by law …"

(D) "… is otherwise subject to collateral attack …"

I'm going to explain these four grounds in a later chapter. For now, I just want you to learn where to get your definitions. In the grand scheme of things, you've not learned much yet, but it's important to apply everything you learn as you learn it. Soon you'll find that you're learning ability will expand.

Next, I'm going to show you how to apply the language of the statute to your claim. Applying the same critical thinking to your own claim as you compare it to the statute will help you convert your claim to one that is expressed clear concise, and succinct. Remember, the less you say, the more they listen. Same with the courts; the less you write, the more attention it gets. First off, get a rough idea of how your claim sounds by writing it out. This is what my claim was:

"I'm filing this motion for relief because I'm incarcerated and have a right to be released. My conviction, sentence, and imprisonment is a violation of the Sixth Amendment to the United States Constitution because I was prejudiced by ineffective assistance of counsel. My court-appointed lawyer was ineffective because he had to work on my case, which was in conflict with another of his clients. Because I was a witness against my lawyer's other client he continually asked me to withdraw my testimony. If my lawyer was working for my benefit, he would have secured a downward departure in my case, at minimum.

I filed a motion asking for a hearing concerning this conflict of interest. Before the hearing, my lawyer talked to me about keeping him as counsel. At the hearing, the judge and my lawyer convinced me that the conflict would not affect my trial. Two hours later, I was compelled to give a statement to authorities. Five hours later, my lawyer visited me in the jail and told me that I had to plead guilty to get protection for my family, even though I'm innocent."

Well, how's that for a good claim? A claim like this will definitely get you into court action. It will also keep you waiting until your sentence is over.

A claim like this uses too many words to say too little. This claim even fails to state an obvious claim that's a structural error. The main problem here is you can convince yourself that you've done well because you've said everything you can. That can't be further from the truth. If you've spent any time at all in a law library, you're familiar with *Haines v Kerner*, 404 U.S. 519. Yes, the controlling Supreme Court pro se doctrine. Because of the pro se doctrine, a claim like this can make a staff attorney look like a real idiot in front of his boss, the judge. This is how it works: you file a verbose claim and that staff attorney has to examine and re-examine it at length because the doctrine allows a liberal construction. Under the doctrine, the staff attorney can't just stop when he finds a claim. He has to continue until he identifies all possible claims. In the event he stops early and the judge rules against you, you then go running to the appellate court and explain what you were talking about, and the panel agrees with you, the judge will appear a bit short of diligent. Believe me, the staff attorney and the judge will take their time so that doesn't happen. Here more than ever less is more, but; clear, concise, and correct is key.

I hope you remember what I said earlier, it's time to teach you to think. The answer to this puzzle will come slowly throughout this book, but by the end you won't need me to give you the answer. Just one more hint before we begin: I often read a book like these four five times to get all I can out of it.

Let's get started.

CHAPTER TWO

STATUTORY PROVISION

This chapter may raise a few questions in your mind. First off, I expect you to know, by now, what a statutory provision is. Second, if you were thinking that this book was about §2255 motions, you're wrong. Not to mention you've just failed your first opportunity at critical thinking. There is a very good reason for writing out your complaint, as we did in Chapter One. The first thing we're going to do is match it to a statutory provision that's an authorized vehicle for relief. Although you'll find many statutes that offer relief, you'll also find that each is specific to certain sets of circumstances. If you're in federal custody, there's a very good chance that the relief you seek is obtainable only through 28 U.S.C. §2255. But, don't take my word for it, take time to read.

Now, with a full reading of 28 U.S.C. §2255, let's compare it with your written complaint. If you're in State custody attacking a future sentence, pay special attention to the prejudice you're suffering. For example, denial of State parole due to a federal detainer. Let's read Section 2255 word for word, and please, take your time. I can guarantee you that every word count, so don't miss any of them. If you can't readily define any word in the statute, look it up. As we go through the statute, we're going to apply every word to your claim, and remember, if something in the statute doesn't fit, find out why or what's missing.

> *Author's Note: "If it doesn't fit, force it." Yeah, we all know the saying ... Well, it won't work here. Forcing a claim into a vehicle that doesn't fit will ruin your chances for relief. It's the worst thing you can do, second only to perjury.*

At this point we're also going to kill two birds with one stone. As I mentioned earlier, my claim used too many words to say too little, so let's work on that. Let's first make sure §2255 fits, then we'll move on.

To qualify for relief under §2255, your claim has to fit squarely in the text of the statute, for example:

Jurisdiction – Are you "imprisoned under a sentence" imposed by "a court established by Act of Congress"? In short, is your current confinement a result of a judgment by a Federal Court?

Claim – Do you claim you have the "right to be released"?

Ground – Is your claim grounded on one of the four sets of circumstances listed in the statute?

Statutory Limitation – Is your claim being raised within one of the four authorized time limitations in §2255(f)?

Are you authorized filing by all other sub-sections of §2255?

If you've answered yes to these five questions, then you can move on. If not, you must consider any facts you've presented that don't fit and/or consider a different vehicle for relief.

I want you to realize that your motion is not a romance novel that the clerk is going to read for entertainment. Your motion is a serious issue for both you and the court, so let's get to the point. You do that by being short and clear. When the court can make a clear determination about what you're saying, you get the fastest response available. Remember also that the court provides a §2255 standard motion for the convenience of both you and the court. If you'll read Rule 2 of the §2255 rules, you'll find that use of the form is required.

> *Author's Note: I've been asked to review hundreds of §2255 motions filed by lawyers. I've even been asked by lawyers to review the §2255s they themselves are about to file. I have discovered that, just like prisoners, you have smart ones and then you have not-so-smart ones. Let me assure you that the smart ones use the form to its fullest extent. The form asks very specific questions to make the process faster, anything extra will only cause delay.*

Let's start by eliminating redundancies. When you fill out the form and send it in, the court knows you're "filing this motion" so you have no need to tell them. "For relief because I'm incarcerated," no kidding. That's in the jurisdictional requirements of the statute. You should get the idea – if what you've said is implied by the filing of your motion, it doesn't need to be in it.

If what you're saying in your motion is not expressly authorized by the statute, it creates a different problem. When you use grounds that don't appear in the statute, you trigger the court's obligation under *Haines v. Kerner*, 404 U.S. 519. Here's one of my all-time favorites: "My conviction, sentence, and imprisonment is a violation of the Sixth Amendment to the United States Constitution because I was prejudiced by ineffective assistance of counsel."

This is what I call a mixed ground. Out of these twenty-six words, I can only use eight of them in a §2255. The rest of them might trigger 28 U.S.C. §2241, which causes the court to take time to try to decipher what you really mean. To give you a hint, "conviction" and "imprisonment" are not found in §2255. Lucky for me, "sentence" is all I need to trigger §2255. Remember, if anything in your claim does not appear in 28 U.S.C. §2255(a), you must remove it or choose a different vehicle.

You must also remove everything that is repeated in your writing. "I was prejudiced by ineffective assistance of counsel" is the same as saying "my court-appointed lawyer was ineffective." No need to say it twice. I also refrain from using "court-appointed counsel" as opposed to "Mr. Bryant." This one little change in wording serves three separate purposes:

(A) It saves space. You've used ten characters as opposed to twenty-three;

(B) You've personalized your statement, so the court won't have to search for which lawyer you're talking about;

(C) "Court-appointed lawyer" is accusatory when you add the word ineffective to it. In essence you're saying, "that inept lawyer you gave me." Let's not accuse the court of malfeasance when you're asking them to rule in your favor.

Let's continue by separating your ground from your supporting facts. Again, we won't be repeating what's codified in §2255(a), so we won't be using the word "sentence." There's no need to repeat any of the four grounds in §2255 either. In separating the ground from the facts, you need to look at the action and who did it. If it's something your lawyer, the government, or the court did, it's a supporting fact. Everything else is either cause or effect.

In looking at what's left of my example, you should notice a major defect: I have no effect. Thus, I have no ground to base my claim for relief.

This is called the "cause and prejudice" standard of review. That is the only standard of review available in a §2255 proceeding where you claim ineffective assistance of counsel. "Cause and

Prejudice" was determined to be required by the Supreme Court in *Strickland v. Washington*, 466 U.S. 668, for relief in a §2255 proceeding. Just to make it easy:

(A) Your claim is the right to be released;

(B) Your ground is most commonly ineffective assistance of counsel;

(C) Counsel's actions are your supporting facts;

(D) Your prejudice is a denial of your right to a fair trial as defined in *Strickland v. Washington*.

Just so you know, I started with 188 words in my claim. I have only four left that I can use in my ground for relief. How did yours come out? Remember, we're only counting subject words, no verbs.

Your claim has just been through a cursory examination of the merit. When or if your motion makes it past the scrutiny of Rule 4, the government is going to put it through a seven-part test. You, most likely, just failed the first step of that test: "cognizability." If you don't think so – and you're holding on to the remainder of your claim – let me go ahead and crush the remnants of your ego by saying "just throw your claim away now so we can build a new one."

> *Author's Note: These first two chapters have been all about breaking your intellectual eggs. Habeas corpus is a complex area of law that can only be based on sound principle.*

> *Remember also that this book is all about what I've learned about advancing a sound claim. When I started; learning, I thought I had it figured out. But, only when I could become humble enough, could I learn what I had to learn.*

Now, then, clear your mind of everything you think you know, so we can start with the basics.

CHAPTER THREE

FORCE OF LAW

"… that the sentence was imposed in violation of the Constitution and/or the laws of the United States …"

This, in my opinion, is the most profound ground for relief listed in §2255. The difficulty in understanding this ground is rooted in the common cliché: "violation of my Constitutional right." Most people have no idea what their Constitutional rights are, let alone how they have suffered a violation of them. The most damaging, yet appropriate, word the government uses against you is "conclusory." When you don't know your Constitutional rights, this word will be used against you, and rightly so.

Exercise in reasoning: There are nine fundamental rights that concern criminal process in the Bill of Rights. Four of the nine are foreclosed on at the end of direct review, if not appealed or if decided unfavorably on direct appeal. That leaves only 5 basic Constitutional rights that can be raised in collateral review. (Author's opinion). Go find them and understand those rights. Also, take a look at *United States v. Frady*, 456 U.S. 152.

When you give 28 U.S.C. §2255 its due textual understanding, you discover that the four grounds are based on violations of:

1) your right under the "Constitution or laws of the United States";

2) the court's jurisdiction to impose such sentence;

3) the statute that particularizes a maximum sentence; or is

4) otherwise subject to collateral attack.

As simple as these four grounds seem, let me assure you that 90% of jailhouse lawyers and probably 60% of street lawyers don't get this right. These grounds, as you see them here, are generalized. Congress didn't have a premonition about your case, and likely you weren't even born when §2255 was enacted.

So, let's get this figured out. Hint: don't tell me about a case you read. If an important "controlling" case has been decided, I already know about it. Habeas advocates will have been advertising their opinions about it for months by the time you heard about it.

When you decide you've been violated by the government – and most of you have, one way or another – you must be able to explain how and what controlling provision it's in violation of. If you believe your Constitutional rights were violated, you must know which one and how. Go study the Bill of Rights, the first ten amendments to the Constitution of the United States. If you claim it's in violation of law, go study the applicable law of conviction. Jurisdiction can be found in Title 28 of the United States Code, and your statute of conviction. Maximum sentence is usually in the statute of conviction or a penalty statute that follows close behind, see 18 U.S.C. §924 as it pertains to 18 U.S.C, §922. The fourth ground is also complicated because it covers things such as statutes that are unconstitutional. Take for example, *Johnson v. United States*, 135 S.Ct. 2551 (2015). Mr. Johnson was convicted under 18 U.S.C. §922(g), a felon in possession of a firearm. At sentencing, he was penalized under 18 U.S.C. §924(e), yes, the Armed Career Criminal Act, A.C.C.A. for short. Mr. Johnson filed his §2255 under the fourth ground because the sentence was authorized by the Constitution and laws of the United States. It was within the court's jurisdiction to impose sentence.

And his sentence did not exceed the statutory limitation of life in prison – which can be violated only if they keep your corpse in the S.H.U. as a circus attraction. Suffice it to say, the sentence was legal. Mr. Johnson, however, successfully claimed that the applicable law was unconstitutionally void for vagueness. Thus, otherwise subject to collateral attack.

Mr. Johnson didn't accomplish this task by making a conclusory claim. He, or whoever helped him, made a studied claim on precise grounds. They preyed upon a history of circuit splits and conflicting decisions in the Supreme Court and provided a sound cognizable synopsis showing vagueness and the Constitutionality of vague statutes. Thus, the residual clause of 18 U.S.C. §924(e) was invalidated as void-for-vagueness by the United States Supreme Court.

> *Author's Note: If you plan to invalidate a statute, consider your questions to the Supreme Court prior to establishing your ground. This is a concept that most lawyers with vast experience don't consider, and for good reason. Keep your sights on reality, fight for what's right, and keep a tight rein on lofty goals.*

When you raise a sound claim for relief, you're going to be brought to court for a hearing, hence the literal translation of habeas corpus. You are guaranteed counsel at that hearing because of court precedent, not the Constitution, so you have no right to effective assistance of counsel at a collateral review hearing. You must know your rights under the Constitution of the United States and the laws passed in pursuance thereof.

Let me say this plainly: if you don't know your rights, you don't have a claim. Basically, if a person can't tell me why he thinks he has a claim. I'll often tell him where to go learn what he needs to know. Never, I repeat, never tell me "I have a case."

CHAPTER FOUR

CONSTITUTIONAL RIGHTS

The Constitutional rights of the accused have become an ambiguous term. This happens because we, as people, fail to learn and apply our rights. Courts and lawyers rarely have to defend violations of these rights, so they have little reason to learn them, either. Because of this, I suggested that you learn them in Chapter Three, and now I realize the complexity of the task I set before you. In this chapter, I'm going to clarify a few of the rights the Constitution reserves for those accused of crimes.

If this chapter seems out of place, it's because I added it after the fact. I added it because of a conversation that resulted in a difference of opinion which I was asked to resolve. The dispute concerned whether a party could re-open a §2255 proceeding years after being denied with a motion based on Fed. R. Crim. P., Rule 15. Of course, Rule 15(b)(2) contains a parenthetical that states "… at any time, even after judgment …." The parties to the dispute coupled these six words with an Eleventh Circuit decision,' dated July 13, 2000, and determined that a motion for leave to amend a §2255 motion would re-open a denied §2255 proceeding. The one who brought the discussion to my attention showed me all the supporting information and a couple of Circuit holdings that he thought supported this view. The unanimous view of the courts was that "… in a §2255 proceeding. Rule 15(c) provides that 'the amendments to a pleading will be considered timely if they relate back to the original claims' … and be considered timely if they 'arose out of the conduct, transaction, or occurrence' set forth in his original §2255 motion."

So, what do you think? Rule 15(c) opens an old §2255 proceeding if the new claim "relates back"? Not a chance. If you could consider this theory as correct it would supplant §2255(h) and 28 U.S.C. §2253. Within about an hour, I was able to dispatch this theory with a single question: What is the definition of "in"? The very first sentence of the theory states, "… in a §2255 proceeding …"

I raise this discussion to show you how critical one word can be. What if the word "in" was replaced with "after"? As you can imagine, it's too early to demand that you apply the principles of this book to learn the principles of this book. Although this has been a good lesson in critical thinking, I'm going to provide you with your Constitutional rights, as the accused, in this chapter.

AMENDMENT 1
Religious and political freedom –

"Congress shall make no law respecting an establishment of religion or prohibiting the free exercise thereof; or abridging the freedom of speech, or of the press; or the right of the people peaceably to assemble, and to petition the Government for a redress of grievances."

In the event you have been exposed to the idea that you have the right to "petition the government" in a criminal proceeding, forget about it. This amendment will be without effect until you are convicted, and therefore does not offer a basis for a claim in a §2255. In a criminal case, the right to due process of law protects your right to be heard.

AMENDMENT 2
Right to bear arms –

"A well-regulated Militia, being necessary to the security of a free State, the right of the people to keep and bear Arms, shall not be infringed."

Any claim you may have had under this amendment was re-addressable at the trial and direct appeal. It offers no basis for claim under §2255.

AMENDMENT 3
Quartering soldiers –

"No Soldier shall, in time of peace be quartered in any house, without the consent of the Owner, nor in time of war, but in a manner to be prescribed by law."

This amendment offers no basis for a claim under §2255.

AMENDMENT 4
Unreasonable searches and seizures –

"The right of the people to be secure in their persons, houses, papers, and effects, against unreasonable searches and seizures, shall not be violated, and no Warrants shall issue, but upon probable cause, supported by Oath or affirmation, and particularly describing the place to be searched, and the persons or things to be seized."

This amendment contains an unlimited number of claims in a criminal trial and direct appeal. You will also find numerous court decisions explaining this amendment and its exclusions one way or another. This amendment provides no basis for a claim under §2255. See *Stone v. Powell,* 428 U.S. 465. This amendment does, however, provide supporting facts for an ineffective assistance of counsel claim, especially where you claim counsel failed to investigate and/or failed to raise your most meaningful issues at trial.

AMENDMENT 5
Criminal actions –

Provisions concerning – Due process of law and just compensation clauses –

"No person shall be held to answer for a capital, or otherwise infamous crime, unless a presentment or indictment of a Grand jury, except in cases arising in the land or naval forces, or in the Militia, when in actual service in time of War or public danger; nor shall any person be subject for the same offense to be twice put in jeopardy of life or limb; nor shall be compelled in any criminal case to be a witness against himself, nor be deprived of life, liberty, or property, without due process of law; nor shall private property be taken for public use, without just compensation."

This is where the "Bill of Rights" has a substantial effect on criminal cases seeking post-conviction relief. Let me explain first how punctuation is used here. As written, this is a list of five identifiable rights. The rights are primarily divided by semi-colons (;), except for three and four, which, in my opinion, should have been separated. Notice between the semi-colons are several commas. These separate parenthetical phrases which explain additional or exceptional circumstances to the right. Take number one for example. It should be read as "no person shall be held to answer for … a crime, unless on … indictment of a Grand jury …" This is one basic right.

2) "… nor shall any person be … twice put in jeopardy …"

3) "nor shall be compelled … to be a witness against himself … (right to remain silent).

4) "nor be deprived if life, liberty, or property, without due process of law …

5) "nor shall private property be taken … without just compensation."

AMENDMENT 6

Rights of the accused –

"In all criminal prosecutions, the accused shall enjoy the right to a speedy and public trial, by an impartial jury of the State and district wherein the crime shall have been committed, which district shall have been previously ascertained by law, and to be informed of the nature and cause of the accusation; to be confronted with the witnesses against him; to have compulsory process for obtaining witnesses in his favor and to have the Assistance of Counsel for his defense."

This amendment contains three basic rights concerning criminal defendants; however, they could be broken into parts to make them more readily understandable:

1) The right to a speedy trial;
2) the right to a public trial;
3) the right to a trial by an impartial jury from the district where the crime was committed;
4) the right to be informed of the nature of the accusation;
5) the right to be informed of the cause of the accusation;
6) the right to be confronted with witnesses against him;
7) the right to compel the attendance of witnesses for his defense;
8) the right to effective assistance of counsel.

AMENDMENT 7

Trial by jury in civil cases –

"In Suits at common law, where the value in controversy shall exceed twenty dollars, the right of trial by jury shall be preserved, and no fact tried by a jury, shall be otherwise re-examined in any Court of the United States, than according to the rules of the common law.

AMENDMENT 8

Bail-Punishment –

"Excessive bail shall not be required, nor excessive fines imposed, nor cruel and unusual punishments inflicted."

This amendment represents a chameleon. The rights it contains apply differently before trial as to after. Excessive bail, for instance, is a pretrial right that no longer exists after a guilty verdict.

AMENDMENT 9

Rights retained by people –

"The enumeration on the Constitution, of certain rights, shall not be construed to deny or disparage others retained by the people."

AMENDMENT 10

Powers reserved to states or people –

"The powers not delegated to the United States by the Constitution, nor prohibited by it to the States, are reserved to the States respectively, or to the people."

AMENDMENT 13

Section 1. [Slavery prohibited.] –

"Neither slavery nor involuntary servitude, except as punishment for crime whereof the party shall have been duly convicted, shall exist within the United States, or any place subject to their jurisdiction."

Section 2. [Power to enforce amendment.] –

"Congress shall have power to enforce this article by appropriate legislation."

This amendment is specific to criminal proceedings because this is where the government's authority to incarcerate you comes from, "… except as a punishment for crime …." It does not, however, reiterate due process is required to avoid a condition of illegal slavery.

AMENDMENT 14

Section 1. [Citizens of the United States.] –

"All persons born or naturalized in the United States, and subject to the jurisdiction thereof, are citizens of the United States and of the State wherein they reside. No State shall make or enforce any law which shall abridge the privileges or immunities of citizens of the United States; nor shall any State deprive any person of life, liberty, or property, without due process of law; nor deny to any person within its jurisdiction the equal protection of the laws."

Section 2. [Representatives – Power to reduce apportionment.] –

"Representatives shall be apportioned among the several States according to their respective numbers, counting the whole number of persons in each State, excluding Indians not taxed. But when the right to vote at any election for the choice of electors for President and Vice-President of the United States, Representatives in Congress, the Executive and Judicial offices of a State, or the members of the Legislature thereof, is denied to any of the male inhabitants of such State, being twenty-one years of age, and citizens of the United States, or in any way abridged, except for participation in rebellion, or other crime, the basis of representation therein shall be reduced in the proportion which the number of such male citizens shall bear to the whole number of male citizens twenty-one years of age in such State."

Section 3. [Disqualification to hold office.] –

"No person shall be a Senator or Representative in Congress, or elector of President and Vice-President, or hold any office, civil or military, under the United States, or under any State, who, having previously taken an oath, as a member of Congress, or as an officer of the United States, or as a member of any State Legislature, or as an executive or judicial officer of any State, to support the constitution of the United States, shall have engaged in insurrection or rebellion against the same, or given aid or comfort to the enemies thereof. But Congress may by a vote of two-thirds of each House, remove such disability."

Section 4. [Public debt not to be questioned – Debts of the Confederacy and claims not to be paid.]

"The validity of the public debt of the United States, authorized by law, including debts incurred for payment of pensions and bounties for services in suppressing insurrection or rebellion, shall not be questioned. But neither the United States nor any State shall assume or pay any debt or obligation incurred in aid of insurrection or rebellion against the United States, or any claim for the loss or emancipation of any slave; but all such debts, obligations and claims shall be held illegal and void."

Section 5. [Power to enforce amendment.] –

"The Congress shall have the power to enforce, by appropriate legislation, the provisions of this article."

Pay special attention to this one if you're a State prisoner. This amendment contains the equal protection of law clause.

CHAPTER FIVE

FIRST WRITE

Now that you have an understanding of what will and won't work, let's get started. In building a sound claim from the ground up, the first thing I want you to do is write your claim with the lessons of the first four chapters in mind.

When you begin, I want you to be yourself, just like you're writing a letter to a loved one. I want you to write it like the person you are talking to is a child, who has no idea how you got to become a prisoner. Write it as though the recipient knows nothing about your case. Start with the conduct you're accused of, the part you played, and the part you're actually convicted for.

Make this letter a time-line. Start every point with the time and date of the occurrence. You can – and I suggest you do – use your docket sheet to assist your memory during this task.

A word of warning: If you're looking to play on a technicality or present false claims and testimony to the court, you're likely to find the trouble you're looking for. Keep in mind that a standard motion for §2255 relief is structured as an affidavit, a sworn statement. The facts alleged in your filing, if not proven false by the record, must be presumed as true. This sounds like you can slip one by, but that's not the case here. The principle has a detrimental effect to your case if you make one false statement. In fact, you ruin your credibility with the court, falsus in uno; falsus in omnibus.

This principle is so critical to your case that you must be careful that you don't even simply overstate your claim. I know from cases I've read over the years that making statements that you're not sure of is just as damaging as presenting false statements. In cases of serious Constitutional violations, we, as people, tend to view our cases as a guaranteed win. Nothing is further from the truth. That guaranteed win still has to be presented accurately. In making it simple, if your judge knew what you know, you probably wouldn't be where you are. Step back and realize that your judge has not worked the case like you have; he or she is simply looking for a quick resolve to your claim, if one can be found. If you characterize your claim as one where relief is guaranteed with nothing more to be said from the government, your only guarantee is a quick loss. No matter what, you must take an approach of humility and present your claim methodically and honestly.

Work diligently to maintain credibility with the court. Proceed as though you're telling your story to someone who has no details of it. Show the merits of your claim and the defects of the government's counterclaims. Don't make personal and insulting remarks, let the government's case speak for itself.

Scrupulous accuracy is the key to presenting a clear claim. Refraining from making false statements is not enough; you must also refrain from making statements you're not sure of. Always err on the side of caution if you must, even speak on the side of understating your claim, and stay away from exaggeration. Absolute negatives are difficult – not impossible – to prove, and are hard to be sure of. You should rarely permit yourself an unqualified "never." Do not present a claim with something like; "a conviction like this is never Constitutional." If you're younger than 240 years old and were not seated on every jury in America, you have no way to be sure of a statement like that. Introduce your claim with something like "As far as I have been able to discover …" or "I confidently believe …" Inaccuracies can result from deliberate misstatement or carelessness. Either way, you will suffer great loss of credibility from which it is hard to recover.

While you're performing this first draft, it's important to use paragraphs to separate ideas. (I even label my paragraphs in my first draft, much like I do a book, as a quick reference.) The first sentence of each paragraph is as important as your note or a sub-heading. Your topic sentence, as we'll call it, will guide you and the next reader through your filing – it gives a complete preview of the thought that's about to be discussed in the paragraph. Paragraph breaks should not occur randomly, inserted simply because the last paragraph was getting too long. They should occur when you are moving on to a new sub-point and wish to signal a change in topic.

Use guide words in your topic sentence, "Although I was present at the scene, I was not involved in the alleged conduct." Notice the first word here. It's used to connect two separate thoughts; 1) I was there; 2) I was not involved.

In helping readers follow from one thought to the next – both between and within paragraphs – guide words are indispensable. In my previous example, I admit to my presence, but I also show that my mere presence is not indicative of guilt. You will find many guide words and phrases in use today: moreover, however, although, on the other hand, nonetheless, to prove the point, and many others. Most legal writers prefer they not be used to start a sentence, I, however, disagree. I don't recommend you start every topic sentence with one, but I do suggest you use one where needed to get your reader's attention. These words and phrases turn the reader's head in the direction you want the reader to look.

In modern literature, you find the best guide words are single-syllable conjunctions: and, but, nor, or, so, and yet. Professional writers use them at the start of a sentence and so should you. The myth that you never begin a sentence with a conjunction is just out of place in today's writing. Look at any newspaper, novel, or non-fiction work and you're likely to find several sentences per page beginning with one of these connectives. You will have a difficult time of achieving a flowing narrative or argument without them.

As a writer of fiction novels also, I make a point of getting a reader's attention and holding it by leaving critical details open. This tactic makes it difficult to put a book down, a perpetual page-turner as it's called. Don't do this to a court. A judge is a different kind of reader who reads for a specific purpose; that is to get critical information. In each paragraph, give a topic sentence so the reader knows what point to look for; end the paragraph with a strong sentence of conclusion that conforms with the topic or a resulting sentence.

The practice I'm suggesting allows the reader to discover the purpose of each paragraph at the beginning, and to maintain their attention through to the conclusion. Because of this purpose, the most useful type of paragraph – especially in legal writing – is one in which:

1. the topic sentence is at the beginning;

2. the sentences that immediately follow explain, establish, or develop the statement on the topic sentence; and

3. the final sentence – in the paragraph – either emphasizes the thought of the topic sentence or states some important outcomes or consequence.

Do not end your paragraph with an unimportant detail. Your last sentence should be an unmistakable definitive statement that's supported by the previous paragraph.

Try to compare your paragraph to a stair case, reaching for your goal. See each sentence as a step. Each should serve the purpose of leading the reader to the next sentence, that collectively makes an important point.

"Although I was present at the scene, I was not involved in the alleged conduct."

In the paragraph that follows a topic sentence like this, each should chronicle progressive events that show mere presence is not evidence of guilt. Example:

"Although I was present at the scene, I was not involved in the alleged conduct. At 8:00 A.M., I parked my car in front of room number six, occupied by my co-worker. As I knocked on the door, I heard another car park next to mine. The driver inadvertently blew the horn, which I mistook as a greeting, to me. I involuntarily offered a reciprocal wave of the hand as a counter-greeting. The officer in the parking lot, who witnessed the wave, assumed we were acquainted. When undercover officers swooped in to make the arrest, I too was apprehended as a suspect. My presence at the motel and innocent wave are not overt acts of conspiracy."

AS you can see here, one sentence leads to the next. Each is required to get from topic sentence to my conclusion. I want the reader to know that being there – at a public establishment – is not proof of guilt. Just as each sentence relates to the next, so should your paragraphs. Your next topic sentence should introduce the next thought describing the event that immediately follows the conclusion of the previous; "… make the arrest …" for instance:

"We were all hand-cuffed and placed in separate police cars."

Again, notice the conjunction of two thoughts separated by "and."

CHAPTER SIX

THOUGHT ORGANIZATION

As I write this book, so should you write your claim. I engage in three different styles of writing, novel fiction, legal, and instructional such as you hold in your hand. I wish I was given a dollar for each time I've been scolded about my use of adjectives, be it as it may, they have their place. Of course, you will find other differences in writing styles that seriously affect legal writing especially. We, as people, generally write in a narrative form, such as in novel fiction. To do so we write a story from the beginning to the end just as sure as we write from left to right. Well, it's time to switch gears. When you write legal papers, motions, briefs, etc., your goal is to reach an objective rather than entertain. Just as I write this book with the intent to advance your thinking; you should write to inform, convince, and reach your goal.

Let's get a clue. Ask yourself; what do I want? At the end of any petition, motion, complaint, or suit you will find a conclusion. This, in some filings, is referred to as a prayer for relief. Regardless of what you label it as, the idea's the same; it's the result you want to gain from your filing. When I say get a clue, I mean that very literally. Figure it out and write it down.

If you're filing any type of habeas corpus petition, the desired result is in the name. If you don't know what habeas corpus means, go look it up; that's going to be your clue. Now then, let's figure out how to get what you want. If you've been listening, you may well have come to the conclusion that I want you to start your writing from the end of it. That would be correct; know what you want, the desired result will affect the statutory vehicle you use.

On the off chance that you're reading this book while you're writing your paragraphs, as we discussed earlier, keep in mind that you may have to add more as you go along. If you study the Supreme Court decision in *Strickland v. Washington*, 466 U.S. at 668 (1984), you will find that more than one claim can be derived from the same set of operative facts or paragraphs.

Let's take your list of paragraphs, each contains a short statement of fact. Now, let's put a number to each one, not just any number, start at number ten, then twenty, thirty … and so on. Number by tens, because that will leave space to add more paragraphs in between. All computer programmers will understand this principle. When you re-write your paragraphs, and you will later, you can follow my favorite habit of writing one double-spaced paragraph per page, until they're perfected.

Now then, let's inspect our paragraphs for readability. Keep in mind that we will encounter two types of reading throughout our lives: one) is silent read; and two) is open read or reading aloud. You may prepare for either form in legal writing, but as a pro se litigant, you're more likely to be required to explain it in open court than a professional lawyer is. Because of this one fact, I like to prepare everything as though I'm giving a lecture. My sentences will usually be short and complete, containing a single point. Structure your sentences so you can read aloud from beginning to end before you need to take a breath, comfortably. In my opinion, your opening, or instant motion, is no place to use successive parenthetic expressions. One or two short alternatives or insertions between commas are acceptable, but keep it short enough to read period to period without taking a breath.

Read and reread your work. It's easy to forget your goal as you ramble on through endless facts. It's also easy to produce a robotic-sounding statement when you keep strict adherence to grammatical rules. We all speak in a comfortable vernacular to express ourselves in a clear and fluid manner. I suggest that you write as you speak, in a professional setting; keep in mind that those of you who worked in the more "colorful" settings should use additional caution.

Let's start with a clear head. Lay all the grammatical rules aside when you read. Read for clarity. Ask yourself if you have to decipher a meaning or is it provided in a plain and simple manner. Do you respond favorably to the subject or does it raise questions? Remember; a paragraph makes a point. It should never be clouded with question.

> *Author's Note: These are the basic principles I follow for writing lecture notes. I believe that every pro se litigant engaged in legal writing can learn a lot from this method. If your instincts are sound, you can infer principles from our likes and dislikes. This process will very likely be more consistent than "rules" you remember from middle school.*

Provided that you have followed all the steps thus far, you're well on your way to having a clear factual basis established. Now let's look at how they relate to the remaining rights you have after the direct appeal stage. Hence, the "understanding of law as well as facts." *Monroe v. United States*. 463 F.2d 1032 (1972 CA 5 Fla.) That's right, if your facts, as they relate to law, fail to constitute a Constitutional violation, you have no claim. Remember also that "A defendant who enters a plea of guilty waives all non-jurisdictional challenges to the constitutionality of the conviction." *Wilson v. United States*, 962 F.2d 996, 997 (11th Cir. 1992).

In an earlier chapter, you were directed to learn your Constitutional rights. More importantly, those that remain actionable after direct appeal. You will find that differences in right exist between defendants that proceed to trial and those that enter guilty pleas. One right that exists in both is a claim of ineffective assistance of counsel; although the approach and claim limitations are a bit different after a plea of guilty.

Time for another list. Make a list of your rights that remain, as you see them. Take each, one at a time, and compare them to your facts contained in your paragraphs. See if the comparison constitutes a claim. OK, we have a claim. Compare your claim to the statutory text of the vehicle you intend to use (§2255). Example: The Sixth Amendment guarantees the right to the assistance of counsel; *Strickland v. Washington*, 466 U.S. 668 defines the standards of effective assistance to include a duty to investigate a criminal case for possible defenses; My lawyer failed to investigate my case by refusing to interview the four witnesses and/or co-defendants who were at the scene; neither the witnesses nor I were called to the stand to provide testimony concerning whether we were acquainted: I was convicted by a jury's finding of guilt; after leaving the courtroom, following sentencing, my lawyer said he was coming to the jail to discuss appeal, but never did; On the 28th day, I wrote the court a letter concerning my appeal, which the court construed as my notice of appeal; the appeal was dismissed, sua sponte, as untimely, a procedural default.

I'm sure by now you've heard the term "ineffective assistance of counsel," right? Indeed, it's I.A.C., however, it's not a claim sufficient to warrant release or reversal. I.A.C. claims are subject to a two-part test, which I'll cover more thoroughly in the next chapter. What I want you to see now are the Constitutional violations in this example. The very first one is I.A.C. for failure to investigate; it is a constitutional claim, but by itself it doesn't give rise to a claim. What I.A.C. does do is give you cause for procedural default. For example:

> *"My lawyer refused to interview four witnesses. Because of the lack of investigation, I was deprived of my right to a compulsory process for obtaining witnesses. I was prejudiced because counsel's actions rendered the trial process fundamentally unfair."*

Ordinarily, being deprived of your right to present witnesses is an appealable issue. The next problem is that since no appeal occurred, the claim would be procedurally barred. But, notice that in this scenario there was no appeal because counsel failed to file a notice and/or failed to provide advice concerning appeal. Counsel's ineffectiveness provided cause to raise this procedurally defaulted claim in a §2255 motion.

Exercise: In this scenario, how many claims can be raised in a §2255 motion? The answer is three, covered in a later chapter.

As the light bulb in your head begins to flash, consider the following:

1) You must take each claim through the test of textual interpretation. Do this by applying every word of the remedial statute you anticipate using.

2) Apply the full extent of the government's standard defenses to your claim. Please, don't assume you know; look these up.

- Cognizable

- Procedural default

- Forfeiture waiver

- Waiver

- Issue preclusion

- Statute of limitations

- Merit of claim

Once your claims are solidified through these two tests, you are now ready to separate your claims and match them to the necessary supporting facts.

You may remember that I said "more than one claim can be derived from the same set of operative facts." Well, here I've identified three, but the supporting facts will vary. Take, for example, that the claim of being deprived of your witnesses will require you to show witnesses existed. However, the claim of being deprived of counsel at the appeal notification stage should start at the jury verdict.

Back to one of my most basic principles of legal writing; Keep It Short and Simple (KISS). Remember also that this book is about what I've recently learned, not what I've always practiced. I would say I'm one of the leading authorities on the subject of contrast in this area, because I have had success with both long and short filings. I can guarantee you the results are better and faster when you use short, concise filings. My point here is, don't add a paragraph that's not needed. If it doesn't provide necessary support, omit it.

Now, with all this finally behind us, you can begin to get your thoughts together. We've already established that you believe events have transpired that warrant your release. We've identified your rights and how they're violated. You can now go forward and prepare the grounds for your motion. Start at the end result and work backward. I can think of nothing more defeating than working for hours and then discovering that your efforts lead to an undesired destination.

Once you've separated each ground from one another, you begin to support it. You'll be using facts and events from your case, to show the court that a path different than authorized process was followed. And that it deprived you of a fair trial. Once you've supported your ground with your facts (paragraphs), read it forward and backward, remove all surplusage, and fill in any missing details. I suggest having someone else read it also, to see if they get a clear picture.

Author's note: When filing a §2255, be sure you don't quote law or case, and definitely don't tell the court about your rights. They already know. A memorandum of law is a waste of time. Again, they already know the law, and nothing in your memorandum becomes a part of the record. Remember, this is the time to build the record, so add affidavits of witnesses and other tangible evidence the court doesn't have, such as letters and notes. This is not the time to re-litigate your criminal case, it's the time to prove it wasn't conducted properly.

CHAPTER SEVEN

INEFFECTIVE COUNSEL

Hell, we've all heard the ole cliché, "I had ineffective assistance of counsel." As true as that statement is likely to be, you still have to know how to prove it. You know the drill, as you may remember, the famous, or quite possibly infamous, quote: "That depends on what your definition of 'is' is." Look it up. I found nothing in the statutes where we looked first, right? I found nothing in the rules. Then I turned to Black's Law Dictionary, where I was referred to, "assistance of counsel." There I found:

> *"ineffective assistance of counsel – A representation in which the lawyer cannot devote full effort to the defendant, usu. because of a conflict of interest."*

How is that for vague? Now we have to define "full effort" … ? Wait, let's refer to some case law. The Supreme Court spelled out ineffective assistance of counsel in *Strickland v. Washington*, 466 U.S. 668 (1984). Not only did the high Court define it, but also showed how to test for it.

In Strickland, the Court held that: "a convicted defendant alleging ineffective assistance of counsel must show not only that counsel was not functioning as the counsel guaranteed by the Sixth Amendment so as to provide reasonably effective assistance, but also that counsel's errors were so serious as to deprive the defendant of a fair trial because of a reasonable probability that, but for counsel's unprofessional errors, the results would have been different …"

This quote from Strickland is anything but straight forward. Ordinarily, this paragraph should send anyone to seek out more definitions. Luckily for us, the Supreme Court cleaned it up with some lengthy discussion so even the layman could apply this cornerstone precedent in all applications. I do recommend that anyone who is going to practice habeas law study *Strickland* as often as possible. Here is my brief understanding of *Strickland*:

The Test:

1) The Sixth Amendment right to counsel is the right to effective assistance of counsel, and the benchmark for judging any claim of ineffectiveness must be whether counsel's conduct so undermined the proper functioning of the adversarial process that the trial cannot be relied on as having produced a just result.

2) A convicted defendant's claim that counsel's assistance was so defective as to require reversal of a conviction or setting aside of a death sentence requires that the defendant show, first, that counsel's performance was deficient, and second, that the deficient performance prejudiced the defense so as to deprive the defendant of a fair trial.

a) The proper standard for judging attorney performance is that of reasonably effective assistance, considering all the circumstances. When a convicted defendant complains of the ineffectiveness of counsel's assistance, the defendant must show that counsel's representation fell below an objective standard of reasonableness.

b) With regard to the required showing of prejudice, the proper standard requires the defendant to show that there is a reasonable probability that, but for counsel's unprofessional errors, the result of the proceeding would have been different. A reasonable probability is a probability sufficient to undermine confidence in the outcome.

A court hearing an ineffectiveness claim must consider the totality of the evidence before the judge or jury.

After reading this small part of *Strickland*, I can only imagine how harsh a task you may believe this has set before you. Please understand what I have come to know: there is great wisdom in the holding of this cornerstone case. Imagine for a moment that every error counsel could possibly make constituted ineffective assistance and any single error required reversal. There would be no need for court or prison, because lawyers are people. As such, they're just as fallible as you and I. We may want to refrain from holding them to such a critical standard, at least until we ourselves can walk on water.

Prejudiced -

> Although you can find more specific definitions in the dictionary, the *Strickland* definition is controlling: "… prejudiced the defense so as to deprive the defendant of a fair trial."

This is a two-headed snake. After trial, prejudice means denied fair trial. After plea agreement means denied trial altogether, thus denied fair trial. Under *Strickland*, your only possible prejudice is that you were denied the adversarial testing of trial, somehow. After a trial, you must show what made your trial unfair, and how. After plea agreement, you have to show how and why your entry into the plea agreement was unfair, thus denying you a trial.

> 3) "A number of practical considerations are important for the application of the standards set forth above. The standards do not establish mechanical rules; the ultimate focus of inquiry must be on the fundamental fairness of the proceeding whose result is being challenged. A court need not first determine whether counsel's performance was deficient before examining the prejudice suffered by the defendant as a result of the alleged deficiencies. If it is easier to dispose of an ineffectiveness claim on the ground of lack of sufficient prejudice, that course should be followed."

This one statement amplifies the meaning of a two-part test. Both your "cause" and "prejudice" arguments must be sufficiently strong to get any kind of relief.

STANDARD FOR I.A.C.
466 U.S. 684

"[1] For these reasons, we granted certiorari to consider the standards by which to judge a contention that the Constitution requires that a criminal judgment be overturned because of the actual ineffective assistance of counsel. 462 U.S. 1105, 77 L Ed 1332, 103 S Ct 2451 (1983). We agree with the Court of Appeals that the exhaustion rule requiring dismissal of mixed petitions, though to be strictly enforced, is not jurisdictional. See *Rose v. Lundy*, 455 US, at 515-520, 71 L Ed 2d 379, 102 S Ct 1198. We therefore address the merits of the constitutional issue.

[2][3] In a long line of cases that includes *Powell v Alabama*, 287 U.S. 45, 77 L Ed 158, 53 S Ct 55, 84 A.L.R. 527 (1932), *Johnson v. Zerbst*, 304 U.S. 458, 82 L Ed 1161, 58 S Ct 1019, 146 A.L.R. 357 (1938), and *Gideon v. Wainwright*, 372, U.S. 335, 9 L Ed 2d 799, 83 S Ct 792, 23 Ohio Ops 2d 258, 93 A.L.R. 2d 733 (1963), this Court has recognized that the Sixth Amendment right to counsel exists, and is needed, in order to protect the fundamental right to a fair trial. The Constitution guarantees a fair trial through

466 U.S. 685

the Due Process Clauses, but it defines the basic elements of a fair trial largely through several provisions of the Sixth Amendment, including the Counsel Clause:

In all criminal prosecutions, the accused shall enjoy the right to a speedy and public trial, by an impartial jury of the State and district wherein the crime shall have been committed, which the district shall have been previously ascertained by law, and to be informed of the nature and cause of the accusation; to be confronted with the witnesses against him; to have compulsory process for obtaining witnesses in his favor, and to have the Assistance of Counsel for his defense.

Thus, a fair trial is one in which evidence subject to adversarial testing is presented to an impartial tribunal for resolution of issues defined in advance of the proceeding. The right to counsel plays a crucial role in the adversarial system embodied in the Sixth Amendment, since access to counsel's skill and knowledge is necessary to accord defendants the "ample opportunity to meet the case of the prosecution" to which they are entitled. *Adams v. United States* ex rel. McCann, 317 U.S. 269, 275, 276, 87 L Ed 268, 63 S Ct 236, 143 A.L.R. 435 (1942); see *Powell v. Alabama*, supra, at 68-69, 77 L Ed 158, 53 S Ct 55, 84 A.L.R. 527.

Because of the vital importance of counsel's assistance, this court has held that, with certain exceptions, a person accused of a federal or state crime has the right to have counsel appointed if retained counsel cannot be obtained. See *Argersinger v. Hamlin*, 407 U.S. 25, 32 L Ed 2d 530, 92 S Ct 2006 (1972); *Gideon v. Wainwright*, supra; *Johnson v. Zerbst*, supra. That a person who happens to be a lawyer is present at trial alongside the accused, however, is not enough to satisfy the constitutional command. The Sixth Amendment recognizes the right to assistance of counsel because it envisions counsel's playing a role that is critical

to the ability of the adversarial system to produce just results. An accused is entitled to be assisted by an attorney, whether retained or appointed, who plays the role necessary to ensure that the trial is fair.

466 U.S. 686

[6][7] For that reason, the Court has recognized that "the right to counsel is the right to the effective assistance of counsel." *McMann v. Richardson*, 397 U.S. 759, 771 n 14, 25 L Ed 2d 763, 90 S Ct 1441 (1970). Government violates the right to effective assistance of counsel when it interferes in certain ways with the ability of counsel to make independent decisions about how to conduct the defense. See, e.g., *Geders v. United States*, 425 U.S. 80, 47 L Ed 2d 592, 96 S Ct 1330 (1976)(bar on attorney-client consultation during overnight recess); *Herring v. New York*, 422 U.S. 853, 45 L Ed 2d 593, 95 S Ct 2550 (1975 Mbar on summation at bench trial); *Brooks v. Tennessee*, 406 U.S. 605, 612-613, 32 L Ed 2d 358, 92 S Ct 1891 (1972)(requirement that defendant be first defense witness); *Ferguson v. Georgia*, 365 U.S. 570, 593-596, 5 L Ed 2d 783, 81 S Ct 756 (1961)(bar on direct examination of defendant). Counsel, however, can also deprive a defendant of the right to effective assistance, simply by failing to render "adequate legal assistance," *Cuyler v. Sullivan*, 446 US, at 344, 64 L Ed 2d 333, 100 S Ct 1708. Id., at 345-350, 64 L Ed 333, 100 S Ct 1708 (actual conflict of interest adversely affecting lawyer's performance renders assistance ineffective).

[8] The Court has not elaborated on the meaning of the constitutional requirement of effective assistance in the latter class of cases – that is, those presenting claims of "actual ineffectiveness." In giving meaning to the requirement, however, we must take its purpose – to ensure a fair trial – as the guide. The benchmark for judging any claim of ineffectiveness must be whether counsel's conduct so

undermined that proper functioning of the adversarial process that the trial cannot be relied on as having produced a just result."

466 U.S. 687
REASONABLY EFFECTIVE

[11] As all the Federal Courts of Appeals have now held, the proper standard for attorney performance is that of reasonably effective assistance. See *Trapnell v. United States*, 725 F.2d, at 151-152.

The Court indirectly recognized as much when it stated in *McMann v. Richardson*, supra, at 770, 771, 25 L Ed 2d 763, 90 S Ct 1441, that a guilty plea cannot be attacked as based on inadequate legal advice unless counsel was not "a reasonably competent attorney" and the advice was not "within the range of competence demanded of attorneys in criminal cases." See also *Cuyler v. Sullivan*, supra, at 344, 64 L Ed 2d 333, 100 S Ct 1708. When a convicted defendant

466 U.S. 688

complains of the ineffectiveness of counsel's assistance, the defendant must show that counsel's representation fell below an objective standard of reasonableness.

More specific guidelines are not appropriate. The Sixth Amendment refers simply to "counsel," not specifying particular requirements of effective assistance. It relies instead on the legal profession's maintenance of standards sufficient to justify the law's presumption that counsel will fulfill the role in the adversary process that the Amendment envisions. See *Michel v. Louisiana*, 350 U.S. 91, 100-101, 100 L Ed 83, 76 S Ct 158 (1955). The proper measure of attorney performance remains simply reasonableness under prevailing professional norms.

Representation of a criminal defendant entails certain basic duties. Counsel's function is to assist the defendant, and hence counsel owes the client a debt of loyalty, a duty to avoid conflicts of interest. See *Cuyler v. Sullivan*, supra, at 346, 64 L Ed 2d 333, 100 S Ct 1708. From counsel's function as assistant to the defendant derived the overarching duty to advocate the defendant's cause and the more particular duties to consult with the defendant on important decisions and to keep the defendant informed of important developments in the course of the prosecution. Counsel also has a duty to bring to bear such skill and knowledge as will render the trial a reliable adversarial testing process. See *Powell v. Alabama*, 287 US, at 68-69, 77 L Ed 158, 53 S Ct 55, 84 A.L.R. 527.

These basic duties neither exhaustively define the obligations of counsel nor form a checklist for judicial evaluation of attorney performance. In any case presenting an ineffectiveness claim, the performance inquiry must be whether counsel's assistance was reasonable considering all the circumstances. Prevailing norms of practice as reflected in American Bar Association standards and the like, e.g., *ABA Standards for Criminal Justice 4-1.1 to 4-8.6* (2d Ed 1980)("The Defense Function"), are guides to determining what is reasonable, but they are only guides. No particular set of detailed rules for counsel's conduct can satisfactorily take

466 U.S. 689

account of the variety of circumstances faced by defense counsel or the range of legitimate decisions regarding how best to represent a criminal defendant. Any such set of rules would interfere with the constitutionally protected independence of counsel and restrict the wide latitude counsel must have in making tactical decisions. See *United States v. Decoster*, 199 U.S. App DC, at 371, 624

F.2d, at 208. Indeed, the existence of detailed guidelines for representation could distract counsel from the overriding mission of vigorous advocacy of the defendant's cause. Moreover, the purpose of the effective assistance guarantee of the Sixth Amendment is not to improve the quality of legal representation, although that is a goal of considerable importance to the legal system. The purpose is simply to ensure that criminal defendants receive a fair trial.

[15] Judicial scrutiny of counsel's performance must be highly deferential. It is all too tempting for a defendant to second guess counsel's assistance after conviction or adverse sentence, and it is all too easy for a court, examining counsel's defense after it has proved unsuccessful, to conclude that a particular act or omission of counsel was unreasonable. Cf. *Engle v. Isaac*, 456 U.S. 107, 133-134, 71 L Ed 2d 783, 102 S Ct 1558 (1982). A fair assessment of attorney performance requires that every effort be made to eliminate the distorting effects of hindsight, to reconstruct the circumstances of counsel's challenged conduct, and to evaluate the conduct from counsel's perspective at the time. Because of the difficulties inherent in making the evaluation, a court must indulge a strong presumption that counsel's conduct falls within the wide range of reasonable professional assistance; that is, the defendant must overcome the presumption that, under the circumstances, the challenged action "might be considered sound trial strategy." See *Michel v. Louisiana*, supra, at 101, 100 L Ed 83, 76 S Ct 158. There are countless ways to provide effective assistance in any case. Even the best criminal defense attorneys would not defend a particular client in the same way."

466 U.S. 690

ACTUAL INEFFECTIVENESS

[16][17] Thus, a court deciding an actual ineffectiveness claim must judge the reasonableness of counsel's challenged conduct on the facts of the particular case, viewed as of the time of counsels conduct.

A convicted defendant making a claim of ineffective assistance must identify the acts or omissions of counsel that are alleged not to have been the result of reasonable professional judgment. The court must then determine whether, in light of all the circumstances, the identified acts or omissions were outside the wide range of professionally competent assistance. In making that determination, the court should keep in mind that counsel's function, as elaborated in prevailing professional norms, is to make the adversarial testing process work in the particular case. At the same time, the court should recognize that counsel is strongly presumed to have rendered adequate assistance and made all significant decisions in the exercise of reasonable professional judgment."

INVESTIGATION

[18] These standards require no special amplification in order to define counsel's duty to investigate, the duty at issue in this case. As the Court of Appeals concluded, strategic choices made after thorough investigation of law and facts relevant to plausible options are virtually unchallengeable; and strategic

466 U.S. 691

choices made after less than complete investigation are reasonable precisely to the extent that reasonable professional judgments support the limitations on investigation. In other words, counsel has a duty to make reasonable investigations or to make a reasonable decision that makes particular investigations unnecessary. In any ineffectiveness case, a particular decision not to investigate must be directly assessed for reasonableness in all the circumstances, applying a heavy measure of deference to counsel's judgments.

The reasonableness of counsel's actions may be determined or substantially influenced by the defendant's own statements or actions. Counsel's actions are usually based, quite properly, on informed strategic choices made by the defendant and on information supplied by the defendant. In particular, what investigation decisions are reasonable depends critically on such information. For example, when the facts that support a certain potential line of defense are generally known to counsel because of what the defendant has said, the need for further investigation may be considerably diminished or eliminated altogether. And when a defendant has given counsel reason to believe that pursuing certain investigations would be fruitless or even harmful, counsel's failure to pursue those investigations may not be later challenged as unreasonable. In short, inquiry into counsel's conversations with the defendant may be critical to a proper assessment of counsel's investigation decisions, just as it may be critical to a proper assessment of counsel's other litigation decisions. See *United States v. Decoster*, supra, at 372-373, 624 F.2d, at 209-210."

PREJUDICE NOT REQUIRED
466 U.S. 692

"[22] In certain Sixth Amendment contexts, prejudice is presumed. Actual or constructive denial of the assistance of counsel altogether is legally presumed to result in prejudice. So are various kinds of state interference with counsel's assistance. See *United States v. Cronic*, ante, at 659, and n 25, 80 L Ed 2d 657, 104 S Ct 2039. Prejudice in these circumstances is so likely that case-by-case inquiry into prejudice is not worth the cost. Ante, at 658, 80 L Ed 2d 657, 104 S Ct 2039. Moreover, such circumstances involve impairments of the Sixth Amendment right that are easy to identify and, for that reason and because the prosecution is directly responsible, easy for the government to prevent.

[23] One type of actual ineffectiveness claim warrants a similar, though more limited, presumption of prejudice. In *Cuyler v. Sullivan*. 446 US, at 345-350, 64 L Ed 2d 333, 100 S Ct 1708, the Court held that prejudice is presumed when counsel is burdened by an actual conflict of interest. In those circumstances, counsel breaches the duty of loyalty, perhaps the most basic of counsel's duties. Moreover, it is difficult to measure the precise effect on the defense of representation corrupted by conflict in interests. Given the obligation of counsel to avoid conflicts of interest and the ability of trial courts to make early inquiry in certain situations likely to give rise to conflicts, see, e.g., Fed Rule Crim Proc 44(c), it is reasonable for the criminal justice system to maintain a fairly rigid rule of presumed prejudice for conflicts of interest. Even so, the rule is not quite the per se rule of prejudice that exists for the Sixth Amendment claims mentioned above. Prejudice is presumed only if the defendant demonstrates that counsel "actively represented conflicting interests" and that "an actual conflict of interest adversely affected his lawyer's performance." *Cuyler v. Sullivan*, supra, at 350, 348, 64 L Ed 2d 333, 100 S Ct 1708."

For those who intend to continue expanding your understanding of ineffective assistance of counsel, I suggest you read all of Strickland's opinion. I suggest you study, at length, the materials I've provided here. You must also be able to stay up to date with new Supreme Court and en banc precedents. I myself thought I had it all figured out until June 23, 2017, when the Supreme Court made a new ruling that individualized the prejudice prong, *Jae Lee v. United States*, (June 23, 2017)(Case No.: 16-327); holding that:

"We cannot agree that it would be irrational for a defendant in Lee's position to reject the plea offer in favor of trial. But for his attorney's incompetence, Lee would have known that

accepting the plea agreement would certainly lead to deportation. Going to trial? Almost certainly. If deportation were the 'determinative issue' for an individual in plea discussions, as it was for Lee; if that individual had strong connections to this country and no other, as did Lee; and if the consequences of taking a chance at trial were not markedly harsher than pleading, as in this case, that 'almost' could make all the difference. Balanced against holding on to some chance of avoiding deportation was a year or two more of prison time. See Id., at 6. Not everyone in Lee's position would make the choice to reject the plea. But we cannot say it would be irrational to do so."

What's important to notice is that the Lee decision in no way affects the *Strickland* holding; it does, however, change my personal understanding of *Strickland*. Had I have been the first to review the Lee case, I would have declined to file. That's because in my narrow belief and understanding – of both Mr. Lee's case and the *Strickland* holding – Mr. Lee would have failed to show adequate prejudice. I believed, contrary to sound advice, that Mr. Lee would have to show the probability of different outcome (guilt). When, in fact, as Lee clarified, he only had to show he was deprived of the guaranteed trial due to counsel's error, not that the outcome of the trial would have been different. He only had to show that he would have demanded trial absent counsel's unprofessional errors.

CHAPTER EIGHT

PROCEDURAL DEFAULT

This is the last preparatory chapter before we begin exploring the principles of advancing your thinking; thus your own claims. As elementary as procedural default may seem to many of you, it warrants its own chapter because many courts get it wrong, and you're no better.

"… claims are procedurally defaulted." This line is the same as the one I find in almost every Response I've read. This is, in fact, probably the most common response by every U.S. Attorney in America engaged in habeas and civil litigations lodged by pro se petitioners. I'm aware that I listed procedural default as an issue in a previous chapter; but I promise you the subject warrants further discussion.

It's important to consider the possible defenses to your claim as you construct your claim. When your consideration goes beyond your initial filing, you can construct your claim in a way that leads your opponent to argue in an arena that favors your position. As we study the next three cases, I want you to realize the importance of all possible outcomes. Just as you shouldn't engage in sky-diving without considering where you're going to land, you shouldn't launch a claim you're not prepared to defend.

United States v. Frady, 456 U.S. 152, is a very good example of a procedural default, which is commonly used in government responses around the country. In this case, Mr. Frady filed a motion under 28 U.S.C. §2255, trying to redress a plain error in his trial. In his criminal case, the court's jury instruction on malice compelled the jury to presume malice and thereby wrongfully eliminate any possibility of a manslaughter verdict. If true, an error like this is a "plain error," readdressable under Federal Rules of Criminal Procedure, Rule 52(b). When you read Rule 52(b), you discover that its applicability is unequivocally reserved for direct appeal.

The Supreme Court rightfully noted that "The Court of Appeals' use of Rule 52(b)'s 'plain error' standard to review respondent's §2255 motion was contrary to long-established law. Because, it was intended for use on direct appeal, such standard is out of place when a prisoner launches a collateral attack against a conviction after society's legitimate interest in the finality of the judgment has been perfected by the expiration of time allowed for direct review or by the affirmance of the conviction on appeal."

Mr. Frady's errors are, for the purpose of this chapter, illustrated to highlight how his claims are procedurally defaulted. Nineteen years after his crime, Mr. Frady complains he was convicted by a jury erroneously instructed on the meaning of malice. At trial, Mr. Frady made no objection to the instruction, nor did he raise the issue on direct appeal.

Mr. Frady initiates an action by filing a motion under 28 U.S.C. §2255 seeking the vacation of his sentence because the jury instructions used at his trial in 1963 were defective. The district court denied his §2255 motion, stating that he should have challenged the jury instruction on direct appeal.

The Court of Appeals reversed. The appellate court held that the proper standard to apply to Frady's claim is the "plain error" standard governing relief on direct appeal from errors not objected to at trial, rather than the "Cause and Actual Prejudice" standard enunciated in *Wainwright v. Sykes*, 433 U.S. 72, etc. Over a vigorous dissent, the full Court of Appeals denied the government a rehearing en banc.

Rule 52(b) was intended to afford a means for the prompt redress of miscarriages of justice. By its terms, recourse may be had to the Rule only on appeal from a trial infected with error so 'plain' the trial judge and prosecutor were derelict in countenancing it, even absent the defendant's timely assistance in detecting it.

Because the rule is intended for use on direct appeal, the "plain error" standard is out of place when a prisoner launches a collateral attack against a criminal conviction after "society's legitimate interests in finality of the judgment has been perfected by the expiration of the time allowed for direct appeal. In Mr. Frady's case, the Court of Appeals applied the "plain error" standard of review, in essence allowing him a second appeal, 15 years after his first appeal had been decided.

> *Author's Note: It's my personal belief that Mr. Frady attempted to exploit a change in local law that led to an ambiguity in procedure. He somehow got past the Court of Appeals, then was called to respond in the Supreme Court. In the Supreme Court, his ruse was revealed for what it was, and reversed, but only after wasting an unreasonable amount of judicial resources.*

As we explore procedural default defenses, keep in mind also that there are exceptions to that rule. Over the last 240 years, the combined wisdom of lawmakers has engineered a system that consistently delivers just results in criminal cases. Again, the system is not impervious to exceptions. As the thinking of people evolves and the complexities of technology expand, so does the sets of circumstances require judgment. In a more recent case, the Eleventh Circuit Court of Appeals faced the possibility of just such an exception.

In the case of *McKay v. United States*, 657 F.3d 1190 (11th Cir. 2011), Mr. McKay appealed the denial of his first §2255. He claimed that he was erroneously sentenced as a career offender because, in light of subsequent case law, his prior conviction for carrying a concealed weapon is not a "crima of violence."

Under the procedural default rule, "a defendant generally must advance an available challenge to a criminal conviction or sentence on direct appeal or else the defendant is barred from presenting that claim in a §2255 proceeding." Lynn, 365 F.3d at 1234. As the Supreme Court has explained, this rule "is neither a statutory nor a constitutional requirement, but it is a doctrine adhered to by the courts to conserve judicial resources and to respect the law's important interest in the finality of judgments." *Massaro v. United States*, 538 U.S. 500, 504. In Mr. McKay's case, it's beyond dispute that his claims are procedurally defaulted because he failed to advance his claim on direct appeal – as a matter of record, he never filed for an appeal at all.

Mr. McKay's procedural default can be excused, however, if one of the two exceptions to the procedural default rule applies: (1) for cause and prejudice; or (2) for a miscarriage of justice, or actual innocence. See *Lynn*, 365 F.3d at 1234. Under the cause and prejudice exception, a §2255 movant can avoid application of the procedural default bar by "show[ing] cause for not raising the claim of error on direct appeal *and* actual prejudice from the alleged error." Id. Under the actual innocence exception – as interpreted by current Supreme Court doctrine – a movant's procedural default is excused if he can show that he is actually innocent either of the crime of conviction or, in the capital sentencing context, of the sentence itself. See *Dretke v. Haley*, 541 US. 386, 388 124 S.Ct. 1847, 158 L.Ed. 2d 659 (2004). Because *McKay* does not argue on appeal that the cause and prejudice exception applies – nor for that matter did he do so at district court – we do not address this exception. We thus limit ourselves to answering whether the actual innocence exception applies to excuse McKay's procedural default, and so pause to examine this exception's contours.

The actual innocence exception has been applied in two distinct contexts: first, in the face of a claim of actual innocence from the crime of conviction and, second, in the face of a claim of actual innocence of a sentence. See *Sibley v. Culliver*, 377 F.3d 1196, 1205-06 (11th Cir. 2004). To show actual innocence of the crime of conviction, a movant "must show that it is more likely than not that no reasonable juror would have found [him] guilty beyond a reasonable doubt" in light of the new evidence of innocence. *Schlup v. Delo*, 513 U.S. 298, 327 115 S.Ct. 851, 130 L.Ed. 2d 808 (1995); *see also id.* at 332 (O'Connor, J., concurring]). To show actual innocence of a capital sentence, a movant "must show by clear and convincing evidence that, but for a constitutional error, no reasonable juror would have found [him] eligible for the death penalty under the applicable state law." *Sawyer v. Whitley*, 505 U.S. 333, 336, 112 S.Ct. 2514, 120 L. Ed. 2d 269 (1992); *see also Sibley*, 377 F.3d at 1205 (describing how a movant claiming actual innocence of his capital sentence must show that "he is 'innocent' of the death penalty because none of the aggravating factors legally necessary for invocation of the death penalty applied").

Neither the Supreme Court nor this Court has yet ruled on whether *Sawyer's* actual innocence of sentence exception extends to the noncapital sentencing context. Several of our sister circuits, however, have spoken on the issue but have reached divergent conclusions. The Second and Fourth Circuits have held that the actual innocence of sentence exception does apply in the noncapital sentencing context. See *Spence v. Superintendent, Great Meadow Corr. Facility*, 219 F.3d 162, 171 (2d Cir. 2000); *United States v. Maybeck*, 23 F.3d 888, 892-93 (4th Cir. 1994). The Fourth Circuit, however, limits its application to claims of actual innocence of career or habitual offender sentences. *United States v. Mikalajunas*, 186 F.3d 490, 495 (4th Cir. 1999). The Eighth and Tenth Circuits, on the other hand, have explicitly held that the actual innocence of sentence exception is limited to the capital sentencing context. See *Embry v. Hershberger*, 131 F.3d 739, 740th Cir. 1997)(en banc)("[W]e think that Sawyer, in terms, applies only to the sentencing phase of death cases."); *United States v. Richards*, 5 F.3d 1369, 1371 (10th Cir. 1993)("A person cannot be actually innocent of a noncapital sentence …").

Despite the lack of binding precedent on this question, the Supreme Court and this Court have articulated several principals that guide our resolution of this case. First, and most importantly, for purposes of the actual innocence exception, "'actual innocence' means *factual* innocence, not mere legal insufficiency." *Bousley v. United States*, 523 U.S. 614, 623 118 S.Ct. 1604, 140 L.Ed. 2d 828 (1998)(emphasis added);; *Sawyer*, 505 U.S. at 339 ("[T]he miscarriage of justice exception is concerned with actual as compared to legal innocence."); *Johnson v. Alabama*, 256 F.3d 1156, 1171 (11th Cir. Cir. 2001). This is true whether that allegation of actual innocence is of the crime or of the sentence. *Bousley*, 523 U.S. at 623 (involving claim of actual innocence of the crime); *Sawyer*, 505 U.S. at 339 (involving claim of actual innocence of the sentence).

Second, as it has been repeatedly emphasized, the actual innocence exception is a narrow exception. See, e.g.. *Sawyer*, 505 U.S. at 340 (describing approvingly how, in previous cases, the Court had "emphasized the narrow scope of the fundamental miscarriage of justice exception"); see also id. at 341 ("bear[ing] in mind that the exception for 'actual innocence' is a very narrow exception"); *McCleskey v. Zant*, 499 U.S. 467, 502 111 S.Ct. 1454, 113 L.Ed. 2d 517 (1991)(referring to the actual innocence exception as "[t]hat narrow exception"); *Schlup*, 513 U.S. at 333 (O'Connor, J., concurring)'(describing the actual innocence exception as a "safety valve for the extraordinary case (quoting *Harris v. Reed*, 489 U.S. 225, 271 109 S.Ct. 1038, 113 L. Ed. 2d 308 (1989)(O'Connor, J., concurring))(internal quotation marks omitted)); *Johnson*, 256 F.3d at 1171 (describing the actual innocence exception as "exceedingly narrow in scope"). Indeed, the very reason the miscarriage of justice exception was linked to a movant's actual innocence was to ensure that this exception "would remain *'rare'* and would only be applied in the 'extraordinary case.'" *Schlup*, 513 U.S. at 321 (emphasis added).

Third, as the Supreme Court has specifically instructed, we must exercise restraint when determining whether to expand the exceptions to the procedural default rule. See *Haley*, 541 U.S. at 394 ("[I]t is precisely because the various exceptions to the procedural default doctrine are judge-made rules that courts as their stewards must exercise restraint, adding to or expanding them only when necessary."). The Court has explained that "[t]o hold otherwise would be to license district courts to riddle the cause and prejudice standard with ad hoc exceptions whenever they perceive an error to be 'clear' or departure from the rules expedient. "13 Id. at 394-95. "Such an approach," the Court observed, "would have the unhappy effect of prolonging the pendency of federal habeas applications as each new exception is tested in the courts of appeals." Id. at 395.

With these principals in mind, we face the question of whether the actual innocence of sentence exception applies to McKay's claim that he was erroneously sentenced as a career offender because one of his prior convictions does not qualify as a "crime of violence." To answer this question, we need not enter the debate regarding whether the actual innocence exception extends to the noncapital sentencing context. Even assuming that this exception does extend beyond the capital sentencing context, it still does not apply to McKay because his claim is one of legal, rather that factual, innocence and thus fails to fall within the actual innocence exception's purview. See *Bousely*, 523 U.S. at 623; *Sawyer*, 505 U.S. at 339.

Although it didn't work out well for Mr. McKay, there are a few meaningful exceptions. This also leads to the question of whether you procedurally bar your exception to procedural default.

As you can imagine, justice requires that someone who is actually innocent must be released no matter what). Right? To answer this question, let's review the Supreme Court's opinion in *McQuiggin v. Perkins*, 569 U.S., (2013).

Decisions of this Court support Perkins' view of the significance of a convincing actual innocence claim. We have not resolved whether a prisoner may be entitled to habeas relief based on a freestanding claim of actual innocence. *Herrera v. Collins*, 506 U.S. 390, 404-05, 113 S.Ct. 853, 122 L.Ed. 2d 203 (1993). We have recognized, however, that a prisoner "otherwise subject to defenses of abusive or successive use of the writ [of habeas corpus] may have his federal constitutional claim considered on the merits if he makes a proper showing of actual innocence." Id. at 404, 113 S.Ct. 853, 122 L.Ed. 2d 203 (citing *Sawyer v. Whitley*, 505 U.S. 333, 112 S.Ct. 2514, 120 L.Ed. 2d 269 (1992)). See also *Murray v. Carrier*, 477 U.S. 478, 496, 106 S.Ct. 2639, 91 L.Ed. 2d 397 (1986)("[W]e think that in an extraordinary case, where a constitutional violation has probably resulted in the conviction of one who is actually innocent, a federal habeas court may grant the writ even in the absence of a showing of cause for the procedural default.") In other words, a credible showing of actual innocence may allow a prisoner to pursue his constitutional claims (here, ineffective assistance of counsel) on the merits notwithstanding the existence of a procedural bar to relief. "This rule, or fundamental miscarriage of justice exception, is grounded in the 'equitable discretion' of habeas courts to see that federal constitutional errors do not result in the incarceration of innocent persons." *Herrera*, 506 U.S. at 404, 113 S.Ct. 853,122 L.Ed. 2d 203.

The miscarriage of justice exception, our decisions bear out, survived AEDPA's passage. In *Calderon v. Thompson*, 523 U.S. 538, 118 S.Ct. 1489, 140 L. Ed. 2d 728 (1998), we applied the exception to hold that a federal court may, consistent with AEDPA, recall its mandate in order to revisit the merits of a decision. Id., at 558, 118 S.Ct. 1489, 140 L.Ed. 2d 728 ("The miscarriage of justice standard is altogether consistent ... with AEDPA's central concern that the merits of concluded criminal proceedings not be revisited in the absence of a strong showing of actual innocence."). In *Bousley v. United States*, 523 U.S. 614, 622 118 S.Ct. 1604, 140 L.Ed. 2d 828 (1998), we held, in the context of §2255, that actual innocence may overcome a prisoner's failure to raise a constitutional objection on direct review. Most recently, in *House*, we reiterated that a prisoner's proof of actual innocence may provide a gateway for federal habeas review of a procedurally defaulted claim of constitutional error. 547 U.S., at 537-538, 126 S.Ct. 2064, 165 L.Ed. 2d 1.

Considering a petitioner's diligence, not discretely, but as part of the assessment whether actual innocence has been convincingly shown, attends to the State's concern that it will be prejudiced by a prisoner's untoward delay in proffering new evidence. The State fears that a prisoner might "lie in wait and use stale evidence to collaterally attack his conviction ... when an elderly witness has died and cannot appear at a hearing to rebut new evidence." Brief for Petitioner 25. The timing of such a petition, however, should seriously undermine the credibility of the actual-innocence claim. Moreover, the deceased witness' prior testimony, which would have been subject to cross-examination, could be introduced in the event of a new trial. See *Crawford v. Washington*, 541 U.S. 36, 53-54, 124 S.Ct. 1354, 158 L.Ed. 2d 177 (2004) (recognizing exception to the Confrontation Clause where witness is unavailable and the defendant had prior opportunity for cross-examination). And frivolous petitions should occasion instant dismissal. See 28 U.S.C. §2254 Rule 4. Focusing on the merits of a petitioner's actual-innocence claim and taking account of delay in that context, rather than treating timeliness as a threshold inquiry, is tuned to the rationale underlying the miscarriage of justice exception – i.e., ensuring "that federal constitutional errors do not result in the incarceration of innocent persons." *Herrera*, 506 U.S., at 404, 113 S.Ct. 853, 122 L.Ed. 2d 203.

We hold that actual innocence, if proved, serves as a gateway through which a petitioner may pass whether the impediment is a procedural bar, as it was in *Schlup* and *House*, or, as in this case, expiration of the statute of limitations. We caution, however, that tenable actual-innocence gateway pleas are rare: "[A] petitioner does not meet the threshold requirement unless he persuades the district court that, in light of the new evidence, no juror, acting reasonably, would have voted to find him guilty beyond a reasonable doubt."

Schlup, 513 U.S., at 329, 115 S.Ct. 851, 130 L.Ed. 2d 808; see House, 547 U.S., at 538, 126 S.Ct. 2064, 165 L.Ed. 2d. 1 (emphasizing that the Schlup standard is "demanding" and seldom met). And in making an assessment of the kind Schlup envisioned, "the timing of the [petition]" is a factor bearing on the "reliability of th[e] evidence" purporting to show actual innocence. Schlup, 513 U.S., at 332, 115 S.Ct. 851, 130 L.Ed. 2d 808.

We vacate the Court of Appeals' judgment and remand the case. Our opinion clarifies that a federal habeas court, faced with an actual innocence gateway claim, should count unjustifiable delay on a habeas petitioner's part, not as an absolute barrier to relief, but as a factor in determining whether actual innocence has been reliably shown. See Brief for Respondent 45 (habeas court "could ... hold the unjustified delay against the petitioner when making credibility findings as to whether the [actual-innocence] exception has been met").

I trust you will realize that what we've covered so far is not all-inclusive. I'm sure you'll find more obstacles as your ability to learn grows.

PART II
CHAPTER NINE

ARGUING EFFECTIVELY

Before I go into the actual structure of legal writing, there are a few basic principles you must be aware of. The first being jurisdiction of the court you're writing to. You will find that there is nothing more frustrating than trying to make your case in the wrong court.

JURISDICTION

In the event you decide to give a notice of appeal before you have a final judgment from a district court, you will get this dreaded response from the Court of Appeals: "Dismissed for a lack of jurisdiction." This order will come quickly and rightfully so, you're asking the Court of Appeals to break the law. See 18 U.S.C. §3742, 28 U.S.C. §1291, and 28 U.S.C. §2253. As you can imagine, nothing is accomplished by presenting even an airtight claim in the wrong court. That's like going to a local post office to resolve a traffic ticket.

So it is with courts of law, whether it be a Municipal Magistrate Judge or a Supreme Court Justice, each has specific limits of authority to act – jurisdictional limitations – under the applicable laws. You will find that the first duty of any and all courts who receive motions or petitions is to determine its jurisdiction to resolve the matter you present. If the court does not have the authority to act in your case, you don't just have a weak case, you have no case at all.

As I have discovered – from studying some of the greatest legal minds in history – all deficiencies in your case will be pointed out by the government. In the event they fail to argue or protest a particular point, the defect will then be considered waived. But a defect in jurisdiction is a different matter entirely. The government has no interest in pointing out jurisdictional defects in criminal cases. However, if you're challenging the court's jurisdiction to impose a sentence in a post-conviction proceeding, procedural default and the court's jurisdiction will be the first thing raised by the government. Notwithstanding the government's position on the matter in most courts, including all federal courts, absence of jurisdiction is different from other defects: a lack of jurisdiction cannot be waived. See Federal Rules of Criminal Procedure, Rule 12(b)(2). What's more Is that in the event neither party raises a jurisdictional defect, the court itself can and must notice the defect.

> *Author's note: I personally follow my own practice of confirming the court's jurisdiction to hear a matter before I write anything. When I'm addressing the Court of Appeals or the Supreme Court; I write out my own theory of the court's jurisdiction right after I write the questions presented. Remember; clear, concise issue first, where to present it immediately follows. Because putting your issue in the wrong court is just as effective as placing it in the waste basket.*

As you begin to write your Jurisdictional Statement, keep in mind that the people you're addressing do this for a living. I can tell you from personal experience, and several conversations, that Jeff Atkins is a polite and very knowledgeable man. He does not need you to teach him law. The last thing you want to do is tell the court what statute gives them jurisdiction to hear the case; they already know.

When writing your own personal Jurisdictional Statement, do just that; make it personal. Always start with you, to wit:

"This court has jurisdiction to issue a Certificate of Appealability in Mr. Riggs's case because the district court denied his §2255 in violation of Clisby v. Jones, See 28 U.S.C. §2253."

Take notice of the "who, what, and why" of this example. As you can see, I want the court to "… issue a Certificate of Appealability …"; for who, "… in Mr. Riggs's case …"; based on what, "… because the district court denied his §2255 …"; why, this denial was, "… in violation of *Clisby v. Jones* …." As you can also see, I refer the reader to the applicable controlling statute but I don't quote it. Why? They already know. What they don't know is what happened in my case. Again, tell them about what happened in your case. Point them to the law you feel you can depend on, but don't try to teach it to them.

KNOW YOUR OWN CASE

I am currently waiting for the court to designate the record in a §2255 appeal. The man I am assisting is completely innocent, a fact admitted to in his pre-sentence report. When I filed his §2255, I showed the sentencing court where the law forbids his sentence and conviction. The district court denied the §2255 motion immediately without issuing a show cause order. The district court brazenly violated the Eleventh Circuit's holding in *Clisby v. Jones*; and failed to address the issue of a Certificate of Appealability. As you can see, we have an innocent man in prison in violation of the Thirteenth Amendment, a district court violating every rule and law conceivable, and the author of the book you hold fighting vehemently to get justice. All of you experienced habeas practitioners should be asking, why? The answer is simple; the defendant didn't know his own case.

As happened in this case, the defendant, being ignorant of the law, was lulled into trusting that a lawyer could represent his case without his input. Once the defendant's trust was obtained, she made a conscious choice to follow the predetermined path of least resistance, conviction by guilty plea.

Had the defendant studied or simply read the statute of conviction – over the 26 months it took to herd him into a guilty plea – he would have discovered that it didn't criminalize the conduct that the government accused, he wouldn't be in prison and he wouldn't be my example right now. The fact is, right now he's doing push-ups rather than studying his case.

Have you ever bought a new car? If you have, you've likely been offered credit life insurance. In most cases such as I've experienced, one question to a car salesman concerning life insurance, and the conversation becomes completely misguided. At the end, a consumer is likely not going to buy anything because the salesman knows nothing about life insurance. Although better dressed, a lawyer is much like a car salesman who's trying to sell something he knows nothing about. On the rare occasion that your lawyer is trying to defend your interests in a criminal case, he will need you to fill him in on all the details. Your lawyer, in most cases, doesn't know you, nor was he or she involved in the alleged conduct. You must help.

In the post-conviction arena, just as in other types of civil litigation, you don't have a right to effective assistance of counsel. Thus, you must present your own case if you can't afford counsel. But, either way, the facts start with you. In all habeas cases, when it comes time for a hearing, a lawyer will be involved one way or another; it's your responsibility to arm your lawyer with the necessary material. In habeas cases, lawyers are appointed to indigent petitioners for hearings, to preserve order and judicial resources. It's common for courts to listen to lawyers because of their training, and therefore can be expected to know more about the legal and factual aspects of the case than anyone else. But, if it becomes clear that this is not true, the court's attention will resort to what it knows to be true; the record that convicted you. If you or your counsel is asked about a fact in the record that you're ignorant of; or your opponent has referred to a relevant case you've failed to become familiar with, you can't expect the court to give your contentions much weight.

Early on we went over developing your factual basis. In the beginning of this very chapter I mentioned the questions you'll be presenting as the first element; you must be able to support a reasonable answer to your questions. Therefore, your first responsibility is to become an expert on the facts and law of your own case.

In a habeas or appellate proceeding, knowing your case means knowing the record. I can promise you that there is no way of knowing in advance what damage a gap in your knowledge of the record can do in open court. As many have said in the past, don't underestimate how important the facts may be in your case. Let me express clearly that you will be depending on the law, but which law applies depends greatly on the facts of your own case. Even in appeal, you must have a clear comprehension of what facts have been previously determined, and what facts are still unresolved. Additionally, get an idea of what relief you can ask for while you're learning your case. You don't want to fall short of relief that will have a meaningful effect on the outcome of your case.

KNOW YOUR OPPONENT

Boxing students are not allowed to enter the competition for the World heavyweight championship. Besides the obvious propensity of getting yourself killed in the ring; a beginner doesn't know enough about boxing to pose a meaningful effort against a champion. He will lose and lose quickly. Thus, is your chance of winning an argument in court when you're unfamiliar with the argument. It's very important to know your opponent's position, sometimes just as important as knowing your own position, especially when the case involves an equally supported position that's contrary to your own.

You must learn your adversary's case as well as your own. When you consider the points that may be raised by the other side; you get a clear understanding of the opposing arguments that you can accept, but show to be irrelevant, and which points must be vigorously disproved on their merits. If you're the initiating party, such as most of you will be, you must decide which of your opponent's points are so important that they must be addressed in your initial filing, and which ones you can wait until you file your reply.

Example:

Ground One:

"Defense counsel, Mr. Jackson, was required to perform his duties under a debilitating conflict of interest." (My position)

Supporting Facts:

1) Mr. Jackson was appointed to represent me and my codefendant at the same time.

2) My codefendant, Danny Young, was the leader/organizer of the wire fraud conspiracy.

3) I was recruited by Mr. Young, whom I had come to know a great deal about.

4) The government had a great interest in the substantial assistance that I could have provided against Mr. Young.

5) Mr. Jackson refused to negotiate a plea agreement that included substantial assistance on my behalf, and refused to file a motion to be relieved as counsel for conflict of interest.

(Facts that support my position)
The movant is not required to prove prejudice where a conflict of interest is apparent.

(This is rebuttal to the government's position, stated preemptively)

As you can see in this example, the Movant presents a sound claim. He supports his claim with well-refined facts of his case. He is clearly an expert in the facts of his case, so the government won't dare to refute the facts. The government, in this example, will, however, attack the procedure you're using. As you can see, the Movant set out the "cause," the first prong of *Strickland*. He then supported it with strong facts presented in a short, concise, and succinct manner. The government will immediately go to prong number 2. This argument can be anticipated, so the Movant addressed it preemptively. "The Movant is not required to prove prejudice ...." I can only imagine a young assistant United States attorney reading his first §2255 motion. I can see his head starting to swell as he reads a pro se litigant's first legal argument that sets out the cause of his case. The new assistant, planning to use his law degree to victimize an unwitting opponent by attacking the beginner's failure to address the "prejudice" prong. As his head continues to swell like a balloon reaching its full capacity, he reads paragraph six of the prisoner's supporting facts. That one single paragraph has an effect on the government's anticipated argument that's only rivaled by the effect of a sharp needle assaulting a tightly filled balloon.

The Movant in the example, did very well in his presentation because he made his strong point, and made it clear. He then used one paragraph to counter any possible attack by using the court's own standards. As you can imagine, any standardized argument would present only a hollow position on the government's part. Bear in mind, however, that the government employs smart lawyers. Lawyers that tend to develop new arguments as they go along. You must constantly ask yourself how you would outsmart someone just like you. Don't get overconfident in this small victory. You are arguing with very intelligent people. You must continually consider that other meaningful theories are coming; be prepared.

CHAPTER TEN

KNOW THE CONTROLLING STANDARDS

The individual issues involved in your claim for relief may be subject to varying presumptions and burdens of proof. In your criminal case (trial), the government is required to establish guilt beyond a reasonable doubt. Where you, as an appellant, seek to overturn a judgment of guilt in the district court, on the basis of an erroneous jury instruction to which there was no objection; you will be required to establish not just error, but plain error. A Movant who seeks to vacate or set aside a sentence in a 28 U.S.C. §2255 proceeding must show both "cause and prejudice" as a standard. A party who attempts to set aside a sentence of a district court, because it's contrary to the law or Constitution, must often show not only that the application of law and rule favors reversal, but that the government's application is not even within the bounds of reason.

When the standards set by previous court decision – from the Supreme Court or the Court of Appeals for your circuit – favors your side of the case, make that point known at the beginning of your claim in issue, and remind the court often throughout your pleadings, I reiterate my initial ground as history in every pleading that follows, one way or another. Don't let the argument evolve into an assumption that you and your adversary are equally positioned when in fact the standard of review favors you.

The Respondent in most post-conviction relief proceedings, i.e. the government, ordinarily treat the standard of review in a boiler plate fashion, kind of a one size fits all theory. If the respondent (government) is fighting against your position stating a clearly erroneous standard, make a big deal about it. Point out that the respondent is attempting to redefine an accepted standard of law and rule, or that they are asking the court to supplant an accepted standard of law and rule, or that they are asking the court to supplant an accepted standard with a theory of their own. State this clearly, not only in the standard of review section of your reply, but in your introduction and arguments also.

When your opponent shows the court a standard of decision that's contrary to your own, and they will, acknowledge the difficulty, but demonstrate unequivocally why the standard you presented is paramount. In your reply to the government's opposition, cite the case in which the petitioner met the standard of review and compare it to your own. In a case like the example in Chapter Nine, seek out a case from your circuit where the movant won at appeal who cited the standard you rely on, such as the *Strickland* standard.

The standard of decision is just as important as a court's jurisdiction and should be considered when framing your issues, especially at appeal. Raising a minor issue that's reviewed for an abuse-of-discretion, as opposed to your more serious issues serves to divert the court's attention from the crux of your petition. You may often avoid the more lenient standard of review by framing your claim differently – as by refraining from arguing that the lower court abused its discretion, but that it had made an error of law in its judgment.

DON'T EXAGGERATE YOUR CASE

One thing I've witnessed time and again is exaggeration so a winning precedent would fit the claim. This is a mistake. Often after working long and hard on learning the facts of the case, then becoming an expert in the applicable law, you discover that the precedent you've picked out almost fits. All you have to do is leave out a couple of small facts. Don't try it. A diligent lawyer will not only catch it, but they will monopolize on the attempt and nothing else you say will matter.

As I've said before, it's impossible to win your case by dodging or minimizing the facts against you. If you can't win your case without doing this, then you can't win your case and should refrain from filing it altogether.

Scrupulous accuracy isn't just about being honest or never making a false statement, but also refraining from making statements you're not sure of. So err on the side of caution, understate your case if you must. And never exaggerate facts or cases to make a point, no matter how beneficial it may seem.

FIRST THINGS FIRST

You have ninety seconds … GO! As you may remember from "Post-Conviction Relief: The Appeal," my opinion, and that of many others, is that you have only ninety seconds to grab the attention of your reader. So, put your best argument up front. I like to provide a short but solid background and provocative questions right up front. In a §2255 motion, I make a captivating statement with a provocative question as to the first supporting fact. Then I go on to support my statement with the facts – at the end or as my last fact I then answer the question I posed. I want the reader to know my position. It's easier to get what I want when I provide a correct and just position for them to agree with, than it is to make them guess what I want. So, when it's logically permissible, put your best foot forward. Remember, first impressions make a lasting mark on the reader's mind that will be difficult to dismiss. Also remember that when the first impression is negative, it's just as difficult to dismiss, or more so. When a person takes a sip of spoiled milk, it's often impossible to get them to drink further; as so is a clerk or judge who starts reading a motion. Because judicial attention is highest in the beginning, start positive when you can.

On the flip side, of course, the requirements of reason sometimes demand that you first discuss a point that is not your strongest. For example, it's most often that a jurisdictional question must be addressed first. It makes no sense to start a discussion of the merits when your opponent first raised a jurisdictional defect in your filing. When defending a jurisdictional issue, always present your position in a positive manner first, then refute your opponent's position second. Start positive. Refuting first puts you in a defensive posture; refuting last leaves your reader focused on your opponent's failures rather than your own.

Arguing for your opponent

I have, and you will, never see a case where the government has no argument. As a matter of fact, arguing with a lawyer is a lot like mud wrestling with a pig; always remember that a pig likes mud. When you keep in mind that a good lawyer will run to a good debate – like a moth to a flame – you will realize the need to raise his or her arguments and refute them in your pleadings. I have learned through continual study that preemptive arguing is essential for many reasons. Here are five:

1) A court that thinks of your opponent's objections even before your opponent will believe that you've overlooked the obvious problems with your position;

2) where obvious objections are involved, responding only after your opponent raises them makes it seem as though you are reluctant, rather than eager, to confront them;

3) by systematically resolving counterarguments, you turn the tables and put your opponent on the defensive;

4) when you take the opportunity to introduce your opponent's argument in your own terms, you establish the initial facts that he or she is likely to leave out; and

5) when you present the entire case and all its facts, you appear trustworthy and deserving of all appropriate relief.

PRODUCTIVE REPLY

A reply is not just a required elementary step, it's a powerful tool of sound reason. Just as a debate requires, at a minimum, two opposing positions, so does an argument require two opposing parties. As such, your opponent has presented opposing theories and arguments. When your opponent has made a reasonable argument to your position, and it was well-received as convincing, you must reply.

You must frame your reply according to the structure of your opponent's response. Consider this: the human brain is one of the most complex computing devices on the planet, and as any other, if you put junk in, you will get junk out. Imagine for a moment that you approach an adding machine. You want to calculate two plus two, but you see the number 6298340 on the display. What must you do first? If the clear button comes to mind, you're on the right track. So must you clear your reader's mind.

If you've received a copy of the government's response, please note that the first thing mentioned are the reasons why the court is prohibited from reaching the merits of your claim. You guessed it; you're going to have to hit the clear button first. This is especially true when your opponent has persuasively argued that the court lacks jurisdiction or that the statute of limitations on your claim has expired. You will better understand this tactic by considering the overly burdensome workload of the court. Judges don't like to engage in more work than necessary to resolve a case. If they have a fair reason to avoid the question of whether a claim has been raised, they will, to preserve judicial resources. Today, judges are well-known to skip over all the merits of your case to first resolve a question of jurisdiction. When your opponent makes a convincing jurisdictional argument in its response, address that issue first – no matter where it appears in the response – you must clear this issue from their minds to make space for the merits you've presented.

Don't forget that once you've made space by dispatching the jurisdictional argument, you must fill that space in by reaffirming the merits of your case. Proceed immediately to your own position of the case, your major premise, and your (the true) version of the central facts. In the words of Harold R. Medina, The Oral Argument on Appeal, 20 ABA J. 139, 142-43 (1934),

> *"Nothing could be a more serious mistake than merely to answer arguments counsel for the appellant. These arguments may be skillfully designed to lead counsel for the respondent off into the woods or they may lead him there unintentionally. The proper line of attack for counsel for the respondent to adopt is to proceed to demonstrate by his discussion of the law and the facts that the judgment is right and that it should be affirmed. All other considerations are secondary."*

As you can see this quote seems productive to the prosecution, but the sound principles work both ways. Bottom line, present your case in a positive light, let this be your own personal standard.

CHAPTER 11

PLAN OF ATTACK

After having the opportunity to study the strategy of offense as a soldier, a prisoner, and a habeas advocate, I've learned to attack at many points. Some of the most effective military offensives have been based on a multiple point theory of attack. The motto of the United States Army's light infantry is Divide and Conquer. The most cunning force I've ever faced was my children in a water balloon battle. I still wonder today how my oldest son got me with a water hose. The answer is simple; my attention was divided between less damaging threats. So, as it is with legal arguments.

As we consider how to construct your argument, let's start by selecting the easiest ground to defend that favors your side of the case. In other words, when a new leading decision comes out, and it's not in your favor, don't rush to the court of appeals declaring that the Supreme Court is wrong. You'll have much better luck showing the court how the case is not applicable to your situation. Argue that it is distinguishable. If you're arguing that a new rule should be established – as in *McCarthan v. Director of Goodwill Industries-Suncoast, Inc.*, 851 F.3d 1076 – and it's a case of first impression, make your proposed rule as narrow as possible that still favors your position. You best understand this by reading the case of *Carol Anne Bond v. United States*, U.S. Supreme Court (2013). In that case, the Court asked counsel, during oral argument, if he was asking that the Court make an "as applied ruling." This little question made the difference between winning or losing. If counsel would have asked the United States Supreme Court to hold the statute unconstitutional in every case, he would have to prove that it was unconstitutional in every case. But, if he asks, as he did, for an as applied ruling, he only had to prove it was unconstitutional in Mrs. Bond's case.

You can point out that you would win either way but specify what the rule should be. Don't present your case in a way that's problematic, meaning don't propose a change in rule or law that will create more work for the court.

Don't let the government distract you from your main point. The government will make a very impressive showing, vehemently attacking your smaller points in an attempt to drive you to less defensible ground. If you claim your position is that the case is distinguishable, don't get pushed into arguing that it should be overturned. And, above all, don't let the government get away with re-characterizing your claim to make it more extreme (this is the most common danger)'. If, for example, you show that: "The lack of counsel during §2255 development warrants liberal construction," don't ignore the government's response that: "a movant has no constitutional right to counsel." You must address that the government re-characterized the claim and that they failed to address your original claim, thereby waiving any argument later.

Don't try to defend a loser. If a rule of law or procedure favoring your outcome is difficult to square with the facts of your case, forget about it. It will cost you too much time and effort to defend it against the court's application of reason. If you decide to make a claim that's not reasonable, you damage your whole case by seeming that you're desperate.

Rarely will all the points of rule and law agree with your position. Make known the points that are against you openly. If you're the moving party or an appellant, be the first to point out the obvious ones. In your opening brief, raise them candidly and explain why they don't dispose of your case. Don't leave them to the government to bring to the court's attention. Being up front in the very beginning has some benefits: One, the court knows you're not trying to hide anything; two, it shows that you have carefully considered these points but don't regard them as significant.

Be mindful of excessively weak claims. Weak claims only take time and attention away from your stronger claims. Petitioning the court in a "shot gun" approach also serves as a bad sign of your judgment and reduces the court's confidence in your stronger claims. As the old saying goes: "it's like the 'thirteenth stroke of a clock'; not only wrong in itself, but also casting doubt on all that precedes it."

The most important thing you will do in any proceeding – whether §2255, appeal, or certiorari – is selecting the claims that you'll advance. A pro se litigant advancing a good claim will beat a great prosecutor defending a bad position most of the time. In most cases, a great prosecutor will concede when he knows the law. It's the bad ones you must be concerned with (lawyers). Give a great deal of thought to what your strongest claims are, and then what order they should be presented in. Extreme emotion about a particular trial point can cloud the judgment about what your strongest claims really are.

Take for example, the pro se litigant who knows they violated the search and seizure rules to find the dope, but, he's so disturbed with the police who broke down the door that he ignores the lawyer's ineffectiveness when he didn't move for a suppression hearing.

Scattered, weak claims are a waste of time. You give the impression of insecurity and desperation. The court will likely take offense. If your strongest claims won't win, your weaker surely will not, either. It's study and practice that teaches an advocate to know which are. Pick your best reasons you should win that will stand alone. I personally don't like the "if this claim is good, then this one will be, too" theory. I want independent claims that need only supporting facts for their support. For example:

1) Breach of Contract;

2) Ineffective Assistance of Counsel;

3) Denied Counsel at a Critical Stage.

Of course, each of these claims require supporting facts, and some of the facts may even be the same, but none of them requires the others to stand.

Pro se litigants are more likely than not to multiply points. Some of the excessive claims are nothing more than previous claims stated differently. When you find that two or more claims use exactly the same supporting facts, it's time to analyze your claims to determine if they are the same. Analyze your claims to see what you can consolidate or eliminate. You never want to repeat a claim stated differently; you will appear less than diligent, and you will bore the court.

Don't let your right as a pro se litigant deprive you of a speedy resolution. Although you have a right to liberal construction, you still must present your claims clearly if you want them resolved before your sentence is over. It's often difficult for a court to glean the facts and law favoring your claim from a wordy and confusing petition, motion, or brief. Most often, judges won't take the time or trouble to decode your pleadings. They will, however, send them down to the law clerks to work on when they get bored. Remember, the court has many other cases and it's up to you to stay on the judge's desk as opposed to the clerk's dusty in-box.

Don't waste the court's time. After taking the time to identify and abandon your weak and/or repetitive claims, you don't want to undo what you've accomplished by presenting the remaining claims in camouflage. Don't hide your claims among points you address in a confusing or needlessly expansive manner. Your claims must be presented clear and brisk and left undisturbed once the content has been presented. You're not writing a book; you have no need to fill pages. The most important thing 1 do in all my work is make my point on page one.

Page limits are established in rules for the United States Court of Appeals and the Supreme Court for the United States. My practice is to stay as far away from the page limitations as possible. "Possible" being the operative word. When filing in the district courts, I follow the appellate court rules if no others apply. Remember also that you are not a slave to the rules; don't think that your petition, motion, or brief is concise because you're under the page limit. Also, refrain from adding more information because it's too short. Make your point, make it effectively, and always make it quickly. I can tell you, as an avid reader myself, that I don't read books that can't keep my attention long enough to readily finish.

CHAPTER TWELVE

PUTTING IT ALL TOGETHER

If you're reading this, you're nearly half-way through. Now, I want you to imagine that I started this book right here, without a title. Exactly, it would be holding the T.V. room door open because no one cares what's in it. The obvious truth is that I titled this book "Post-Conviction Relief: ..." showing you without question what we're talking about, and "... Advancing Your Claim" tells you what level in the series you can expect. I did that – title the book – so you would know if you want to read it, and/or if it applied to your needs as soon as you look at the cover. Let's face it; we're people, we get bored quickly. Guess what? Judges are people, too (well, except mine).

What I'm saying is: tell the judge what's going on right off. Don't leave him or her to guess while you pelt their minds with facts, laws, and case citations. I'm very fond of how the Supreme Court does it; questions first.

The Court knows right off what they're expected to answer. Yes, I do this in other courts whose rules don't forbid the practice. Yes, just like a paragraph, introduce your pleading with the questions you want answered up front, then give the answer you want in the ending. Everything else must support your resolution. Nothing else should be added. In short, state the issues first.

When you write your questions; guide them with facts. Some of the simplest of questions can draw the worst answers when undirected by the issues at hand. Example:

"Is the tire shop duty-bound to return Mr. Doe's car to him in good running order, once paid?"

Seems obvious, right? Well, not exactly. This simple question has too many variable, or unknown, facts. Any reasonable court would require an evidentiary hearing just to establish a sound question that's supported by controlling facts. The question is better presented like this:

"On March 1, 2017, Mr. Doe had his car towed to A-l Tire Shop, where he requested an evaluation for an engine overhaul. After the evaluation cost was paid, Mr. Doe refused the estimate and retrieved his car. Was the tire shop obligated to overhaul the engine for the cost of an evaluation?"

As you can see here, I provided enough facts concerning what was expected. This makes your question clear and easy to answer in the beginning. You must always fill in the facts that narrow the issue to only what must be decided. If you read the question and are able to answer it one way or another immediately, it's probably a good question. But, if you have to ask questions first, you're absolutely wrong. Remember also that to win an argument concerning your issue, it helps to be supported by law and previous decisions. If you think that a Judge will make a whimsical decision and scour case authorities to find support, you would be wrong. Most commonly, the principle and authorities will lead an honorable judge to his or her conclusion, rather than merely provide later support for a conclusion arrived at by the judge's independent sense of morality. It's important to show that your issue is supported, not only by law but also by previous precedent that reached a reasonable result.

Before I get into putting your claims on paper, let's discuss your ending. The most convincing conclusions make a statement that compels the reader to do something; not just anything, but what you're asking. "For the foregoing reasons," or anything like that, won't work. It should briefly remind the reader what your principle arguments are, and then describe why the rule of law favors your resolve. Explain exactly what relief you want and show that anything different would constitute injustice.

ELEMENTS OF A BRIEF

As we explore the briefing process, keep in mind that the practice is used or should be used, no matter which court you're addressing. Also, keep in mind that the process of submitting arguments in writing dates back to ancient Rome. That means that I'm probably not providing any significant change to the process. What I'm doing is attempting to provide laymen a practicable method to present your arguments where counsel is not a guarantee. As you can imagine, I also had to learn what I am explaining to you now; so if you're an avid reader, you may have been exposed to some of this material in the past. What I ask of you is that, as you learn, share your new-found knowledge. Let's make a difference.

MEANING OF LAW

For those of you who are locked up, you may already know where I'm going with this. The textual interpretation of law is complicated, and there exists no all-encompassing way to make it easy. Therefore, you must first learn why you're here.

The law requires that you be identified as engaging in conduct that is determined to be criminal by an act of a legislative body, i.e. Congress. Unfortunately, it usually works the other way around. Take the Controlled Substance statutes in title 21 U.S.C. for example; as statutes were enacted to control the distribution of certain drugs, law enforcement went hunting for those who had possession of those drugs. A fine example is the Eighteenth Amendment, which was ratified in 1919. The Eighteenth Amendment banned the manufacture, sale, transportation, etc., of all intoxicating liquors which Congress defined as containing 0.5 percent alcohol. The true effect of the Eighteenth Amendment was that it propelled organized criminal enterprises/ that bootlegged liquors or opened disguised bars, into mainstream commerce.

A commonly misused statute is 21 U.S.C. §846, the drug conspiracy statute. In most cases, a local officer gets lucky and arrests a drug user. The user is most often offered a deal to forego conviction. The deal is: provide ten alternative arrests and go free or mitigate sentence exposure.

This is done by use of the User's phone record. The law enforcement agency simply alleges a conspiracy case rather than simple possession, transfers the case to the federal government, then everyone in the user's contact list becomes a con-conspirator. All a judge requires to convict all the innocent victims, is a finding of good reason for the court to determine the initial arrestee is credible. This is most often done when the original arrestee swears to a prepared statement as to each con-conspirator (victim) and a threat of five to forty years in prison. In the more difficult cases of the innocent who wants to go to trial, the court makes it extremely difficult for the victim to prove his innocence. The fact is that the court only profits from convictions, not justice. Notice in the above scenarios you find no actual drug possession. The original arrestee need only claim that the victim talked about drugs. This theory is best exemplified by our current administration. President Donald Trump and U.S. Attorney General Jeff Sessions have declared the need for more convictions, with no discussion of justice or fighting crime. For these reasons, you must learn the textual interpretation of the applicable statutes. Just as we studied 28 U.S.C. §2255 in an earlier chapter, you must learn the meaning of your statute of conviction and penalty statute. Currently they are seeking to employ the Death Penalty for drug offenses.

It's important to understand the meaning of the text before you come to an unwavering conclusion. You must read the entire subsection, and the Congressional notes, not just the part at issue. Often you will find statutes and rules that can be understood as having more than one meaning. In that event, the court will want to define the application further to give meaning to the context of the document in which it appears. Often, you will find the meaning you're looking for in a provision that follows.

Here are some simple rules that I've learned:

- Words are presumed to be understood in their ordinary meaning.

- Unless specifically designated otherwise, a word or phrase is assumed to have the same meaning throughout a document.

- A document should be construed as to provide an interpretation that renders its provisions harmoniously, and not contradictory.

- an interpretation should not be adopted if it renders the provision in question redundant, unlawful, or invalid. Especially as it relates to other statutes and rules.

- If possible, every word should have purpose; no word should be read as extra.

- Acts of Congress – and other legislative bodies – should be interpreted in a way that avoids placing their Constitutionality in doubt.

In the event your argument depends on the proper reading of a criminal statute, always begin with the words of its text to establish your premise. Move on to how the law or the wording of the statute affects you and your case as the minor premise. Finally, make your point and relief clear in your conclusion.

Where you and your opponent present an equally sound argument, both based on the text of the statute; the court will resort to the next step to resolve the issue. In cases such as this, judges often use legislative history. Since we're prepared for such things we can use legislative history as well. Considering also the time required to thoroughly review the history of a major act or Congress, I suggest you start early and read it more than once. In the event the government fails to bring up the legislative history, be the first, but keep it short. You can simply state that: "The clarity of the text is confirmed by the legislative history."

CHAPTER THIRTEEN

SUPPORTING DECISIONS

A.K.A., Caselaw; Earlier decisions of courts are very helpful when arguing a point that is supported by both parties. As I've touched on before, neither our judicial system nor those who run it are perfect. I've been witness to court decisions that outright violate the law and Constitution; only because that's how a Superior Court decided the matter in an earlier case. This occurs because there are two kinds of authorities (case law); governing – which the court must follow, and persuasive – which the court could follow.

Governing authorities are more important and should get more of your time and effort. In the event you're preparing your first brief for the Court of Appeals or a reply in the district, the most important authority you can use is caselaw from the Circuit Court whose circuit you're in. The next most important is the court immediately superior to the court you're filing in. You will accomplish nothing by arguing Supreme Court precedent in a district court where the Court of Appeals holds a different view. If, however, the Court of Appeals has not addressed the point, Supreme Court opinions will be the most important.

If, however, you feel that the decision directly above is wrong, you should argue that point. But, remember when a governing authority is flatly against you; you will lose at the district and the Circuit. You must be prepared to go all the way to the Supreme Court. The downside is that if you have other meritorious grounds – on which you could win – they may be denied also, without reaching the merits. When you know you're right and you're prepared to put your best foot forward, and start walking, see *Welch v. United States*, _____ U.S. _____ (2016); *Yates v. United States*, _____ U.S. _____ (2015).

On the less risky side, when you have additional claims, raise the issue lightly. If, for example, you're preparing a reply to the government's response, that raises the defunct authority, in the district court that's bound by a prior Court of Appeals precedent; it's of little use to argue it at length. Simply state that the decision mistakes the law; that way you will have placed your view in the record. In the event you get an adverse ruling, you must do the same before the panel of the Court of Appeals so there will be no doubt of your right to raise that issue in your rehearing or rehearing en banc.

Don't fall into the category of average, by ignoring non-governing precedents. Nor should you forget the hierarchy of persuasiveness as most advocates do. The most compelling, i.e. persuasive non-governing case authorities are the dicta – which only has validity because of the authority of the person who makes the statement – of governing courts and the holdings of governing courts in similar cases. This group of authorities should be quoted as persuasive but be sure to identify that they are only dicta. Next in line are the final decisions of courts of equal authority whose law governs your case. In the United States, you have one Court of Appeals that's divided into Thirteen circuits. All circuits divide the workload that's distributed among panels, which are groups of three circuit judges, in most cases. Ordinarily, one panel will not rule against another panel in the same circuit. Finally, are the holdings of trial courts in your district.

Among this multitude of authority, they too are divided by their level of influence. The most convincing, in each of the previous categories, are the ones where litigants, situated just like you, lost in the district, but were corrected in the circuit. In almost every §2255 case, you must seek out victories in the circuit only, unless the district decision is exactly like your case and was issued by the same judge. Be sure to point out that ruling against your position would result in a reversal just like the case you're quoting. The next most important are the ones where movants have won, being granted relief and the Court of Appeals affirms the victory. Point this fact out to the court, stating in your reply that "Your Honor, if you rule in my favor, you will be affirmed in the Court of Appeals."

Another deeply rooted principle is the date of the ruling you depend on. I've observed, much too often, pro se litigants find an old cite book and quote old holdings, sometimes even overruled. Be sure the case you're quoting is indeed persuasive. This occurs most often when it's recent. Rule of thumb; old cases may remain controlling, where persuasive cases are a lot like left-over fish and visiting relatives – they all start to stink in time.

PRESENTATION OF CASE CITATIONS

This is a hot subject in legal writing. Why? Because most people screw this up one way or another. Try to imagine for a moment, a fire chief who dispatches his men to a structure fire that is fully involved. Yes, your criminal case is that serious if you're innocent. Now take it a step further by imagining the chief giving his men water but sending them in the wrong direction. That's what happens when you present case law incorrectly. Take for example *Strickland v. Washington*, 466 U.S. 668 (1984). In that case, the government, i.e. *Strickland*, won. I use *Strickland* regularly in §2255 cases that I prepare for other prisoners, so, what? Am I helping the enemy? Hardly. It's how you present your case citation that matters. As a matter of fact, *Strickland* is often the governing case I use in ineffective assistance of counsel cases, because it contains passages that say precisely what I want my major premise to be. Let's take for example that I intend to present a ground showing that counsel didn't investigate a case where an alibi defense existed. You can bet I'm going to quote *Strickland*. That's because, although *Strickland* (the government) won, the Supreme Court still defined counsel's obligation to investigate. As you can conclude by now, my syllogism will begin with this as my major premise:

> "... Counsel has a duty to make reasonable investigations or to make a reasonable decision that makes particular investigation unnecessary." *Strickland v. Washington*, 466 U.S. 668, 691.

Minor premise:

> "Counsel is ineffective when he decides not to interview witnesses as support to determine that existing witness testimony warrants no further investigation into the actual innocence defense."

Now that you can see how powerful a governing authority can be, let me explain how it should be presented.

In the previous example, you see that I quoted exactly what the court said in *Strickland* – noted by the quotation marks ("") – I then listed the case location immediately after the ending punctuation. As you can imagine, a controlling case passage can become just as much a cliché as "My Constitutional Rights" have become. Therefore, in your writing, you show the court where you found the passage, i.e. the numbers and letters that follow the case name. But what I consider to be the most important is what comes before the case name. What comes before the case name is your fire chief, that one word or combination of words tells the court exactly how you intend to apply the case to your argument. As you probably noticed earlier, I placed absolutely nothing before the case name in my example. That too has a purpose.

What comes before the case name is called a "signal," be it a word, letters, or phrase, it tells the reader how you're applying the case. This is one application where liberal construction under *Haines v. Kerner*, 404 U.S. 519, will hurt your case. Always remember that, in collateral proceedings, the court is your first adversary. The court's job in collateral proceedings is to preserve the finality of the conviction. When a court finds a misused "signal" word, your brief becomes their playground. Immediately, they liberally construe your pleading into something that offers no relief. Although the courts will deny this fact; remember that the numbers don't lie. This is what I've learned:

1) Signals of Support.
No Signal at all – The case cited is quoted, and directly states the proposition; is followed by the digest location; identifies any authority it refers to in the text. I use no signal when I'm quoting the words of a governing case directly, followed by the digest location for the exact paragraph where it's found.

e.g. – The case cited quotes the proposition; in addition, other cases state the same thing, but it would be of no help to list them.

Accord – "Accord" is commonly used when two or more sources state or support the proposition, but the text quotes, or refers to, only one; the other sources are then introduced by "accord." Similarly, the law of one jurisdiction may be cited as being in accord with the law of another. I routinely quote a Supreme Court case – I use as my major premise – then I list one case that "accords" with it from the circuit I'm filing in. Also remember when filing in the district, to use cases by the judge you're in front of.

See – Cited authority supports your proposition. "See" is used in the place of no Signal [" "] when the proposition is not directly stated by the authority but obviously follows from it; it is inferred that the authority is in agreement with the proposition you're supporting with it.

See also – Signals that the authority provides additional material that supports your proposition. "See also" is commonly used then citing an authority supporting your proposition but follows a previously quoted authority that directly supports your proposition. I suggest you use a parenthetical phrase that explains the relevance of the additional authority or its material.

cf – Cited authority supports a proposition different from the main proposition but is sufficiently analogous to lend support. "Cf" literally means "compare." The citation's relevance will usually be clear to the reader only if it's explained. Parenthetical explanations are required.

2) Signals that present a comparison
Compare; and; with; [and] – Comparing authorities will offer support when you're suggesting a particular method of reasoning you want the court to follow. When used as a signal, "compare" must be used in conjunction with "with"; the "with" is preceded by a comma, as is "and" when used. The relevance of the comparison will usually be clear to the reader only if it is explained. Parenthetical explanations following each authority are required.

3) Signals that indicate contradictions
Contra – Cited authorities are in direct contradiction to your proposition. "Contra" is used where "[no signal]" would be used for support, indicating a direct quote to the contrary.

But see – Cited authority clearly supports a proposition contrary to your main proposition. "But see" is used, as in the opposite, where "see" would be used for support.

But cf. – Cited authority supports a proposition analogous to the contrary of your main proposition. Requires explanation.

When compounding negative signals, one following another, "But" must be omitted from those that follow the primary negative authority. The creation of a double negative in signals has the same effect as a double negative in grammar. "Ain't not" won't work.

ARRANGING AUTHORITIES

In the event – and I strongly discourage a beginner's attempt – you feel the need to compound authorities and signals by stringing citations separated by semi-colons; you must put them in the proper order. Where one authority is obviously offering more support or authority than others cited within a signal, or no signal, it must be the first listed. I strongly suggest that cases within a signal be arranged according to the courts issuing the cited opinion. I generally use, and preferably quote. Supreme Court cases as my main support. I then go to circuit court opinions that agree with the holding, preferably from the circuit I'm filing in. And last. I'll list decisions handed down by the judge I'm dealing with. Remember that when quoting first, you use no signal, the next supporting case that doesn't use the quote directly will require the first signal word.

SECTION THREE
CHAPTER FOURTEEN

REPLIES

What's the purpose of a brief or reply? Ah, the age-old question. I've heard time and again, over the years, how a memorandum should be used rather than a brief. Let me take a moment to clear this up for you … WRONG! Don't remind the court about the law. Don't pretend to know what you do not, i.e. the law. The people you're dealing with will dominate you in a pure question of law. Stand on your own ground. The facts, that's what belongs to you. The actual purpose of a brief or a reply is to make the court's job easier. The court's job, in your case, is to determine the facts as they relate to the law, so let's give them the facts. Anything else is a secondary initiative. You achieve this goal by presenting the facts in a short, simple, and straightforward brief written in plain English.

You will find that several people have written books on brief writing – including this one – but what's important is that your facts be presented clearly and quickly. So, as I've suggested before, read everything you can, and confirm everything. Dismiss the nonsense and above all, take no one's opinion for granted concerning your case.

Keep in mind that an effective brief cannot be a patchwork of paragraphs you get from one source or another; your brief must form a clear explanation of your facts and your theory of the case under the law. Your brief should be a clear road map that guides the court to the result you're asking for. In this section, I'm going to provide the structure that I've learned works. I have taken the time to learn from many sources; from experienced lawyers, scholars of law, and a dearly departed Supreme Court Justice. I do suggest that if you happen to form a better idea, go bury it somewhere. It has no place in court.

CONFIDENCE IN ENGLISH

What would you think of a lawyer who showed up at a visit trying to talk to you with a mouth full of snuff, or maybe without even bringing a pen and paper? Confidence? Hardly. A lawyer has only one tool to express his thoughts; language. Lawyers spend years honing the best speaking and writing skills of probably any other profession in the legal world. You are likely not a lawyer.

You, regardless of your education or profession, most likely don't share the same love of words, nor do you use them exactly. Naturally, this is not a skill you can acquire overnight, nor can it be done in the month or so you have to prepare your brief or reply.

> *Author's Note: If you plan to assist other inmates on a regular basis; realize that learning to speak and write can be lifelong projects, so begin to learn now. You can learn an effective prose by reading regularly. Get a dictionary and look up words you don't know. You will learn exact word usage that way. So, get out of the T.V. room and read a book. At least one a week.*

Be careful of what you read on a regular basis. You can read Shakespeare once among months of tabloids and you will write like the tabloids. Don't read briefs by lawyers, either. Lawyers are condemned to a life of reading legal digests, as a profession, which are only a step above the tabloids. Many judges will tell you that, to become a good legal writer, you must spend your time reading good prose, not legal materials. So, start reading good articles in mainstream publications like respectable magazines that address a general audience. So, get out of the law library and read some current articles.

The advantage of putting the case in your own words – fully contained in a comprehensible reply brief – is that it provides a complete description of your side of the case to retro-readers and it serves as a definitive reminder of your positive case to forward readers. Either way your position of the case will be the last complete presentation the court or clerk will read.

> *Author's Note: Some of the greatest legal minds in history believed that since there are probably more forward readers than there are retro, a writer should refute any well-presented points raised by an adversary first. Otherwise, in the case of a weak response, begin with a quick summary of your own case, and then show the inadequacy of your opponent's response.*

Remember also the things you can't present in a reply brief: no new arguments, claims, or grounds; just because you forgot them or you didn't have room in your initial filing does not give you leave to add them in your reply. Recap your case, reply to any new materials or issues raised by the government, and then bring it to a close.

3) Many of you reading this book now may be in a collateral proceeding. It's important for you to know that everything in your filings are presumed as true, unless they are refuted by the record, so please consult the record often. I always quote the record when possible. And, don't argue the law. You're likely not qualified to stand toe-to-toe with these people, stick to the facts. That's what I do.

CHAPTER SIXTEEN

STARTING YOUR DRAFT

Please don't misconstrue my humor as to have a religious connotation. But, on the seventh day, it's time to write rather than rest – barring any restraints established by your faith, of course. You should remember that   I said your outline could be collapsed or expanded. And, please don't take this as my own, originally established rule; I've learned a lot of how I write from my high school literature teacher, the late Randy Simmons. Also consider that many of the principles in writing have been refined by learning from others, such as Antonin Scalia, Brian Gardner, and others. What is my own is my way of applying what I've learned, which brings me to you. I'm about to share with you how I structure my writing. No matter how innovative this may seem to you, let me assure you that it's nothing new. People have been expressing themselves in legal writing since as early as ancient Rome. So, as we go through this section, don't be afraid to develop your own way of expressing yourself, as long as you stay within the boundaries of the rules.

I chose day seven to start writing because most often the court gives thirty (30) days to reply.

My personal preference is to mail my completed work out one week before it's due, just in case you get locked down because of a hurricane. Today is September 10th, 2017, and I know people who are locked down because Hurricane Irma is ravishing Florida. All this in mind leaves me twenty – one (21) days to reply: I think for one third; I write for one third; and finally, I read, revise, and type for one third. I set these strict timelines because my hardest task is getting started. I don't know about other authors, but me personally, I have to force myself to begin writing each and every day. And I love writing. So, establish your schedule, and force yourself to write according to the schedule you have established.

> *Author's Note: Start every element on a new page. You will be changing things and you don't want to rewrite what you normally wouldn't need to.*

QUESTIONS

Anything I write has a purpose. In legal writing, I seek resolution to a question, and I want the court to answer the questions. Your primary concern is to present sound questions. The resolution you propose in your writing must answer the questions that you present, and the answers must be fair and legal. Remember, no difference equals no relief.

BODY OF YOUR ARGUMENT

I hope you noticed that I've departed from the rules. Don't worry, the order in which I prepare is not my order of presentation. I move to the body of my argument immediately after writing my questions because of their obvious relation. My questions briefly present my issues, and my argument answers those issues in detail.

Once you've answered your own questions, determine, from your factual basis, what facts you must include in a statement of facts to support your argument.

INTRODUCTION

Moving on to the first impression of your filing: After the court reviews your issue and glances over the arguments, the judge is likely to investigate what the cause of your filing is. If you've read any of my previous publications, or my filings, you'll find I'm notorious for being straight to the point; "Mr. Riggs was prejudiced by ineffective assistance of trial counsel which caused the incarceration of an innocent defendant. Thus, he files his reply to the 'Government's Response to Mr. Riggs' §2255' in an effort to correct the oversites in the government's brief ..."

One thing that's important to remember when writing an introduction; it's short, kind of a brief to a brief. If you intend to become a careful writer, you have to learn when to stop writing once you've started. Introduce your brief and its purpose; don't reiterate your case-in-chief in your introduction.

At the end of day seven you should have completed your questions, your arguments, and your introduction. Great, go play handball, read a book or whatever. Just stay out of the S.H.U. What I like to do at the end of these three elements is to lay them aside and get my mind off the case. On day eight, it's time to put your elements in order; questions, introduction, then the arguments. Read what you have and see if you get a clear picture. Read as though you're someone else, so you don't leave pertinent information out. Now let's make it better. Revise your work. Yes, a rewrite. I suggest a rewrite because people hate to copy something that's already complete. When you want your work brief, concise, and succinct, all you have to do is rewrite it. You will find all the useless stuff in it, because you don't want to rewrite it.

ELEMENTS

Once you're done with the rewrite, take the next 48 hours completing your brief. Fill in all the blank spots. Refer to Federal Rule of Appellate Procedure, Rule 28 for guidance. Pay close attention to your Statement of Facts, Conclusion – where you specify the relief you want – and your Summary of your Arguments. When you write the "Summary of the Arguments," pay special attention to clarity. Summarizing sharpens your perspective of what you're saying, and you might feel the need to revise your arguments; that's normal. Do as you must and write a new summary to match.

On day ten, bright and early in the morning, find something to do that's not case related. I want you to forget that brief for the next 48 hours. On day eleven is when the work starts. I want you to pretend to be the enemy for just one day. Remember the duty of a judge – preserve the finality of the judgment – as you perform a critical reading of your own work. You can even enlist friends in this part, if you feel so inclined. In this step, you need to find what the judge is looking for – a reason to deny the action. This is where I find so many civil attorneys fail; they fail because they assume fairness in the proceeding as in all other civil cases. However, what they fail to realize is that the judge has a duty to remain biased, favoring the integrity of the court. In any collateral proceeding to a criminal conviction, the judge has a duty to preserve the finality of your conviction, the judgment.

First, read your questions; do they seem easy to answer in your favor? Does the implied answer follow the law? Are they being adequately supported?

Second, read the summary of the argument; do you present a good, clear argument? Does the argument follow the law?

Third, read the Conclusion; do you make a reasonable request? Is the proposed question legal? Will the proposed resolution create legal issues in other cases to follow?

Now let's go back and read the whole brief, reply, or motion from the beginning. Remember you're going to do this as though you want to deny your own work. Let's do this one element at a time. And, make sure you take good notes.

> *Author's note: This book is being written for a variety of applications; replies for §2255's, §2254's, §2241's, appeals, and other writings in federal courts. As I go through this exercise. I'll be listing elements required in all the above listed*

applications. So, some won't apply to your writing. It's your duty to know which under the rules are, so pay attention.

ANSWERS

As mentioned earlier, no court in America – except the Supreme Court of the United States – makes mention of presenting questions for review in their rules. Thus, you have no support in rule or law to present your questions for review as the first thing the judge sees. If it's of any consolation, I've done this in every federal court across the country and not received one reprimand. But, because I present questions for review in such splendid isolation from all other material, I set myself apart from all other advocates. Therefore, your questions must be deserving of the grandeur you suggest. As discussed earlier, your questions must invoke an immediate answer from everyone who reads them. Nonsensical questions will lead to a superficial read by someone gleaning through your brief looking for any reason to deny it.

The outcome of the case can be directed by the court's understanding of the issues. Any judge will be reading the questions as a preview to the issues of the case. Therefore, the judge will be reading the questions to: first, determine if they are presenting the issue fairly; and second, to determine if you present a clear issue that's supported by sound facts.

As a pro se litigant, you will find difficulty in capturing the court's attention. So, you want to develop a premise that will pull a court's attention to your theory of the case. You do this by asking provocative questions that demand an immediate answer in one's mind.

INTERESTED PARTIES AND CORPORATE DISCLOSURE

When filing, in either the Court of Appeals, or the Supreme Court of the United States, a Certificate of Interested Parties is required. See Federal Rules of Appellate procedure (11th Cir. Local) Rule 26.1 and Rules for the Supreme Court of the United States, Rule 24(l)(b). This element is required on these two applications but is not required nor desired in any other federal court. I don't use them anywhere other than required by rule.

TABLE OF CONTENTS

This element contains more than I could possibly describe here. But it's primarily just as it sounds; it's a road map to your theory – basically, a finding tool. Consider also that a judge or clerk is going to look at your Table of Contents just like you look at the table of this book. One, it tells you if it contains what is necessary. And two, it gives you an opinion to whether the book is constructed soundly. A court, on the other hand, uses the table to get a preview of your argument and to see if you arrived at your theory in a reasonable, syllogistic manner. So, let's look to see if your Section Headings and Subsections are full informative sentences. Remember, this book is about stepping out of the kiddie pool and "Advancing Your Claim," so instead of just listing your "Arguments": Section Heading, follow it with particular Subsections, and appropriate headings, i.e.,

Note that in the example, I indented my Section Heading and then indented my Subsection even more. Notice also that my Subsection is a full and informative sentence. Moreover, in my Table of Contents, both my Section Heading ("Arguments") and my Subsection heading (full informative sentence) appears in an outline-style, illustrated in a progressive indentation, displaying the hierarchy of my argument. Be sure you provide a difference in your indentation between Section and Subsection, which is indented more.

TABLE OF AUTHORITIES

This is sometimes added to the Table of Contents by some advocates, even seasoned lawyers. Don't make that mistake. This one mistake often leads to misnumbering the table, more than any other. The Table of Authorities should be listed in your Table of Contents as a different table, never combine the two. Next, while you're still impersonating a judge, see how careful a writer you're dealing with. Did he use recent or controlling precedent cases? Did he Shepardize his authorities? Are the quoted authorities relevant to the proposed arguments?

STATEMENT OF JURISDICTION

This element is one I provide in every filing. In the Supreme Court and the Court of Appeals, it's set out in the rules with a full description of its contents. But I also provide a brief statement to the district courts by providing the statute or rule that provides the court with the authority to provide the relief I'm requesting.

INTRODUCTION OR PRELIMINARY STATEMENT

This element is only used in district courts, therefore not recommended in any court where you give statements of facts in the case, or summaries. I use this element predominantly to rebut my opponent when he files a messy response, or to present questions in a primary motion. This is also a very good place to set out a Summary of the Arguments presented in a reply in a district court. When using this element in a §2255 proceeding, stick to the facts. Sarcasm and personal attacks are not well received. For those of you on appeal, check your rules for the requirement of a "Statement of the Issues Presented for Review."

STATEMENT OF THE CASE

This element in some courts is called the "Proceedings Below." This element is used in some circuits of the Court of Appeals; be sure to check your local rules. When reading this section, look for arguments; one single argument is grounds to hang it up. This element, where required, is nothing more than a list of court proceedings that lead to the case at hand; how the case got where it is. Including this element incorrectly in a Writ of Certiorari will result in instant denial.

STATEMENT OF THE FACTS

Provided you've been as studious as you should be, given your current tenure you've discovered that 90% of this book concerns a critical presentation of your facts. Therefore, in this section, your evaluation of those facts should be just as critical in this stage of preparation.

In almost all sets of court rules, a "statement of facts" is required near the beginning this is called the Statement of the Case in the Rules of the Supreme Court. Your facts should be set out as a narration without argument, and in a chronological order. Two things a court will be looking for here are facts that are left out or misstatements of facts. In either case, you will lose credibility in the court. These are critical mistakes. As you evaluate this element, perhaps you should also pretend to be the prosecutor as well, because I can assure you he will be looking at the filing as well. Both the court and the government will be looking at the facts, because nothing is easier than pointing out your errors. And, nothing is more damaging to your credibility than making a mistake in your own facts.

When your position is that you're disputing erroneous facts, and that issue raises a genuine basis for argument, you must use your Statement of Facts to correct the error. So, to say that you can't raise an argument in your Statement of Facts is not to say that it cannot be different from the government's assertion of the facts. Needless to say, your statement should be set out to persuade the court concerning the truth. In most criminal cases, the government will omit facts to make you seem culpable. Clear this up by making sure the court knows why you were there, rather than just that you were, without explanation.

A complete Statement of the Facts includes facts that seem harmful to your case. Those facts will come out anyway, and if you run from them, or omit them, you do nothing but give the government an opportunity to claim your word can't be trusted.

In your evaluation of this element, determine if it tells a complete story. You're looking for a good timeline of events that's presented in chronological order, that's a sequence of all the necessary facts. Are the facts presented by time, day by day, and hour by hour?

As you can see, I've had you look at your Statement of Facts in all directions. That's because nothing is more important than a proper presentation of your facts. Here again, I'm going to provide a positive method of presenting your facts. And, remember this is advancing your claim, so it is a bit different from other books I've written for beginners.

Dates are very important to your facts, but too many confuse your reader. A few dates will be important, but never repeat one in a successive event that happened on the same day. It's much more acceptable to your reader to use "The next morning," "That afternoon," etc. Keep in mind that putting a date in front of every statement adds unnecessary text and leads your reader to believe that you're moving on to the next subject, causing confusion.

If you're filing a reply, you must counter the government's presentation with a full counterstatement of the facts. It's a guarantee that the government will tell a story in a way that is best for their own theory of the case, regardless of the truth. If you don't tell the story your own way, you give your acquiescence to the government's position, leaving absolutely no reason to file a reply in the first place.

To overcome the possibility that the court will assume the government's Statement of Facts is true, and fail to read yours, start yours with a brief introduction indicating that the government's statement is incorrect or incomplete. In a reply, this is preferred, not only because of the tactical advantage of telling the court the real story, but also because you want your reply to be self-contained – a complete document the court can refer to for all aspects of your case.

SUMMARY OF THE ARGUMENTS

This is not an introduction, nor is it a replacement for a Statement of Issues; the Summary of the Arguments is not only a preview of what's to come, it's just what it says; it's a summary of the arguments under the individual topics. I often refrain from giving a lengthy summary because a court will often read the argument anyway. Therefore, I only add it if the rules require it. Then I try to keep each topic to only two or three short paragraphs a piece.

ARGUMENTS

OK, here we are; this is the big one. If I've told you 500 times, I've not told you enough. A *pro se* litigant wins by presenting the facts of the case. As you evaluate this section, I want you to consider one thing; are you being honest? If you're a novice trying to sound like a lawyer, you're not being honest with the court or yourself.

I can't stress to you enough how easy it is to screw up in a purely legal question. I don't care how many cases you string along or whose lawyer you got it from, it's likely going to be a mistake. Arguing law requires the efforts of an expert, and just recently, I was witness to an Eleventh Circuit

Court judge who exclaimed that he had been wrong for 18 years. You attempting to sound like a lawyer is what the court is looking for to deny you relief. Don't try it.

Again, present a clear reading of the facts, explain how the law relates to the facts of your case, and finally, show one or two governing cases that agree with you. Above all, keep it brief, and move on to the next court if you must. The more you say now, the more the government will bring up later.

CONCLUSION

Most rules require a Conclusion in which you specify the relief you seek. This is what you should do, but don't stop there. In a short statement, tell the court how it should rule. Without just repeating your section titles, you should use one or two paragraphs that summarize your winning syllogism in a fresh, new statement. Make yourself clear: "the real facts are …" "the controlling law says …" "previous courts hold …" "This court should grant the requested relief." Make this your last kick at a stubborn mule, and make it good.

APPENDIX

Above all, your appendix should include every court entry you reference. Don't depend on the government to do the right thing, because they won't. If you've quoted parts of law that are lengthy, add those also. What's also important is that the Appendix is only used in the Court of Appeals or the Supreme Court. Don't use it in the district, just attach as necessary.

CHAPTER SEVENTEEN

REVISING A BRIEF

The morning of day twelve, you should have a fist full of notes and, quite possibly, certain paragraphs of your work rewritten for a second time. Now it's time to read for clarity. Making a good, clear statement should be your primary concern. Set aside all other characteristics of writing to make room for clarity. One of my worst pet peeves, as an author, is to repeat any word in a paragraph. But, in legal writing, the same word should be used to refer to a particular concept, although elegance of style would avoid such repetition in favor of long lists of synonyms. Never use a word that a judge or a clerk may have to look up, especially if it's critical to your point. This means that nothing important should be in a footnote. As a matter of fact, 1 don't use footnotes at all in my own work.

Your quest for clarity means that you should shun legalistic lingo such as "wherefore now." Who uses that at a party?! Make your points and ask for your specified relief in a blunt, straight forward manner. Above all, don't use words you don't understand.

Clarity is sufficiently justified where it guarantees you will be understood. Keep in mind that when you're clear, it's harder for your adversary (government) or the court to re-characterize your claims. Think of it like this; if you get a response that's hard to understand, it's hard to understand for everyone involved. When this happens, as I advised earlier, you can simply brush it aside and give your theory of the case clearly. So, write clearly and this won't happen to you. Neither the government nor the court can distort what you're saying if it's clear,

SECTION HEADINGS

Divide your work in sections to keep it simple. I've learned to avoid using: Section, then Subsection, then Numbered Paragraphs. My most common practice now is to section my work "Arguments," then identify each argument with a statement "The district court erred by failing to resolve all habeas issues." Imagine for a moment I used a subheading like "Habeas Issues." The latter, or the Wrong Choice, leaves the court to wonder what my argument is. The previous, however, makes clear that the court erred and how.

Because I'm going to be brief – and I'm only arguing the facts and how they relate to the applicable law – I can afford to start each section at the top of its own page and still come in well under the page and word limitations. Notice when a court wants you to understand a lengthy brief or report, they use a single identification method, such as a P.S.R. Any identified number will reference one paragraph and that number will appear nowhere else.

When I was going through the criminal trial process, I wrote a thirteen-page brief just as a lawyer would. It was very systematic, and each paragraph was easily identifiable. At that time, I had been abandoned by counsel and the court refused to appoint counsel leaving me to defend my brief on my own. Both the court and the government's attorney used duplicate paragraph identifiers to try to confuse me. The court even suggested I meant to mix the two.

I share this experience because I learned from it. Today I number each and every paragraph with a number that's never duplicated anywhere in the brief. I start with the first paragraph that follows the Jurisdictional Statement. This method – although not preferred by the government – leaves every paragraph in your brief identified by a singular numerical system. No two paragraphs are numbered the same, thus unique.

BORING?

Judges don't read boring briefs. So, if your brief bores you, imagine what you're doing to the judge. You must keep the court's interest. Think back to a movie you've watched 50 times. That's right, you'd rather mop your cell. Your work is a movie. It's either new and interesting, or it's a rerun to that judge or clerk. Again, don't try to teach them the law, believe me when I say that they have been through years of study and practice in the field of law, so any lesson you're giving is not only boring, but also offensive. What's new to a judge is the facts, so make them interesting. One thing that I can guarantee is that your judge or clerk has never been arrested, never hauled into a criminal court as a defendant, and you wouldn't be in prison if your claim and facts had been properly presented before, so let's present your facts.

True crime drama is a multi-billion-dollar business. Why? Because it's interesting to those who have never been there. So, let's tell your story in your brief. Be clear, but also be entertaining. If you go back to my earlier description of an arrest scenario, you'll have a good idea about how you should tell your story.

TAKING IT TO PRINT

Well, here we are; day fourteen. It's almost over. Now you have a handful of notes, ten thousand little marks on your brief, and you're ready to give it one more read. Once you get all your fine tuning done, it's time to type. You don't want to take anything away from its clarity by doing a bad job of typing, so let's go over some basics. Again, less is more when you emphasize something on a written page. It's very easy to lose the forest for the trees when you over-use any type of emphasis. So, bold, underline, and capitalize your Section Headings; bold and underline (Upper and lower case) your Sub-Sections; and finally, bold print your citations (cases). Nothing else and no other emphasis.

Footnotes? Don't. Now, let's go on to the actual typing. A good-looking document draws many a dollar from consumers. When you read an instructional book, you automatically dismiss the credibility of someone who can't spell. The same is true for convincing your court that your view is correct. A poorly typed brief or motion won't invite a reader to indulge willingly. I know that you're likely very limited concerning resources but put your best foot forward. And, for those submitting hand-written work, remember *Boag v. MacDougall*, 454 U.S. 364, where the plaintiff wrote his petition on toilet paper in the S.H.U.

SECTION FOUR

INTRODUCTION

It's abnormal for me, as an author, to introduce a specific section of a publication. This section, however, is deserving of just such attention. My primary concern is to make you aware of the obvious; ninety percent of all post-conviction relief books are written based completely on theory, how habeas corpus is supposed to work. I also include much of the normal theory in my books that address beginners. But, this section, of this book, is for those of you who need the facts instead of the fairy tale. So, let's be clear, I am not a lawyer, although I am well-studied, I harbor an unparalleled disdain for that profession.

At the tender age when ideals and passions are developed, I joined the United States Army, taking an oath to uphold and defend the Constitution of the United States against all enemies, foreign and domestic. Even before I began my study of law, I viewed our government's Constitution as a device that protected the people from any possible overzealousness of our very own government. As a soldier, it was my duty to uphold and defend the law that protected the people of the United States from any and all governmental encroachment upon the freedom of fellow Americans. Consider the words of our third president, Thomas Jefferson; "the people have two enemies, criminals and government, so let's bind the second with the chains of the Constitution so they don't become a legalized version of the first." Although this is a famous quote of a President of the United States, this is not a direct quote. This is the belief that resides in my heart still today, years after high school. I defend those who cannot defend themselves.

An alternative oath, once taken, commits a lawyer to the service of the Court. He, as an officer of the Court, is bound to assist in the expedient resolution of criminal proceedings. In any criminal proceeding, you will discover the Court's efforts are to reach an expedient plea of guilty, rather than the just resolution of a controversy. Perhaps this is why an appointed lawyer will advise a client to plea guilty before he or she has requested the discovery. It is my experience that the Court preys upon the people – when it desires to convict in violation of the Constitution of the United States – and lawyers are duty-bound to assist as they uphold their respective oath.

At the age of seventeen I took an oath. That oath had no expiration date, it is a life-long commitment as a patriot to my country – once a soldier, always a soldier; a guardian to the people. It is my humble opinion that taking a secondary oath – to prey upon the intellectually weak of our nation – is an act of treason, for a soldier.

In this section, I forego the fairy tales that lawyers base their legal theories on. Instead, I provide you with the experience of an advocate, perhaps even an activist, who fights from the trenches where the intellectually elite cast their victims. See Case No.: 2:16-cv-709-RDP-HGD, in the Northern District of Alabama, via LEXIS NEXIS for more details.

CHAPTER EIGHTEEN

§2255: A CLOSER LOOK

This, and the chapters that follow, are written for those of you who, like myself, are unwilling to accept defeat. As with anyone who applies himself in the field of advocacy while confined, you will become a magnet who attracts all those who were victimized. You will also be hated by those who are legitimately imprisoned, although they too will seek you out for sentence reductions. I encourage you to fight for those who cannot and educate those who can learn. Assist anyone with a claim, notwithstanding bias or prejudice. The experience you will acquire will be invaluable to you.

A BRIEF HISTORY OF THE PENAL SYSTEM

To obtain a candid understanding of 28 U.S.C. §2255, you must possess a clear understanding of our penal system. The contemporaneous view of habeas corpus is that of an archaic tool that's no longer needed. The propaganda of today falsely informs the people of America that imprisonment is a necessary expenditure that's levied on the people without financial benefit. We as citizens are led to believe that imprisonment is such a wasteful expense that no one in government would possibly consider incarcerating an innocent, or even over-sentence a prisoner.

In the very beginning of our nation, long-term prisoners were unnecessary. As opposed to today's interpretation of crime; as little as one hundred years ago, a citizen's conduct required a victim, a witness, and discernable damage or injury to be considered criminal. In the Nineteenth Century and part of the Twentieth, an example of crime included conduct such as murder, rape, armed bank robbery, and horse theft. In those earlier days, as late as 1950, a criminal was hanged by the neck until dead. In those developmental years of this country, our society also faced petty offenses. Petty offenses, such as minor theft, were sentenced to labor at the discretion of the one damaged – still, no prison necessary.

With other such lesser offenses as slander, libel, and some torts, American citizens often settled the dispute among themselves, with a little help from Sam Colt. Even when a dispute was settled with gunfire – which most often resulted in at least one homicide – no charges were brought if at least one witness declared it a fair fight … again, no prison necessary.

When slaves (African, Indian, Chinese, and Mexican) or lesser-esteemed people were involved in a dispute with citizens, the citizen would most often just shoot the slave and drag the corpse to the edge of the property for disposal, just as any other deceased cattle. A thorough student of history will also find that there was no Constitutional provision that granted the United States the authority to imprison a U.S. citizen. As a matter of fact, the Constitution only provided jurisdiction to punish counterfeiting, piracies, and felonies on the high seas.

As you can see, the federal jurisdiction over criminal conduct is very limited under the Constitution of the United States. Moreover, the jurisdiction of the United States is limited to its military personnel, those involved in interstate and foreign commerce, and the enumerated offenses in Article One, Section Eight of the Constitution. You will also discover that the United States was authorized to "punish," but not specifically to incarcerate. As a matter of fact, there were no federal prisons in 1789 when the Constitution was enacted. The bottom line is that punishment meant: death as a deterrent or servitude until such time as the cost of damage was satisfied.

Which brings me to Article One, Section Nine, Clause Two, which states:

"The privilege of the Writ of Habeas Corpus shall not be suspended, unless when in cases of rebellion or invasion the public safety may require it."

For those of you who forgot, habeas corpus is the right to take action against unlawful detention. So, let's consider that the United States has no police power or authority to incarcerate, under the Constitution; yet it contains a provision to take legal action against unlawful detention in its very first article. The truth is that the United States government was empowered to bring equality among the states and to provide national security. The right to habeas corpus was particularized to provide an appellate review for citizens incarcerated – or committed to a condition of servitude – by the authority of the several states, later codified as 28 U.S.C. §2241. It's also noteworthy that the writ of habeas corpus was rarely used because those incarcerated or committed to servitude were not usually citizens.

The problems with habeas corpus didn't begin until 1865. On January 31, 1865, the Thirteenth Amendment was finally passed by Congress. On February 1, 1865, United States president Abraham Lincoln showed his support for the new amendment by handwriting: "Approved February 1, 1865 – Abraham Lincoln." directly on the joint resolution passed by Congress. The new amendment reads as follows:

"Neither slavery nor involuntary servitude, except as punishment for crime whereof the party shall have been duly convicted, shall exist within the United States, or any place subject to their jurisdiction." Ratified on December 6, 1865.

After the enactment of the Thirteenth Amendment, the United States was plagued with thousands of plantations without workers and thousands of workers without food and clothing. Some former slave owners became the employers of the new era. However, many lacked the business background to structure an employment-for-pay system. The next best option – especially for those lacking the capital to finance a business structure – was to employ the Thirteenth Amendment to its fullest extent, "slavery ... as a punishment for crime ..." Many former slave owners simply accused former slaves of crimes to return them to servitude.

Former slaves who were accused of crimes were caught in a catch twenty-two. When they were accused of crimes, they – the former slaves – didn't have a right to due process because they were not citizens. Under the Bill of Rights, enacted in 1791, United States Citizenship was based on the "right of blood" rather than "birthright." Thus, slaves were easily returned to captivity with convictions of crime. Of course, slaves didn't have a right to a writ of habeas corpus because of this problem.

This is an obvious defect in due process that served to reverse the effects of the Thirteenth Amendment. It wasn't until July 9, 1868 that reform began with the ratification of the Fourteenth Amendment. The Fourteenth Amendment brought a final resolution to the slavery issue by granting former slaves, born in America, citizenship and all the rights that came with it. See the first paragraph of the Fourteenth Amendment that reads in part:

"All persons born or naturalized in the United States, and subject to the jurisdiction thereof, are citizens of the United States and of the State wherein they reside."

Once former slave owners learned that the "slavery by conviction" scheme was thwarted by the Fourteenth Amendment, they would hire the former slaves as workers when needed during heavy seasons, in the off-time, former slaves and their families were banished to fend for themselves, ostracized to colonies. Still today, such a community exists in the Northern District of Alabama, referred to on the map only as "Colony." See *Rand McNally's Atlas*, exit 292 off I-65, north of Birmingham, Alabama.

As the years went by, these colonies turned to minority communities where people assisted each other to survive. Having very few resources and being paid only during the work seasons, people of these communities bartered goods and services to ensure basic survival.

The end of the Civil War also brought about required change. During the end of the Nineteenth Century, it was easy to find Confederate soldiers who refused to let the war end. They often made a living robbing banks, stagecoaches, and trains. Crimes unmistakably in federal jurisdiction, many of which warranted hanging, but some called for less severe punishment. No longer military action, their conduct required criminal action and incarceration. Thus, the prison system became needed.

In the early days, a prison was anything but profitable. Tax dollars were few and families didn't send money to spend in the commissary or on the phone. The prisoners were sentenced to hard labor and basically had to work to eat. Nearing the turn of the century came changes in technology that caused a decline in the labor market. Even minor changes in resources caused severe repercussions in the colonies. Lost employment of even a few caused minorities to go without food for their families. Thus, in desperation they resorted to crime to feed their children.

The beginning of the Great Depression marked one of the biggest spikes in crime in America. This also sparked the government's use of propaganda to demonize those dangerous criminals who simply tried to feed their families. As conditions got worse, prison officials learned to rent out their ample source of labor to the highest bidder.

Another contributing factor that must be considered is the influx of veterans returning from war. Returning veterans marked the greatest increase of incarceration of "acceptable" American citizens, most of which were suffering the psychological effects of battle (P.T.S.D.). This new trend of incarceration marked the beginning of a literate prison population. Following the end of World War One (1918), prisoners began to file for writs of habeas corpus.

CHAPTER NINETEEN

THE HABEAS HOAX

The beginning of the Twentieth Century marked an increase in prison population. Thus, the need to structure a prison scheme that was self-sustaining. Innovative wardens and government officials enacted plans and policies that, when adopted, diverted tax dollars to offset the cost of incarceration along with streamlining the lease of prison labor into a profitable endeavor. Once labor contracts were secured, the prisoner work force became a necessity in our country; criminal conduct and justice were no longer the concern, only conviction and incarceration. With the additional labor force requirements – to make license plates and other items used by the government – on the rise, literate prisoners began the conflict by applying for writs of habeas corpus.

In the early days, a petition for the common-law writ, of habeas corpus, was fairly simple to file. Anyone who could read and write could apply for relief. Due to the sharp increase in petitions between 1937 and 1945, the Courts and Congress began to seek a resolution. Prior to 1948, state and federal prisoners alike filed exactly the same way, under the Constitutional provision of Article One, Section. Nine.

In the effort to streamline the conviction process, Congress and the Supreme Court engaged in the concerted effort together. By June 29, 1940, the Supreme Court prescribed rules for the district court to follow in all criminal proceedings. These rules were intended to expedite a just resolution in all criminal cases, or were they? Read this rule:

FEDERAL RULE OF CRIMINAL PROCEDURE, Rule 2:

> *"These rules are to be interpreted to provide for the just determination of every criminal proceeding, to secure simplicity in procedure and fairness in administration, and to eliminate unjustifiable expense and delay."*

This rule defines the purpose of the rules as establishing a "just determination," this couldn't be further from the truth for a defendant. The purpose of the rules was to create a conviction assembly line, the process we have today. Many of you heard your appointed lawyer say, "Just plead guilty. It's easier to beat the case in habeas corpus court." Yes, as you now know, your lawyer lied to you.

At or around the same time, Congress enacted the Federal Rules of Criminal Procedure – which now allow a defendant to just plea out, saving the court the cost of trial – The Seventy-Ninth Congress was working diligently on a plan to legally suspend habeas corpus.

By June 1948, Congress did it, it codified habeas corpus as 28 U.S.C. §2241, stating that:

> *"Section consolidates Section 451, 452, and 453 of the Title 28 U.S.C., 1940 ed., with changes in phraseology necessary to effect the consolidation.*

> *Words 'for the purpose of an inquiry into the cause of restraint of liberty' in former 28 U.S.C. §452 were omitted as merely descriptive of the writ."*

As you can see here, laws were merged, words were omitted, and definitions changed. Thus, the writ of habeas corpus – now codified 28 U.S.C. §2241 – no longer defines conviction and sentence as detention. In an additional deception, Congress went a step further by enacting 28 U.S.C. §2241 and §2243. These statutes particularize a very clear purpose and strict time limits -for the issuance of a writ of habeas corpus, to end unlawful detention. Of course, without the people of America being made aware of the fact that conviction and sentence were no longer considered detention.

On the very same day, Congress enacted 28 U.S.C. §2241 as the common law writ of habeas corpus; they, diligently working behind the scene to enact 28 U.S.C. §2255. The Seventy ninth Congress stated that:

> *"This section restates, clarifies, and simplifies the procedure in the nature of an ancient writ of error coram nobis. It provides an expeditious remedy for correcting erroneous sentences without resort to habeas corpus. It has the approval of the judicial conference of the United States. Its principal provisions are incorporated in H.R. 4233, Seventy Ninth Congress."*

As you can see, Congress has been a busy bee, changing laws and meanings concerning habeas corpus. One of the most damaging results was the denial of a speedy resolution. In 28 U.S.C. §2255(b), it states in pertinent part that:

> *"unless the motion and the files and records of the case conclusively show that the prisoner is entitled to no relief, the Court shall cause notice thereof to be served upon the United States attorney, grant a prompt hearing thereon, determine the issue and makes findings of fact and conclusions of law with respect thereto."*

Now then, what's most important for you to realize is that on June 25, 1948, Congress separated prisoners from the right to file for habeas corpus writs. In the alternative, they provided a statutory remedy as "an expeditious remedy for correcting erroneous sentences ..." rather than "... inquiry into the cause of restraint of liberty ..." Another disturbing difference is that, on that same day Congress separated prisoners from a defined time limit to resolve the issue.

In 28 U.S.C. §2243, the law requires that:

> *"A court, justice or judge entertaining an application for a writ of habeas corpus shall forthwith award the writ or issue an order directing the respondent to show cause why the writ should not be granted ..."*

> *"The writ, or order to show cause shall be directed to the person having custody of the person detained. It shall be returned within three days unless for good cause additional time, not exceeding twenty days, is allowed." See 28 U.S.C. §2243.*

As a result, Congress has effectively transferred our right to demand proof that our detention is legal into a one-time opportunity to prove our very own government tricked us. Please notice the transition concerning the burden of proof from the court and government to the prisoner. Look up the word "prestidigitation."

The next most troubling result is that you don't have a right to be released based on due process error. But, only if you can prove the sentence and conviction is unlawful. Thus, you remain in custody until you prove it. The court and government then only need to stall the proceedings until the end of your sentence.

FEDERAL COURT RULES

As you can see, this concerted effect of legal prestidigitation is complicated because Congress knows that it cannot suspend "the privilege of the Writ of Habeas Corpus." Thus, Congress enacted the post-conviction relief statutes for the sole purpose of shifting the burden of proof from the government to the prisoner. Under the post-conviction relief statutes, the prisoner has a right to prove that he is deserving of a writ of habeas corpus. This burden of proof is, most often, impossible for a layman at law to meet in the one year he is allotted to learn advanced habeas corpus law and practice.

You will also find that, in today's criminal conviction scheme, the government is attempting to incarcerate a more docile prison population. Prisoners who follow the rules are less expensive to control. Also, selecting the more educated people of our communities means that the prisoner will be more likely to have outside financial support. Thus, the criminal conviction scheme allows the harvest of additional funds that are sent in by family and friends to spend in its captive market. Although the why is important, it's most important to you to know how.

As with any other court and procedure, rules are enacted for what the government calls efficient execution of the action. As described earlier, a writ of habeas corpus is controlled by statute. 28 U.S.C. §2255 and §2254 are not habeas corpus writs, but only post-conviction relief statutes – a gateway through which you must pass to get a writ of habeas corpus – which are controlled by rules.

I'm going to give you a brief overview of the rules governing Section 2255 proceedings. You can follow along by reading the rules in your prison law library or my previous book "post-Conviction Relief: The Appeal." What I'm giving you here is the actual practice and operations of the rules the courts follow to legally suspend your right to a writ of habeas corpus.

Rule One – When you seek a true understanding of these rules, you must consider the court's scope of operation. In a 28 U.S.C. §2254 case, the court acts in an appellate capacity to determine if the prisoner's "custody violates the Constitution ..." Rules governing Section 2254 cases, Rule 1(a)(1). In a 28 U.S.C. §2255 case, however, the action is considered an extension to the criminal case, determined by the offending judge. In the §2255 context, the court is effectively reviewing its judgment on a quasi-reconsideration capacity over its own judgment. See rules governing Section 2255 cases, Rule 1(a)(1) " the judgment violates the Constitution ..." Consider also that a federal prisoner who claims that he suffered from a Sixth Amendment violation, because of ineffective assistance of counsel, is not allowed to raise the issue in his direct appeal. See *Massaro v. United States*. 538 U.S. 500 (2003).

Your Constitutional claim – that you suffered constructive denial of counsel due to ineffectiveness – is not appealable in any way. If you read 28 U.S.C. §47, you find that

"No judge shall hear or determine an appeal from the decision of a case or issue tried by him."

Thus, §2255 action is not an appeal for ineffective assistance of counsel. Moreover, if you take some time to review Chapter 253 (appeal) in Title Eighteen, you will discover that the text of all the statutes have been abrogated by the Federal Rules of Criminal procedure. The only remaining appeal available to a federal criminal defendant is a review of sentence under 18 U.S.C. §3742. You may easily discover that the enactment of §2255 not only suspended your right to a writ of habeas corpus, but also deprives you of direct review of an ineffective assistance of counsel claim, a Constitutional violation of the Fifth and Sixth Amendments to the Constitution of the United States. I will provide the resolve to this issue in a later chapter.

Rule Four – I cannot express to you enough that the court's concern – in your criminal and §2255 case – is to preserve the finality of the conviction. What I'm attempting to show you here is how the court, and its personnel – i.e., clerks, prosecutors, defense lawyers (yours), and staff attorneys – use the rules governing §2255 proceedings to delay your winning argument until your sentence is served, and what you can do about it.

What I want you to realize about Rule Four is the beginning of ambiguous language and how it's used against you. As you can see, the first line of defense is the clerk, who of course, "must promptly forward the motion." This is a bad joke, I've been witness to clerks who sit on §2255 motions for months because the word "prompt" is not specifically defined in the statutes or the rules. My practice is: if I don't have a "Show Cause Order" within a month, I move to compel the court; a motion filed in the criminal case.

The next travesty is that the court must fix a time to answer. Please notice again that "fixed time" is not defined anywhere. Remember my Rule Four – thirty days, you move to compel but be prepared for the court to give a lengthy time for the government to respond.

Rule Five – Another crucial time the court is going to play with is your time to reply. In 99% of all §2255 cases, the court will not provide you a time to reply. The court correctly believes, in most cases, that a defendant will fail to reply – thus, lose when the court fails to specify a time. The defendant/movant is misled to believe that the court will order him to reply at a later time. Keep in mind that if the court fails to provide a fixed time, the court is again trying to fool you because of your sound Constitutional claim.

Rule Eight – This rule is the court's most damaging playground for those who have good claims that warrant relief. Once you have been determined to have a valid claim, the court must determine if the case requires an evidentiary hearing.

Basically, what happens here is the judge is reading the last thing filed in the case to determine if it can be dismissed without a proceeding. When the court fails to find reason to dismiss or deny, it's sent back to the staff attorney to determine if it requires an evidentiary hearing. The court's standing order is to review §2255 cases on a basis of speedy resolution. Thus, he or she reviews their workload to glean out all the cases that can be dismissed. The cases with valid claims remain on the bottom of the stack as the latest cases are reviewed for dismissal. Your case will remain on the bottom until you file for a writ of mandamus in the Court of Appeals.

I hope you can understand how the rules are used to complete the suspension of habeas corpus. Your judge knows exactly how long your sentence is; their only concern is whether they can stall that long

CHAPTER TWENTY

§2255: THE QUANTUM LEAP

The enactment of §2255 changed the meaning of relief from unlawful restraint of one's liberty to review of an unlawful sentence. Thus, the government and the Court have effectively diverted your attention away from being deprived of due process and/or structural errors and distracted you with the thought of obtaining relief from an unlawful sentence.

Deciphering the difference between unlawful restraint and unlawful prosecution is as simple as challenging your sentence rather than the process of conviction.

In almost all granted §2255's, the prisoner is released, only to discover that he is still a felon and sometimes must comply with certain registries. §2255 has been a very effective tool, used to grant relief from unlawful restraint but yet maintain the intended conversion of civil rights, which were granted to all American citizens. Thus, continuing the prosecution for a lifetime.

You will soon discover that actual innocence, ineffective assistance of counsel, and deprivation of due process are not actionable under §2255, unless it's the cause and prejudice that go directly to an unlawful sentence. Thus, §2255 is ineffective to challenge Constitutional violations such as the kidnapping of innocent Americans, or the due process violation of constructive denial of counsel. That's why the courts require that a criminal defendant make his claim of ineffective assistance of counsel in a §2255 proceeding; effectively shielding the attorney from further action because his deficiencies were merely the cause for not raising a claim in an earlier proceeding. Yes, judges and prosecutors are lawyers also; they will protect each other at all cost. In one case, the court went as far as to say an attorney who slept through a criminal trial wasn't ineffective; the defendant's guilt thus predetermined.

Always consider that if you're filing under §2255, you must target the authority to impose the sentence. The purpose of this chapter is to give you a focus on targeting the sentence in a §2255 claim, before I move on to challenging the previously mentioned structural errors.

AFTER A TRIAL

In the event you're wondering, being deprived of a fair trial is a Constitutional error. But it is not actionable under §2255; It is the prejudice under Strickland that rendered your sentence unlawful. That violation of due process divested the court of the authority to sentence you. Ineffective assistance of counsel can, and most commonly is, the cause that made your trial proceeding unfair, resulting in a sentence that's unlawful.

A sentence that's based on unreliable or completely erroneous information is also cause that results in an unlawful sentence. *See Gall v. United States, 552 U.S. 38.*

You must target the sentence if you're using §2255. Here are a few examples:

JURISDICTIONAL CLAIMS

The court's lack of jurisdiction is specifically mentioned in the statute as a ground for relief. Please consider the following jurisdictional grounds but remember that this list is not all-inclusive. For more ideas, please review "Post-Conviction Relief: A David and Goliath Story."

- U.S. attorney did not have authority to file information in instant case, and Movant's Waiver of Indictment was not binding and did not confer power on the convicting court to hear the case;

- District court was without power to impose pre-parole eligibility period that exceeded the limitation of ten years set forth by statute;

- If the government fails to comply with the procedural requirements of 21 U.S.C. §851 by failing to file an information concerning the defendant's prior convictions at the appropriate time, the court is without jurisdiction to use those prior convictions to enhance the defendant's sentence under §851;

- A district court is divested if jurisdiction where an information or indictment failed to charge an offense;

- Evidence is insufficient to satisfy the statutes interstate commerce element;

- Insufficient evidence to support Movant's conviction under 18 U.S.C. §924(c)(1) for use of a firearm during and in relation to a drug trafficking offense.

UNCONSTITUTIONAL SENTENCE & CONVICTION

- Government violated due process by failing to disclose exculpatory evidence of a critical witness's recantation, where, absent prosecutorial misconduct. Movant would not have pled guilty;

- Government's suppression of impeaching evidence violated Fifth Amendment;

- The government knowingly presented falsified evidence or allowed it to go uncorrected when it appeared at trial;

- Prosecution's adoption of "shifting and at times misleading position" that resulted in a conviction that "had no legitimate factual or legal basis."

RIGHT TO COUNSEL CLAIMS

- Counsel failed to offer proper jury instructions on Movant's only defense, and that defense had a strong likelihood of success;

- To the detriment of his client, counsel opened the door to the prosecution's introduction of otherwise inadmissible and damaging character evidence;

- Counsel made illogical and incomprehensible comments on the record;

- Counsel acted with inappropriate hostility and paranoia;

- Counsel failed to object to erroneous enhancement at sentencing;

- Counsel failed to object to government's untimely filing of 21 U.S.C. §851 information

- Counsel failed to file a notice of appeal;

- Counsel failed to file a notice of appeal timely;

- Counsel failed to timely file the record on appeal and/or briefing, which resulted in dismissal;

- Counsel failed to raise an obviously winning argument on appeal;

- Counsel failed to conduct any pretrial investigation, failed to hire an investigator to conduct such investigation, and failed to contact potential witnesses;

- Counsel failed to conduct any investigation into an insanity defense after receiving a letter from a psychiatrist who concluded, based on an interview with the defendant immediately following his arrest, that the defendant was manic and psychotic at the time of the crime.

Another counsel deficiency, that warrants its own section, is a conflict of interest claim. Relief under §2255 is available where counsel was laboring under such an actual conflict of interest.

- Court order required defense counsel to advise government witness that her decision not to testify against counsel's client would violate her plea agreement;
- Trial counsel labored under conflict of interest after government witness alleged that trial counsel was engaged in drug trafficking related to the charge for which Movant was on trial.

OUTRIGHT DENIAL OF COUNSEL

- District court failed to appoint alternative and un-conflicted counsel at a pre-trial conflict of interest hearing;
- Counsel was ordered, by the court, to represent his client at a conflict of interest hearing where counsel's interests were in conflict with his clients at the hearing;
- Where district court-imposed sentence in absence of Movant and counsel;
- Where defendant was unrepresented during two days of trial;
- Trial counsel's irreconcilable conflict with Movant resulted in denial of counsel.

AFTER PLEA AGREEMENT

This is where post-conviction relief gets sticky for most federal prisoners. That's because a federal defendant, who has entered a plea of guilty, cannot obtain collateral relief under 28 U.S.C. §2255 based on claims alleging that a violation of rights, Constitutional or otherwise, occurred prior to the guilty plea. Thus, defense lawyers, appointed and paid, use this legal maxim – coupled with the inability to directly attack counsel's performance as a basis – to bring a criminal case to a quick resolve via guilty plea. That's not to say, however, that challenges to the validity of the plea itself are precluded. Personally, I've had a great deal of success overturning plea agreements, even as old as twenty years. Ordinarily, I target structural and plain errors, along with jurisdiction claims in §2255 action, regardless of age, because claims such as those are never foreclosed. Read these examples I've used over the last couple of years.

ATTACKING THE PLEA

- The plea was induced by threats or promises;
- Threats to prosecute a third party;
- The government breached a plea agreement;
- The district court initiated or participated in plea negotiations;
- District court misinformed Movant as to possible maximum sentence he could have received;
- District court failed to advise Movant of his right to appeal his sentence, and there is no evidence that Movant learned of his right to appeal from another source;
- District court failed to inform Movant, before accepting plea, that his federal sentence could be served consecutively to any state sentence subsequently imposed;
- The government breached a plea agreement;
- The government breached a plea agreement when it failed to recommend a sentence below the mandatory minimum;
- District court failed to advise Movant of a term of supervised release;
- The criminal judgment does not comport with the Constitution's mandated due process requirement since the plea was not entered intelligently, knowingly, or voluntarily;
- Defense counsel's inadequate advice at plea negotiation stage denied Movant the Constitutional guarantee of counsel;

For those of you who intend to practice the art of advocacy, such as I have, may I suggest you write and preserve all successful claims you encounter. This list of ideas is hardly a complete list. What I'm doing here is giving you food for thought.

CHAPTER TWENTY-ONE

§2255 AND STRUCTURAL ERRORS

Be aware that this subject is a bit of a sore spot for me at the time that I write this book. Because of my personal concern with this issue, I have been compelled to read tens of thousands of pages on the subject. One troubling constant I've discovered is that courts and lawyers have diluted the availability of resources on the subject. This is done by using complicated writing and language while explaining the mechanics of structural errors. Just as anything else that's hidden in plain sight; this subject's explanation has been camouflaged in complex legal writing. In this chapter, I'll be attempting to explain the complexities of this legal issue in layman's terms. This affects all federal prisoners in a very profound, yet fundamental way, so pay close attention.

Although I have found many examples of what is – and what is not – a structural error, I have not yet found a clear definition. So let's cover that first. A structure is simply a building of something; something unnatural that's made up of parts. Anything you organize, or that is made up of the bringing together of different parts is a structure. Your criminal case is a structure, i.e., arrest, complaint, initial hearing, appointment of counsel … etc. It's also important to identify the essential parts of the structure. If you remember we covered the bill of rights in an earlier chapter, those are essential parts. Next, look at the Federal Rules of Criminal Procedure and the statutes they reference. Those are also essential parts. Now, imagine if one of those parts is broken. Since the part is required to produce the desired structure, a broken part results in a broken structure. A structural error is an error that has a propensity to affect the whole, resulting in an unreliable structure.

Building a house with broken foundation materials can affect the whole house, all the way up to the attic that never sees the broken materials. A marriage founded on a lie will result in an unreliable expectation of the future. And, a Court that breaks the law at any point of the proceeding will taint the entire process, leaving no reasonable expectation of reliability to do justice. To be clear, a structural error is an error that makes the whole trial process unreliable, not to be confused with a trial error that's plain.

CORAM NOBIS

As mentioned in an earlier chapter, the Seventy-Ninth Congress "restates, clarifies, and simplifies the procedure in the nature of an ancient writ of error coram nobis." This one remarkable statement redirects the basic principles of 28 U.S.C. §2255, because coram nobis encompasses claims that go beyond the federal sentence, the ancient writ of error coram nobis is considered an "extraordinary remedy" available only to correct errors "of the most fundamental character." See Morgan, 346 U.S. at 511-12. In light of its "extraordinary" nature, and the mandates of the All Writs Act, coram nobis relief is available only in circumstances in which no statutory remedy is adequate or unavailable.

As you can see, 28 U.S.C. §2255 specifically "simplifies" coram nobis and provides remedy for a wide variety of Constitutional errors. Thus, §2255 provides a statutory remedy to prisoners incarcerated pursuant to a federal conviction and sentence; who are therefore barred from seeking relief in a writ of error coram nobis.

The writ of error coram nobis is not without a place in today's judicial system. Coram nobis is available when the challenged conviction is one that has been obtained as a result of errors "of the most fundamental character" that have "rendered the proceeding itself irregular and invalid." Morgan. The writ of coram nobis was, in its time, unmistakably the remedy for structural errors. In today's system of justice, the writ of error coram nobis is reserved to remedy structural errors after the prisoner has already served the entire sentence and is no longer in custody. I have read several letters from defense lawyers who tell their clients that a structural error can only be rectified in a writ of error coram nobis after the sentence is served. Those lawyers are either misinformed or they're working to preserve the conviction, i.e. lying. I have been fortunate in my filings because I know that 28 U.S.C. §2255 provides relief from a structural error at any time, even outside the one year statutory limitation. Structural errors divest the court of jurisdiction to make a finding of guilt or impose a sentence. In *Finley v. Johnson*, the Fifth Circuit concluded that "a showing of facts establishing an affirmative defense that would result in the defendant's acquittal constitutes a sufficient showing of actual innocence ..." *Rozelle v. Sec. FL. Dept. of Corr.*, 672 F.3d 1000 (11th Cir. 2012).

AFTER A DIRECT APPEAL

Under three very specific circumstances, a federal prisoner will have one extra avenue for relief after direct appeal:

1) the failure of the indictment to charge an offense;
2) ineffective assistance of counsel; and
3) denial of the right to counsel.

These three are bedrock principles in any criminal proceeding. These are fundamental Constitutional rights. They are also rights that no attorney on earth will protect for you, unless you tell him to, and sometimes not even then. In a case where any or all of these violations occur, a prisoner may raise a claim of structural error in a Motion to Vacate under 28 U.S.C. §2255. But, while your court is scratching their head, also file a motion, in the Court of Appeals, to Recall the mandate. If you can show that the structural error is in the record, the Court of Appeals is duty bound to reverse or vacate. Don't forget to send your sentencing court a copy.

STRUCTURAL ERRORS

These errors that are referred to as structural are different from plain errors; because they are not subject to the harmless error review when they are presented in appeal. This includes when brought up in a Motion to Recall the mandate. However, you must read your current court rules to determine timeliness. In the Eleventh Circuit Court of Appeals, Circuit Court Rule 41(c) states in pertinent part that:

> *"When a Motion to Recall the mandate is tendered for filing more than one year after issuance of the Mandate, the Clerk shall not accept the Motion for filing unless the Motion states with specificity why it was not filed sooner."*

In comparing a "plain error" under Federal Rules of Criminal Procedure, Rule 52(b) and "structural errors," you discover that:

Plain Errors – Most often occur in and during the trial itself. They are "plain" and "obvious" in the record and having an effect on the defendant's substantial rights. In most cases, the Court of Appeals cannot correct the forfeited error unless the defendant shows that the error was prejudicial, and thereby satisfies the "affecting substantial rights" prong of Rule 52(b). See *United States v. Olano* 506 U.S. 725.

Structural Errors – Courts have realized that demanding a showing that the error change the outcome would in many cases be asking the impossible. "Another mode of analysis leads to the same conclusion that harmless-error analysis does not apply: In *Fulminante*, we distinguished between, on the one hand, structural defects in the Constitution of the trial mechanism, which defy analysis by "harmless-error" standards', 499 U.S. an 309 ... and, on the other hand, trial errors which occur 'during the presentation of the case to the jury, and which may therefore be quantitatively assessed in the context of other evidence presented, id., 307-308, 113 L. Ed 2d 302, 111 S.Ct. 1246. Denial of the right to a jury verdict of guilt beyond a reasonable doubt is certainly an error of the former sort, the jury guarantee being a "basic protection" whose precise effects are unmeasurable, but without which a criminal trial cannot reliably serve its function. *Rose*, Supra, at 577, 92 L. Ed. 2d 460, 106 S.Ct. 3101. The right to trial by jury reflects, we have said, 'a profound judgment about the way in which law should be enforced and justice administered.' *Duncan v. Louisiana*, 391 U.S. at 155, 20 L. Ed. 2d 491, 88 S.Ct. 1444. The deprivation of that right, with consequences that are necessarily unquantifiable and indeterminate, unquestionably qualifies as 'structural error'." See *Sullivan v. Louisiana*, 508 U.S. 275 at 281, 282 (1993).

I cannot express to you enough how important it is to identify cases exactly like yours when seeking support for yozur argument. A case that's almost right will provide an avenue for the government to pick your argument apart in its response. I also suggest that you only quote direct holdings of a controlling court (any court of appeals if you're raising a novel argument), and of course, remember in an initial §2255, you must frame all case holdings as your own statement, not "quoting law or case citation." You can back your position with case law in your reply.

Keep in mind that the structural error categories are not rigid. In a particular case, more than one rationale may be part of the explanation for why an error is deemed to be structural. For the purpose of determining that an error is structural, however, one point is critical: An error can count as structural even if the error does not lead to fundamental unfairness in every case. Compare the following:

> *"An unconstitutional failure to recuse constitutes structural error even if the judge in question did not cast a deciding vote." Williams v. Pennsylvania. 136 S.Ct. 1899 (Feb. 29, 2016).*

> *"It is not surprising: first, that the U.S. Supreme Court's opinions often refer to the right counsel as fundamental; second, that commentators describe the right as a great engine by which an innocent man can make the truth of his innocence visible; third, that the Court has understood the right to require that the government provided counsel for an indigent defendant accused of all but the least serious crimes; and forth, that the Court has considered the wrongful deprivation of the right to counsel a structural error that so affects the framework within which the trial proceeds that courts may not even ask whether the error harmed the defendant." Luis v. United States. 578 U.S. 136 S.Ct. 1083 (March 30, 2016).*

The Sixth Amendment violation is not subject to harmless-error analysis. Erroneous deprivation of the right to counsel of choice, "with consequences that are necessarily unquantifiable and indeterminate, unquestionably qualifies as 'structural error.'" *Sullivan v. Louisiana*. 508 U.S. 275, 282. It "defies analysis by 'harmless error' standards" because it "affects the framework within which the trial proceeds" and is not "simply an error in the trial process itself." *Arizona v. Fulminante*. 499 U.S. 279. Different attorneys will pursue different strategies with regard to myriad trial matters, and the choice of attorney will affect whether and on what terms the defendant cooperates with the prosecution, plea bargains, or decides to go to trial. It is impossible to know what different choice the rejected counsel would have made, and then to quantify the impact of those different choices on the outcome of the proceedings. This inquiry is not comparable to that required to show that counsel's deficient performance prejudiced the defendant. *United States v. Gonzalez-Lopez* 548 U.S. 140 (2006).

The Supreme Court of the United States, in *Neder v. United States*, 527 U.S. 1 (1999), reaffirms the rule that it would be structural error (not susceptible of "harmless-error" analysis) to "' vitiate all the jury's findings.'" Ante, at 11, 144 L. Ed. 2d, at 48 (quoting *Sullivan v. Louisiana*. 508 U.S. 275,

281, 124 L. Ed. 2d 182, 113 S.Ct. 2078 (1993)). A court cannot, no matter how clear the defendant's culpability, direct a guilty verdict. See *Carpenters v. United States,* 330 U.S. 395, 410, 91 L. Ed. 973, 67 S.Ct. 775 (1947); *Rose v. Clark.* 478 U.S. 570, 578, 92 L. Ed. 2d 460, 106 S.Ct. 3101 (1986); *Arizona v. Fulminante.* 499 U.S. 279, 294, 113 L. Ed. 2d 302, 111 S.Ct. 1246 (1991)(White, J., dissenting), the question that this raises is why, if denying the right to conviction by jury is structural error, taking one of the elements of the crime away from the jury should be treated differently from taking all of them away – since failure to prove one, no less than failure to prove all, utterly prevents conviction.

"The Court holds today that the reasonable-doubt instruction given at Sullivan's trial, which (it is conceded) violates due process under our decision in Cage v. Louisiana. 498 U.S. 39, 112 L. Ed. 2d 339, 111 S.Ct. 328 (1990) (per curiam), amounts to structural error, and thus cannot be harmless regardless of how overwhelming the evidence of Sullivan's guilt. See ante, at 281-282, 124 L. Ed. 2d at 190-191. It grounds this conclusion in its determination that harmless-error analysis cannot be conducted with respect to error of this sort consistent with the Sixth Amendment right to a jury trial. We of course, have long since rejected the argument that, as a general matter, the Sixth Amendment prohibits the application of harmless-error analysis in determining whether Constitutional error had a prejudicial impact on the outcome of a case. See, e.g.. Rose, Supra, at 582, n.11, 92 L.Ed. 2d 460, 106 S.Ct. 3101. The Court concludes that the situation at hand is fundamentally different, though, because in the case of a constitutionally deficient reasonable-doubt instruction, "The entire premise of Chapman [harmless-error] review is simply absent. Ante, at 280, 124 L. Ed. 2d at 189."

SECTION FIVE: MY PROCESS
CHAPTER TWENTY-TWO

TEN MINUTE CASE REVIEW

Your reading of this chapter implies that you desire a deeper understanding of habeas cases. I commend your efforts, however, they're most fruitful when you take your time. What I'm about to share with you are the steps of case review that I use personally. Again, what I'm providing here are the steps that I have found to work; not the fairy tale that the Court wants us to believe. Let's begin.

Step One: I most often start with a brief conversation. Most people, in their first conversation, will want you to hear their whole story. Don't. Remember ten minutes. Don't be afraid to interrupt and ask questions. Streamline the conversation and get to the point. What you want to know is if he has a habeas claim, i.e., cause and prejudice; structural error; jurisdictional error, etc. In this initial conversation, you want the answer to three critical questions:

1) Did the government drop any charges in an agreement to plead guilty?

2) Are you willing to go to trial right now? and

3) Are you willing to spend time learning the law and facts of your case?

If the answer to question one is yes, and you continue, take time to calculate any possible sentence that may follow, and count on the maximum.

The total time needed for this conversation is about ten minutes. If, after that time, you can extrapolate a reasonable habeas claim, move to the next step. If not, don't waste any more time. You'll only hurt your reputation as an advocate.

Author's note: Don't compare yourself to other advocates, and above all, don't gossip about others in the advocacy business. While I'm discussing a case, I will not provide any assessment of another's opinion, that's a waste of time. If you, yourself, are unable to provide a sound legal analysis, you should refrain from helping others.

Step Two: Be aware that the accuracy of the facts you just received have a great propensity to be skewed by emotion. Thus, the previous conversation should serve to drive you to gather more information only

This step, in fact, gathering, begins with a docket sheet. It's time to determine if the facts – as you heard them – warrant further review. Once you have the docket, you must determine if you have a single defendant case or a multiple defendant conspiracy.

With a single defendant case, read each entry one by one until you reach the finding of guilt. Highlight that entry, no matter if it is a jury verdict or a plea of guilt. The finding of guilt is important because it's the point of a criminal case where rights are lost or otherwise converted. The finding of guilt deprives a defendant of the presumption of innocence. Now, start over and read again. Look for motions that challenge jurisdiction or evidence. Most likely, you won't find anything filed in the defendant's favor, i.e. motion for a bill of particulars, etc.

In the event you do find a motion that's not an extension of time, mark it. One I look for specifically is a motion requesting a speedy public trial. This is the most fundamental right if any defendant, if it is not filed – and most lawyers don't – the lawyer was stalling to assist the government.

The most fundamental principles of the trial process are that the government's case is put to the crucible of adversarial testing. That means the evidence set against a defendant is on trial; not the defendant. When a lawyer is trying to convince a defendant that he or she is on trial, the lawyer is already ineffective. Thus, what I look for in a docket are meaningful discovery or challenging motions in the pre-guilt determination stage. You most likely won't find any if you had appointed counsel.

In a multiple defendant case, you must begin by finding the point of guilt. But, this time when you start over with your reading, you're looking for entries with your client's name in them. You will find hundreds of entries in some dockets so dividing them up is important. Highlight the entries that affect your client for easy identification. Now, start over again and read the entries that are important to the case at hand.

Beware, there are some diligent lawyers out there. They are few and far between, but they do exist. It's important for you to acknowledge – even if just to yourself – when you find one who did a good job. In the event you find a lawyer who did all he could, but your client wants to file anyway, it's best for your reputation, and peace of mind, to refuse the case. Remember, you weren't appointed. You have choices.

CHAPTER TWENTY-THREE

TRAINING THE CLIENT

I am truly amazed at how many movants go to court, based on a writ of habeas corpus, and end up with the same or longer sentence. I am very careful to ensure that one of my petitions won't result in a longer sentence. I know I've covered this before, but let's take a closer look at how this happens.

What's most important when training your client is making him or her aware of all possibilities. If you fail to fully advise them of all possible outcomes; you, yourself are no different from the corrupt lawyer who got them convicted in the first place. I begin to train my clients right after I determine that they have a claim. I do this because I don't want to waste hours of time on someone who won't want to file when the time comes.

One of the most important facts in the post-conviction game is that a movant *can* get more time under certain circumstances. Of course, and as discussed earlier, a movant can, and likely will, be prosecuted on any and all counts the government dropped as a result of a plea agreement.

The next area of possibility is that, a movant may face more time on the same charge after his conviction has been set aside, when opposed by a prosecutor who is vindictive. The Supreme Court has held in the past that; after an accused's conviction has been set aside and the accused has received a sentence that is longer than the original sentence, after being convicted in a subsequent trial, it may be presumed that the imposition of the longer sentence was motivated by vindictiveness, Although, vindictiveness violates the due process rights of your client; this fact does not vitiate the effectiveness of the subsequent sentence. What your client needs to be aware of is that: one) some prosecutors are vindictive; and two) this is an appealable issue.

Remember, once a movant wins in any post-conviction proceeding, the court may demand a retrial. In the event a longer sentence is imposed, he may file a direct appeal. What's most important for you to do before you file for post-conviction relief is to make your client aware of the fact that, after the post-conviction relief process, he is once again a defendant in a criminal proceeding (new trial) with all his rights to Direct Appeal restored.

When one can presume vindictiveness, I always anticipate the need to prove vindictiveness. Remember to presume means to rely on the fact without proof. With that in mind, realize that just because you can't always presume vindictiveness doesn't mean that you can't win the appeal, it only means you won't win automatically. Just a hint, if the government or court fails to present new facts or charges upon which to lengthen your sentence, it's imposed vindictively.

In *North Carolina v. Pearce*, 395 U.S. 711 (1969), the accused was sentenced by the trial judge to a prison term of 12 to 15 years after being convicted of assault with the intent to commit rape. Mr. Pearce initiated a post-conviction proceeding years later that resulted in the reversal of his conviction. After retrial and reconviction, he received, from the trial judge, a sentence that the parties agreed amounted to a longer prison term then that originally imposed. In *Rice* – also finalized by the *Pearce* decision – the accused, after pleading guilty to four separate charges of second-degree burglary, being sentenced to prison terms together equaling ten years. After having his convictions set aside in a state Coram Nobis proceeding, he was retried and convicted on three of the four charges, and was sentenced to a prison term equaling twenty-five years, instead. With respect to the Rice case, the Supreme Court referred to a federal district judge's statements that the state's failure in *Rice* to offer any evidence attempting to explain or justify the significant increase in the aggregate sentence was shocking, and that the conclusion was inescapable that the state was punishing the accused for having exercised his post-conviction right to review. Although the situation in *Pearce* was not so dramatically clear, the court continued, the fact remained that neither at the time the longer prison term was imposed nor at any stage in the habeas corpus proceeding in *Pearce* had the state offered any reason or justification for the longer sentence, other than the state's naked power to impose it.

Also consider that in the case of *Alabama v. Smith*. 490 U.S. 794 (1989), the Supreme Court overruled the Rice portion of its holding in *North Carolina v. Pearce*, to the extent that Rice held that a presumption of vindictiveness applies where a second sentence imposed after a trial is heavier than a first sentence imposed after a guilty plea.

Confused? Good! It makes you think. I follow a simple rule of thumb, always prepare to prove vindictiveness on Direct Appeal. You do that by illustrating that neither the government nor the court relied on any new information to increase the sentence. You are simply being punished for exercising your Constitutional right to habeas corpus and your Sixth Amendment right to a public speedy trial. See 18 U.S.C. §242.

If your client is still prepared to go to court after that, continue your client's preparation concerning the facts of his or her case. Also, you will find a full section on preparing for hearings in "Post-Conviction Relief: Secrets Exposed," Corrlinks, Diane@freebirdpublishers.com.

CHAPTER TWENTY-FOUR

FREEDOM OF INFORMATION ACT (FOIA)

Let's not kid ourselves, you are reading a book about advancing your claim, so I'm going to assume you already know how to get a case file. With that considered, I must also tell you that often more information is available. In any situation where defense counsel failed to investigate, it can be real difficult to prove your claim. The most common answer you hear from the court and government is that the movant failed to show particular facts or issues that reflect his counsel failed to investigate, so it stands to reason that, he won't have the evidence to prove that he doesn't have the evidence. Yeah exactly – circular reasoning.

To avoid the problem of failing to prove that counsel didn't investigate, you must have in your possession something that he failed to obtain. This is best achieved by obtaining an affidavit from a witness counsel failed to interview, or something discovered that wasn't in your case file. How? Excellent question. The answer is the Freedom of Information Act.

FOIA AS CODIFIED

The Freedom of Information Act is codified in Title 5 U.S.C. §552, and §552a. In simple terms, the Freedom of Information Act is, established in law, as guidance to all government agencies to provide full agency disclosure to the public. 5 U.S.C. §552. The act is not, however, without exception. You will find that the act is structured to provide virtually every document generated by the agency available to the public in one form or another, unless it falls within one of the act's exemptions.

The FOIA allows you to request documents relating to you, as well as all public documents.

PRIVACY ACT OF 1974

The Privacy Act is closely related to the Freedom of Information Act, in that it restricts individuals from obtaining records that don't pertain to them. 5 U.S.C. §552a, 28 C.F.R. §16.40 through 28 C.F.R. §16.55, 26 U.S.C. §6103, and the Social Securities Act. Due to these restrictions on personal information, you will be required to set out with particularity what documents you seek and proof of who you are.

FORM OF FOIA REQUEST

To obtain documents from a government agency using the Freedom of Information Act, you must write a request letter to the main agency and request the required documents. See *Sample FOIA Request Letter*. Your request letter must be accompanied by a "Certification of Identity." See sample: "Certification of Identity" form that immediately follows the sample letter

Sample FOIA Letter

[Your name and prisoner number]

[Your institution]

[Your address]

[Your Town, State, Zip Code]

[DATE]

U.S. Department of Justice

Freedom of Information and Privacy Staff

(select address from list that follows)

Washington, DC 20530

RE: Freedom of Information Act Request

Dear [Agency name]:

I am invoking my right under the Freedom of Information Act, 5 U.S.C. §552, and the Privacy Act, 5 U.S.C. §552a, to request access to all records related to:

> Make a list of the records you seek, include the agency, the field office, and agent name if available.
>
> Example
>
> Kelly Patrick Riggs, to include but not limited to D.E.A. 6, and 302 reports, Witness Statements, Warrants, Affidavits, Agent Notes, etc. that may have been completed by Agent Cornelius Harris in the Birmingham, AL F.B.I. field office.

I request that you make a determination regarding the release of this information within 20 days pursuant to 5 U.S.C. §552(a)(6)(i).

Moreover, I request a waiver of any possible fee that may or may not be imposed by your office, pursuant to 5 U.S.C. §552(a)(4)(A)(iii), as these documents will go directly to the public's interest in the integrity of the United States criminal justice system.

In the event you deny all or any part of this request, please cite each specific exemption you believe justifies your refusal to release, under the law. For any questions about handling this request, you may contact me at the address listed above.

Sincerely,

_____

[Name]

cc:

P/file

APPEAL FROM A FOIA DENIAL

An appeal from a denial of a FOIA request is governed by 28 CFR §16.8, 5 U.S.C. §§ 552(a)(4) and 552 (a)(6)(A)-(C). If you are dissatisfied with an agency's response to your request, you can appeal the determination to deny any or all of your request to: Freedom of Information Act Appeal, Office of Information and Privacy, U.S. Department of Justice, Flag Building, Suite 570, Washington, DC. 20503. Your appeal must be in writing and must be received by the "Office of Information and Privacy" within 60 days from the date that appears on the agency letter that denied your request.

Your appeal from a FOIA request denial can be formatted as a simple letter stating the facts and arguments in support of your claim "that the agency erred when it denied your request." See the Sample Appeal Letter that follows.

In the event that your appeal is not successful, you have a right to file a civil action in the appropriate federal district court tinder 28 U.S.C. §1331 and 5 U.S.C. §552(a)(4)(B).

[Your name and prisoner number]

[Your institution]

[Your address]

[Your Town, State, Zip Code]

[DATE]

FOIA Appeal

Department of Justice

Flag Building, Suite 570

Washington, DC 20530

RE: FOIA appeal from Case No.: _____

To the Administrator:

Mr. _____ files this appeal under the authority mandated by the enactment of 5 U.S.C. §522 on [Date]. I filed a FOIA request to your agency for information and data related to: [Restate your request here] on [Date], your agency denied my request in part because [Describe the agency's reasons for denial]. Please find copies of my original FOIA request and your agency's response attached hereto.

The requested material is clearly reasonable under the FOIA and I consider your agency's blanket denial policy to be arbitrary and capricious.

[Present a brief statement stating your need for the materials]. Thus, the denial of the FOIA request in this case is clearly a violation of President Obama's Executive Order 2009.

Upon reconsideration, I respectfully request that you reverse the decision to deny my request. Finally, I respectfully request that you grant my appeal so additional litigation won't be necessary to obtain what's rightfully due under federal law.

Respectfully submitted,

_____

[Your Name]

cc: p/file

DEPARTMENT OF JUSTICE COMPONENTS

Deputy Director
Office of Information and Privacy Suite 570,
Flag Building Department of Justice
Washington, DC 20530-0001

Civil Rights Division
Chief, FOIA/PA Branch
Civil Rights
Division Box 65310
Department of Justice
Washington, DC 20035

Executive Office for United States Attorneys
Assistant Director, FOIA/Privacy Unit
Executive Office for United States Attorneys
Room 7200, 600 E Street, NW
Department of Justice
Washington, DC 20530-0001

Federal Bureau of Prisons
Chief, FOIA Section
Office of the Director
FOIA/Privacy Act Requests
Room 738, HOLC Building Bureau of Prisons
Department of Justice
Washington, DC 20534

Director
Freedom of Information
Act/Privacy Act Program
Immigration and Naturalization Service
2nd Floor, 425 Eye Street, NW
Department of Justice
Washington, DC 20536

Tax Division
Senior Division Counsel for FOIA and PA
Matters Tax Division
950 Pennsylvania Avenue, NW
Department of Justice
Washington, DC 20530-0001

United States Parole Commission
FOIA Officer

United States parole Commission Suite 420,
5550 Friendship Boulevard Department of
Justify
Chevy Chase, MD 20815

Civil Division
Freedom of Information/Privacy Act Officer
Civil Division Room 808
901 E Street, NW
Department of Justice
Washington, DC 20530-0001

Drug Enforcement Administration Chief
Freedom of Information Operations Unit Drug
Enforcement Administration Department of
Justice
700 Army Navy Drive
Arlington, VA 22202

Federal Bureau of Investigation Chief, FOIA
PA Section
Federal Bureau of Investigation
935 Pennsylvania Avenue, NW
Department of Justice
Washington, DC 20535-0001

INTERPOL – United States National Central
Bureau
FOIA/PA Specialist
INTERPOL – United States National Central
Bureau
Department of Justice
Washington, DC 20530-0001

Office of the Inspector General
POIA Paralegal Specialist
Office of the Inspector General
Room 4261, 950 Pennsylvania Avenue, NW
Department of Justice
Washington, DC 20530-0001

Office of Justice programs
FOIA Legal Technician Office of Justice
Programs Room 5400, 810 7th Street, NW,
Department of Justice
Washington, DC 20531

United States Marshals Service FOIA/PA
Officer Office of General Counsel
United States Marshals Service
Suite 1250, 600 Army Navy Drive
Department of Justice
Arlington, VA 22202-4210

OTHER FEDERAL AGENCIES

Bureau of Alcohol, Tobacco and Firearms
Chief, Disclosure Division, Room 8400
6550 Massachusetts Avenue, NW,
Washington, DC 20522-6001

Department of State Director
Office of IRM Programs
SA-2, 5th Floor
Washington, DC 20522-6001

National Archives.
FOIA Officer
Office of the General Counsel
8601 Adelphi Road
College Park, MD 20740-6001

United States Secret Service
POIA/PA Officer Suite 3000
950 H Street, NW
Washington, DC 20001

Central Intelligence Agency
POIA and Privacy Coordinator
Washington, DC 20505

Internal Revenue Service
Director, Freedom of Information
Office of Disclosure
1111 Constitution Avenue, NW
Washington, DC 20224

United States Customs Service FOIA
Paralegal Specialist,
ORR Room 34A
1300 Pennsylvania Avenue, NW, Washington,
DC 2022

CHAPTER TWENTY-FIVE

IN THE INTERIM

I've said it many times before, and I say it again; the interpretation of law is a living, breathing, all-consuming creature that continually evolves. Thus, we must continually study to prepare our minds. As recent as March of 2017, I – through no fault of my own – was caught off-guard by a new en banc decision in the Eleventh Circuit.

This occurred shortly after the Supreme Court upheld its *Martinez* and *Trevino* decisions in its ruling handed down in *Buck v. Davis* (2017). Based upon the Supreme Court's position concerning counsel in habeas proceedings; I filed for relief in three cases under 28 U.S.C. §2241(c)(3). In March of 2017, the Eleventh Circuit Court of Appeals, sitting en banc, effectively invalidated 28 U.S.C. §2241 (c)(3). Days later, the United States District Court for the Middle District of Florida, Ocala Division, dismissed all three petitions for a lack of jurisdiction, based on the Eleventh Circuit's holding in *McCarthan v. Director of Goodwill Industries – Suncoast. Inc.* 851 F.3d 1076.

STUDYING THE UPDATES

I say that this record decision caught me off guard because I had no idea it was in litigation, nor did I realize its effects. The reason I was surprised is because of its timing. I ordinarily study all recent changes in the law and precedent to stay informed. This little debacle, however, was unavoidable because *McCarthan* took effect on how things were done before it was published. By the time I made the discovery, all three cases had been dismissed. But I was quite well-prepared for the appeals.

Let me make this as clear as possible; study the quarterly updates. If you are in federal prison, you can access the updates via Lexis Nexus. On the main menu you will find Supreme Court updates, as well as Courts of Appeals updates. Take advantage of this resource. At a minimum, it will sharpen your understanding of what you already know.

SWEAT THE DETAILS

You've studied the case file, you've studied the law, and you've developed your claim. Now you're ready, right? Wrong! Facts. This case is all about the facts and you can't possibly know it all about someone else's case. In my normal process, I develop the points I think are important. I then take my client (victim) to the walking track (if possible) for my first interrogation. This is where I have them fill in all my questions with additional details. In most cases, I have to do this a few times.

Once I think I have it all together, I compare my supporting facts (affidavit and/or supporting facts) to the record to be sure that it's effective to either clarify the record or completely supplant the false information it contains. My goal is to get a response of disbelief out of my client. I want him or her to declare that that's what they're trying to say. Anything less is ineffective on your part.

THE EXTRA MILE

Please don't misunderstand this section as a requirement or even a suggestion. I'm only sharing my own experience. As mentioned earlier, clarity is rewarded. Can you imagine what it would be like if you had to read this book by skipping around random pages? Now imagine if I provided you a hodge-podge sequence of page numbers to follow, yeah, confusion and frustration. I strive to make everything easy on a judge, even reading my work.

Now then, if you look at a 28 U.S.C. §2255 form, you discover a limited amount of space to present your ground for relief and even less by proportion to set out your supporting facts, and I detest the words "See attached."

In going through great lengths to construct a §2255 motion that can be read as a book, like this one, I made my own. (See example at the end of this chapter).

As you can see, I provide adequate space to show my ground. I then left the remainder of that page for my supporting facts. The page that follows is an optional page if more room is needed for your supporting facts. In the event even more room is needed, simply add pages. If you do this for each ground, you will easily have a sequential book format.

I'm including my own custom §2255 that you may use at your own risk. It works for me and likely will work for you. To use the one in this book, simply copy it in a single-side format, increasing its size by 10%. Don't forget to add page numbers.

MOTION UNDER 28 U.S.C. § 2255 TO VACATE, SET ASIDE, OR CORRECT

SENTENCE BY A PERSON IN FEDERAL CUSTODY

United States District Court	District	
Name *(under which you were convicted)*:		Docket or Case No.:
Place of Confinement:	Prisoner No.:	
UNITED STATES OF AMERICA V.	Movant *(include name under which convicted)*	

MOTION

1. (a) Name and location of court which entered the judgment of conviction you are challenging:

   _____

   (b) Criminal docket or case number (if you know): _____

2. (a) Date of the judgment of conviction (if you know): _____

   (b) Date of sentencing: _____

3. Length of sentence: _____

4. Nature of crime (all counts):

5. (a) What was your plea? (Check one)

   (1) Not guilty ☐   (2) Guilty ☐   (3) Nolo contendere (no contest) ☐

   (b) If you entered a guilty plea to one count or indictment, and a not guilty plea to another count or what did you plead guilty to and what did you plead not guilty to?

6. If you went to trial, what kind of trial did you have? (Check one)   Jury ☐   Judge only ☐

7. Did you testify at a pretrial hearing, trial, or post-trial hearing?   Yes ☐   No ☐

8. Did you appeal from the judgment of conviction?   Yes ☐   No ☐

93

9. If you did appeal, answer the following:

   (a) Name of court: _____

   (b) Docket or case number (if you know): _____

   (c) Result: _____

   (d) Date of result (if you know): _____

   (e) Citation to the case (if you know): _____

   (f) Grounds raised:

   (g) Did you file a petition for certiorari in the United States Supreme Court?   Yes ☐   No ☐

      If "Yes," answer the following:

      (1) Docket or case number (if you know): _____

      (2) Result: _____

      (3) Date of result (if you know): _____

      (4) Citation to the case (if you know): _____

      (5) Grounds raised:

10. Other than the direct appeals listed above, have you previously filed any other motions, petitions, or applications, concerning this judgment of conviction in any court?
   Yes ☐   No ☐

11. If your answer to Question 10 was "Yes," give the following information:

   (a) (1) Name of court: _____

      (2) Docket or case number (if you know): _____

      (3) Date of filing (if you know): _____

      (4) Nature of the proceeding: _____

      (5) Grounds raised: _____

(6) Did you receive a hearing where evidence was given on your motion, petition, or application?

Yes ☐ No ☐

(7) Result: _____

(8) Date of result (if you know): _____

(b) If you filed any second motion, petition, or application, give the same information:

(1) Name of court: _____

(2) Docket of case number (if you know): _____

(3) Date of filing (if you know): _____

(4) Nature of the proceeding: _____

(5) Grounds raised:

(6) Did you receive a hearing where evidence was given on your motion, petition, or application?

Yes ☐ No ☐

(7) Result: _____

(8) Date of result (if you know): _____

(c) Did you appeal to a federal appellate court having jurisdiction over the action taken on your motion, petition, or application?

(1) First petition: Yes ☐ No ☐

(2) Second petition: Yes ☐ No ☐

(d) If you did not appeal from the action on any motion, petition, or application, explain briefly why you did not:

12. For this motion, state every ground on which you claim that you are being held in violation of the Constitution, laws, or treaties of the United States. Attach additional pages if you have more than four grounds. State the facts supporting each ground.

GROUND ONE:

(a) Supporting facts (Do not argue or cite law. Just state the specific facts that support your claim.):

GROUND ONE:

(a) Supporting facts (Continued):

(b) **Direct Appeal of Ground One:**

    (1) If you appealed from the judgment of conviction, did you raise this issue?

        Yes ☐   No ☐

    (2) If you did not raise this issue in your direct appeal, explain why:

(c) **Post-Conviction Proceedings:**

    (1) Did you raise this issue in any post-conviction motion, petition, or application?

        Yes ☐   No ☐

    (2) If you answer to Question (c)(1) is "Yes," state:

Type of motion or petition: _____

Name and location of the court where the motion or petition was filed:

Docket or case number (if you know): _____

Date of the court's decision: _____

Result (attach a copy of the court's opinion or order, if available):

---

    (3) Did you receive a hearing on your motion, petition, or application?

        Yes ☐   No ☐

    (4) Did you appeal from the denial of your motion, petition, or application?

        Yes ☐   No ☐

    (5) If your answer to Question (c)(4) is "Yes," did you raise the issue in the appeal?

        Yes ☐   No ☐

    (6) If your answer to Question (c)(4) is "Yes," state:

Name and location of the court where the appeal was filed:

Docket or case number (if you know): _____

Date of the court's decision: _____

Result (attach a copy of the court's opinion or order, if available):

---

    (7) If your answer to Question (c)(4) or Question (c)(5) is "No," explain why you did not appeal or raise this issue:

GROUND TWO:

(a) Supporting facts (Do not argue or cite law. Just state the specific facts that support your claim.):

GROUND TWO:

(a) Supporting facts (Continued):

(b) **Direct Appeal of Ground Two:**

    (1) If you appealed from the judgment of conviction, did you raise this issue?

        Yes ☐   No ☐

    (2) If you did not raise this issue in your direct appeal, explain why:

_____

(c) **Post-Conviction Proceedings:**

    (1) Did you raise this issue in any post-conviction motion, petition, or application?

        Yes ☐   No ☐

    (2) If you answer to Question (c)(1) is "Yes," state:

    Type of motion or petition: _____

    Name and location of the court where the motion or petition was filed:

_____

    Docket or case number (if you know): _____

    Date of the court's decision: _____

    Result (attach a copy of the court's opinion or order, if available):

_____

    (3) Did you receive a hearing on your motion, petition, or application?

        Yes ☐   No ☐

    (4) Did you appeal from the denial of your motion, petition, or application?

        Yes ☐   No ☐

    (5) If your answer to Question (c)(4) is "Yes," did you raise the issue in the appeal?

        Yes ☐   No ☐

    (6) If your answer to Question (c)(4) is "Yes," state:

    Name and location of the court where the appeal was filed:

_____

Docket or case number (if you know): _____

Date of the court's decision: _____

Result (attach a copy of the court's opinion or order, if available):

_____

    (7) If your answer to Question (c)(4) or Question (c)(5) is "No," explain why you did not appeal or raise this issue:

GROUND THREE:

(a) Supporting facts (Do not argue or cite law. Just state the specific facts that support your claim.):

GROUND THREE:

(a) Supporting facts (Continued):

(b) Direct Appeal of Ground Three:

    (1) If you appealed from the judgment of conviction, did you raise this issue?

        Yes ☐   No ☐

    (2) If you did not raise this issue in your direct appeal, explain why:

(c) Post-Conviction Proceedings:

    (1) Did you raise this issue in any post-conviction motion, petition, or application?

        Yes ☐   No ☐

    (2) If you answer to Question (c)(1) is "Yes," state:

Type of motion or petition: _____

Name and location of the court where the motion or petition was filed:

Docket or case number (if you know): _____

Date of the court's decision: _____

Result (attach a copy of the court's opinion or order, if available):

    (3) Did you receive a hearing on your motion, petition, or application?

        Yes ☐   No ☐

    (4) Did you appeal from the denial of your motion, petition, or application?

        Yes ☐   No ☐

    (5) If your answer to Question (c)(4) is "Yes," did you raise the issue in the appeal?

        Yes ☐   No ☐

    (6) If your answer to Question (c)(4) is "Yes," state:

Name and location of the court where the appeal was filed:

Docket or case number (if you know): _____

Date of the court's decision: _____

Result (attach a copy of the court's opinion or order, if available):

    (7) If your answer to Question (c)(4) or Question (c)(5) is "No," explain why you did not appeal or raise this issue:

GROUND FOUR:

(a) Supporting facts (Do not argue or cite law. Just state the specific facts that support your claim.):

GROUND FOUR:

(a) Supporting facts (Continued):

(b) **Direct Appeal of Ground Four:**

    (1) If you appealed from the judgment of conviction, did you raise this issue?

        Yes ☐   No ☐

    (2) If you did not raise this issue in your direct appeal, explain why:

(c) **Post-Conviction Proceedings:**

    (1) Did you raise this issue in any post-conviction motion, petition, or application?

        Yes ☐   No ☐

    (2) If you answer to Question (c)(1) is "Yes," state:

    Type of motion or petition: _____

    Name and location of the court where the motion or petition was filed:

    Docket or case number (if you know): _____

    Date of the court's decision: _____

    Result (attach a copy of the court's opinion or order, if available):

    (3) Did you receive a hearing on your motion, petition, or application?

        Yes ☐   No ☐

    (4) Did you appeal from the denial of your motion, petition, or application?

        Yes ☐   No ☐

    (5) If your answer to Question (c)(4) is "Yes," did you raise the issue in the appeal?

        Yes ☐   No ☐

    (6) If your answer to Question (c)(4) is "Yes," state:

    Name and location of the court where the appeal was filed:

    Docket or case number (if you know): _____

    Date of the court's decision: _____

    Result (attach a copy of the court's opinion or order, if available):

    (7) If your answer to Question (c)(4) or Question (c)(5) is "No," explain why you did not appeal or raise this issue:

13. Is there any ground in this motion that you have <u>not</u> previously presented in some federal court? If so, which ground or grounds have not been presented, and state your reasons for not presenting them:

14. Do you have any motion, petition, or appeal <u>now pending</u> (filed and not decided yet) in any court for the you are challenging?　　Yes ☐　　　No ☐
If "Yes," state the name and location of the court, the docket or case number, the type of proceeding, and the issues raised.

15. Give the name and address, if known, of each attorney who represented you in the following stages of the you are challenging:
(a) At the preliminary hearing:

(b) At the arraignment and plea:

(c) At the trial:

(d) At sentencing:

(e) On appeal:

(f) In any post-conviction proceeding:

(g) On appeal from any ruling against you in a post-conviction proceeding:

16. Were you sentenced on more than one court of an indictment, or on more than one indictment, in the same court and at the same time? Yes ☐ No ☐

17. Do you have any future sentence to serve after you complete the sentence for the judgment that you are challenging? Yes ☐ No ☐

    (a) If so, give name and location of court that imposed the other sentence you will serve in the future:

    _____

    (b) Give the date the other sentence was imposed: _____

    (c) Give the length of the other sentence: _____

    (d) Have you filed, or do you plan to file, any motion, petition, or application that challenges the judgment or sentence to be served in the future? Yes ☐ No ☐

18. TIMELINESS OF MOTION: If your judgment of conviction became final over one year ago, you must explain why the one-year statute of limitations as contained in 28 U.S.C. § 2255 does not bar your motion.*

---

* The Antiterrorism and Effective Death Penalty Act of 1996 ("AEDPA") as contained in 28 U.S.C. § 2255, paragraph 6, provides in part that:

A one-year period of limitation shall apply to a motion under this section. The limitation period shall run from the latest of –

    (1) the date on which the judgment of conviction became final;

    (2) the date on which the impediment to making a motion created by governmental action in violation of the Constitution or laws of the United States is removed, if the movant was prevented from making such a motion by such governmental action;

    (3) the date on which the right asserted was initially recognized by the Supreme Court, if that right has been newly recognized by the Supreme Court and made retroactively applicable to cases on collateral review; or

    (4) the date on which the facts supporting the claim or claims presented could have been discovered through the exercise of due diligence.

Therefore, movant asks that the Court grant the following relief:

_____

or any other relief to which movant may be entitled.

_____
Signature of Attorney (if any)

I declare (or certify, verify, or state) under penalty of perjury that the foregoing is true and correct and that this Motion under 28 U.S.C. § 2255 was placed in the prison mailing system on _____.

                                                                    (month, date, year)

Executed (signed) on _____ (date)

_____
Signature of Movant

If the person signing is not movant, state relationship to movant and explain why movant is not signing this motion.

APPENDIX

FEDERAL RULES OF CIVIL PROCEDURE

Rule 1. Scope and Purpose

These rules govern the procedure in all civil actions and proceedings in the United States district courts, except as stated in Rule 81. They should be construed and administered to secure the just, speedy, and inexpensive determination of

Rule 2. One Form of Action

There is one form of action – the civil action.

Rule 3. Commencing an Action

A civil action is commenced by filing a complaint with the court.

Rule 4. Summons

(a) CONTENTS; AMENDMENTS.
    (1) *Contents*. A summons must:
        (A) name the court and the parties;
        (B) be directed to the defendant;
        (C) state the name and address of the plaintiff's attorney or – if unrepresented – of the plaintiff;
        (D) state the time within which the defendant must appear and defend;
        (E) notify the defendant that a failure to appear and defend will result in a default judgment against the defendant for the relief demanded in the complaint;
        (F) be signed by the clerk; and
        (G) bear the court's seal.
    (2) *Amendments*. The court may permit a summons to be amended.
(b) ISSUANCE. On or after filing the complaint, the plaintiff may present a summons to the clerk for signature and seal. If the summons is properly completed, the clerk must sign, seal, and issue it ti the plaintiff for service on the defendant. A summons – or a copy of a summons that is addressed to multiple defendants – must be issued for each defendant to be served.
(c) SERVICE.
    (1) *In General*. A summons must be served with a copy of the complaint. The plaintiff is responsible for having the summons and complaint served within the time allowed by Rule 4(m) and must furnish the necessary copies to the person who makes service.
    (2) *By Whom*. Any person who is at least 18 years old and not a party may serve a summons and complaint.
    (3) *By a Marshal or Someone Specially Appointed*. At the plaintiff's request, the court may order that service be made by a United States marshal or deputy marshal or by a person specially appointed by the court. The court must so order if the plaintiff is authorized to proceed in *forma pauperis* under 28 U.S.C. § 1915 or as a seaman under 28 U.S.C. § 1916.
(d) WAIVING SERVICE.
    (1) *Requesting a Waiver*. An individual, corporation, or association that is subject to service under Rule 4(e), (f), or (h) has a duty to avoid unnecessary expenses of serving the summons. The plaintiff may notify such a defendant that an action has been commenced and request the defendant waive service of a summons. The notice and request must:
    (A) be in writing and be addressed:

       (i) to the individual defendant; or

       (ii) for a defendant subject to service under Rule 4(h), to an officer, a managing or general agent, or any other agent authorized by appointment or by law to receive service of process;

   (B) name the court where the complaint was filed;

   (C) be accompanied by a copy of the complaint, two copies of a waiver form, and a prepaid means for returning the form;

   (D) inform the defendant, using text prescribed in Form 5, of the consequences of waiving or not waiving service;

   (E) state the date when the request is sent;

   (F) give the defendant a reasonable time of at least 30 days after the request was sent – or at least 60 days if sent to the defendant outside any judicial district of the United States – to return the waiver; and

   (G) be sent by first-class mail or other reliable means.

(2) *Failure to Waive.* If a defendant located within the United States fails, without good cause, to sign and return a waiver requested by a plaintiff located within the United States, the court must impose on the defendant:

   (A) the expenses later incurred in making service; and

   (B) the reasonable expenses, including attorney's fees, of any motion required to collect those service expenses.

(3) *Time to Answer after a Waiver.* A defendant who, before being served with process, timely returns a waiver need not serve an answer to the complaint until 60 days after the request was sent – or until 90 days after it was sent to the defendant outside any judicial district of the United States.

(4) *Results of Filing a Waiver.* When the plaintiff files a waiver, proof of service is not required and these rules apply as if a summons and complaint had been served at the time of filing the waiver.

(5) *Jurisdiction and Venue Not Waived.* Waiving service of a summons does not waive any objection to personal jurisdiction or to venue.

(e) SERVING AN INDIVIDUAL WITHIN A JUDICIAL DISTRICT OF THE UNITED STATES. Unless federal law provides otherwise, an individual – other than a minor, incompetent person, or a person whose waiver has been filed may be served in a judicial district in the United States by:

(1) following state law for serving a summons in an action brought in courts of general jurisdiction in the state where the district court is located or where service is made; or

(2) doing any of the following:

   (A) delivering a copy of the summons and of the complaint to the individual personally;

   (B) leaving a copy of each at the individual's dwelling or usual place of abode with someone of suitable age and discretion who resides there; or

   (C) delivering a copy of each to an agent authorized by appointment or by law to receive service of process.

(f) SERVING AN INDIVIDUAL IN A FOREIGN COUNTRY. Unless federal law provides otherwise, an individual – other than a minor, an incompetent person, or a person whose waiver has been filed – may be served at a place not within any judicial district of the United States:

(1) by any internationally agreed means of service that is reasonably calculated to give notice, such as those authorized by the Hague Convention on the Service Abroad of Judicial and Extrajudicial Documents;

(2) if there is no internationally agreed means, or if an international agreement allows but does not specify other means, by a method that is reasonably calculated to give notice:

(A) as prescribed by the foreign country's law for service in that country in an action in its courts of general jurisdiction;

(B) as the foreign authority directs in response to a letter rogatory or letter of request; or

(C) unless prohibited by the foreign country's law, by:

    (i) delivering a copy of the summons and of the complaint to the individual personally; or

    (ii) using any form of mail that the clerk addresses and sends to the individual and that requires a signed receipt ; or

(3) by other means not prohibited by international agreement, as the court orders.

(g) SERVING A MINOR OR AN INCOMPETENT PERSON. A minor or an incompetent person in a judicial district of the United States must be served by following state law for serving a summons or like process on such a defendant in an action brought in the courts of general jurisdiction of the state where service is made. A minor or an incompetent person who is not within any judicial district of the United States must be served in the manner prescribed by Rule 4(f)(2)(A), (2)(B), or (f)(3).

(h) SERVING A CORPORATION, PARTNERSHIP, OR ASSOCIATION. Unless federal law provides otherwise or the defendant's waiver has been filed, a domestic or foreign corporation, or a partnership or other unincorporated association that is subject to suit under a common name, must be served:

(1) in a judicial district of the United States:

(A) in the manner prescribed by Rule 4(e)(1) for serving an individual; or

(B) by delivering a copy of the summons and of the complaint to an officer, a managing or general agent, or any other agent authorized by appointment or by law to receive service of process and – if the agent is one authorized by statute and the statute so requires – by also mailing a copy of each to the defendant; or

(2) at a place not within any judicial district of the United States, in any manner prescribed by Rule 4(f) for serving an individual, except personal delivery under (f)(2)(C)(i).

(i) SERVING THE UNITED STATES AND ITS AGENCIES, CORPORATIONS, OFFICERS, OR EMPLOYEES.

(1) *United States.* To serve the United States, a party must:

(A)

    (i) deliver a copy of the summons and of the complaint to the United States attorney for the district where the action is brought – or to an assistant United States attorney or clerical employee whom the United States attorney designates in a writing filed with the court clerk – or

    (ii) send a copy of each by registered or certified mail to the civil-process clerk at the United States attorney's office;

(B) send a copy of each by registered or certified mail to the Attorney General of the United States at Washington, D.C.; and

(C) if the action challenges an order of a nonparty agency or officer of the United States, send a copy of each by registered or certified mail to the agency or officer.

(2) *Agency; Corporation: Officer or Employee Sued in an Official Capacity.* To serve a United States agency or corporation, or a United States officer or employee sued only in an official capacity, a party must serve the United States and also send a copy of the summons and of the complaint by registered or certified mail to the agency , corporation, officer, or employee.

(3) *Officer or Employee Sued Individually.* To serve a United States officer or employee sued in an official capacity for an act or omission occurring in connection with duties performed on the United States' behalf (whether or not the officer or employee is also sued in an official capacity), a party must serve the United States and also serve the officer or employee under Rule 4(e), (f), or (g).

(4) *Extending Time.* The court must allow a party the reasonable time to cure its failure to:

(A) serve a person required to be served under Rule 4(i)(2), if the party has served either the United States attorney or the Attorney General of the United States; or

(B) serve the United States under Rule 4(i)(3), if the party has served the United States officer or employee.

(j) SERVING A FOREIGN, STATE, OR LOCAL GOVERNMENT.

(1) *Foreign State*. A foreign state or its political subdivision, agency, or instrumentality must be served in accordance with 28 U.S.C. § 1608.

(2) *State or Local Government*. A state, a municipal corporation, or any other state-created governmental organization that is subject to suit must be served by:

(A) delivering a copy of the summons and of the complaint to its chief executive officer; or

(B) serving a copy of each in the manner prescribed by that state's law for serving a summons or like process on such a defendant.

(k) TERRITORIAL LIMITS OF EFFECTIVE SERVICE.

(1) *In General*. Serving a summons or filing a waiver of service establishes personal jurisdiction offer a defendant:

(A) who is subject to the jurisdiction of a court of general jurisdiction in the state where the district court is located;

(B) who is a party joined under Rule 14 or 19 and is served within a judicial district of the United States and not more than 100 miles from where the summons was issued; or

(C) when authorized by a federal statute.

(2) *Federal Claim Outside State-Court Jurisdiction*. For a claim that arises under federal law, serving a summons or filing a waiver of service establishes personal jurisdiction over a defendant if:

(A) the defendant is not subject to jurisdiction in any state's courts of general jurisdiction; and

(B) exercising jurisdiction is consistent with the United States Constitution and laws.

(l) PROVING SERVICE.

(1) *Affidavit Required*. Unless service is waived, proof of service must be made to the court. Except for service by a United States marshal or deputy marshal, proof must be by the server's affidavit.

(2) *Service Outside the United States*. Service not within any judicial district of the United States must be proved as follows:

(A) if made under Rule 4(f)(1), as provided in the applicable treaty or convention: or

(B) if made under Rule 4(f)(2) or (f)(3), by a receipt signed by the addressee, or by other evidence satisfying the court that the summons and complaint were delivered to the addressee.

(3) *Validity of Service; Amending Proof*. Failure to prove service does not affect the validity of service. The court may permit proof of service to be amended.

(m)TIME LIMIT FOR SERVICE, if a defendant is not served within 120 days after complaint is filed, the court – on motion or on its own after notice to the plaintiff – must dismiss the action without prejudice against the defendant or order that service be made within a specified time. But if the plaintiff shows good cause for the failure, the court must extend the time for service for an appropriate period. This subdivision (m) does not apply to service in a foreign country under Rule 4(f) or 4(j)(1).

(n) ASSURING JURISDICTION OVER PROPERTY OR ASSETS.

(1) *Federal law*. The court may assert jurisdiction over property if authorized by a federal statute. Notice to claimants of the property must be given as provided in the statute or by serving a summons under this rule.

(2) *State law.* On a showing that personal jurisdiction over a defendant cannot be obtained in the district where the action is brought by reasonable efforts to serve a summons under this rule, the court may assert jurisdiction over the defendant's assets found in the district. Jurisdiction is acquired by seizing the assets under the circumstances and in the manner provided by state law in that district.

Rule 4.1. Serving Other Process

(a) IN GENERAL. Process – other than a summons under Rule 4 or a subpoena under Rule 45 – must be served by a United States marshal or deputy marshal or by a person specially appointed for that purpose. It may be served anywhere within the territorial limits of the state where the district court is located and, if authorized by a federal statute, beyond those limits. Proof of service must be made under Rule 4(1).

(b) ENFORCING ORDERS: COMMITTING FOR CIVIL CONTEMPT. An order committing a person for civil contempt of a decree or injunction issued to enforce federal law may be served and enforced in any district. Any other order in a civil-contempt proceeding may be served only in the state where the issuing court is located or elsewhere in the United States within 100 miles from where the order was issued.

Rule 5. Serving and Filing Pleadings and Other Papers

(a) SERVICE: WHEN REQUIRED.
   (1) *In General.* Unless these rules provide otherwise, each of the following papers must be served on every party:
      (A) an order stating that service is required;
      (B) a pleading filed after the original complaint, unless the court orders otherwise under Rule 5(c) because there are numerous defendants;
      (C) a discovery paper required to be served on a party, unless the court orders otherwise;
      (D) a written motion, except on that may be heard ex parte; and
      (E) a written notice, appearance, demand, or offer of judgment, or any similar paper.
   (2) *If a Party Fails to Appear.* No service is required on a party who is in default for failing to appear. But a pleading that asserts a new claim for relief against such a party must be served on that party under Rule 4.
   (3) *Seizing Property.* If an action is begun by seizing property and no person is or need be named as a defendant, any service required before the filing of an appearance, answer, or claim must be made on the person who had custody or possession of the property when it was seized.

(b) SERVICE: HOW MADE.
   (1) *Serving an Attorney.* If a party is represented by an attorney, service under this rule must be made on the attorney unless the court orders service on the party.
   (2) *Service in General.* A paper is served under this rule by:
      (A) handing it to the person;
      (B) leaving it:
         (i) at the person's office with a clerk or other person in charge or, if no one is in charge, in a conspicuous place in the office; or
         (ii) if the person has no office or if the office is closed, at the person's dwelling or usual place of abode with someone of suitable age and discretion who resides there;
      (C) mailing it to the person's last known address – in which event service is complete upon mailing;
      (D) leaving it with the court clerk if the person has no known address;

(E) sending it to a registered user by filing it with the court's electronic-filing system or sending it by other electronic means that the person consented to in writing – in either of which events service is complete upon filing or sending, but is not effective if the filer or sender learns that it did not reach the person to be served; or

(F) delivering it by any other means that the person consented to in writing – in which event service is complete when the person making service delivers it to the agency designated to make delivery.

(3) *Using Court Facilities.* If a local rule so authorizes, a party may use the court's transmission facilities to make service under Rule 5(b)(2)(E).

(c) SERVING NUMEROUS DEFENDANTS.

(1) *In General.* If an action involves an unusually large number of defendants, the court may, on motion or on its own, order that:

(A) defendants' pleadings and replies to them need not he served on other defendants;

(B) any crossclaim, counterclaim, avoidance, or affirmative defense in those pleadings and replies to them will be treated as denied or avoided by all other parties; and

(C) filing any such pleading and serving it on the plaintiff constitutes notice of the pleading to all parties.

(2) *Notifying Parties.* A copy of every such order must he served on the parties as the court directs.

(d) FILING.

(1) *Required Filings; Certificate of Service.*

(A) *Papers after the Complaint.* Any paper after the complaint that is required to be served must be filed no later than a reasonable time after service. But disclosures under Rule 26(a)(1) or (2) and the following discovery requests and responses must not be filed until they are used in the proceeding or the court orders filing: depositions, interrogatories, requests for documents or tangible things or to permit entry onto land, and requests for admission.

(B) *Certificate of Service.* No certificate of service is required when a paper is served by filing it with the court's electronic-filing system. When a paper that is required to be served is served by other means:

(i) if the paper is filed, a certificate of service must be filed with it or within a reasonable time after service; and

(ii) if the paper is not filed, a certificate of service need not be filed unless filing is required by court order or by local rule.

(2) *Nonelectronic Filing.* A paper not filed electronically is filed by delivering it:

(A) to the clerk; or

(B) to a judge who agrees to accept it for filing, and who must then note the filing date on the paper and promptly send it to the clerk.

(3) *Electronic Filing and Signing.*

(A) *By a Represented Person – Generally Required; Exceptions.* A person represented by an attorney must file electronically, unless nonelectronic filing is allowed by the court for good cause or is allowed or required by local rule.

(B) *By an Unrepresented Person – When Allowed or Required.* A person not represented by an attorney:

(i) may file electronically only if allowed by court order or by local rule; and

(ii) may be required to file electronically only by court order, or by a local rule that includes reasonable exceptions.

(C) *Signing.* A filing made through a person's electronicfiling account and authorized by that person, together with that person's name on a signature block, constitutes the person's signature.

(D) *Same as a Written Paper.* A paper filed electronically is a written paper for purposes of these rules.

(4) *Acceptance by the Clerk.* The clerk must not refuse to file a paper solely because it is not in the form prescribed by these rules or by a local rule or practice.

Rule 5.1. Constitutional Challenge to a Statute – Notice, Certification, and Intervention

(a) NOTICE BY A PARTY. A party that files a pleading, written motion, or other paper drawing into question the constitutionality of a federal or state statute must promptly:

(1) file a notice of constitutional question stating the question and identifying the paper that raises it, if:

(A) a federal statute is questioned, and the parties do not include the United States, one of its agencies, or one of its officers or employees in an official capacity; or

(B) a state statute is questioned, and the parties do not include the state, one of its agencies, or one of its officers or employees in an official capacity; and

(2) serve the notice and paper on the Attorney general of the United States if a federal statute is questioned – or on the state attorney general if a state statute is questioned – either by certified or registered mail or by sending it to an electronic address designated by the attorney general for this purpose.

(b) CERTIFICATION BY THE COURT. The court must, under 28 U.S.C. § 2403, certify to the appropriate attorney general that a statute has been questioned.

(c) INTERVENTION; FINAL DECISION ON THE MERITS. Unless the court sets a later time, the attorney general may intervene within 60 days after the notice is filed or after the court certifies the challenge, whichever is earlier. Before the time to intervene expires, the court may reject the constitutional challenge, but may not enter a final judgment holding the statue unconstitutional.

(d) NO FORFEITURE. A party's failure to file and serve the notice, or the court's failure to certify, does not forfeit a constitutional claim or defense that is otherwise timely asserted.

Rule 5.2. Privacy Protection for Filings Made with the Court

(a) REDACTED FILINGS. Unless the court orders otherwise, in an electronic or paper filing with the court that contains an individual's social-security number, taxpayer-identification number, or birth date, the name of an individual known to be a minor, or a financial-account number, a party or nonparty making the filing may include only:

(1) the last four digits of the social-security number and taxpayer-identification number;

(2) the year of the individual's birth;

(3) the minor's initials; and

(4) the last four digits of the financial-account number.

(b) EXEMPTIONS FROM THE REDACTION REQUIREMENT. The redaction requirement does not apply to the following:

(1) a financial-account number that identifies the property allegedly subject to forfeiture in a forfeiture proceeding;

(2) the record of an administrative or agency proceeding;

(3) the official record of a state court proceeding;

(4) the record of a court or tribunal, if that record was not subject to the redaction requirement when originally filed;

(5) a filing covered by Rule 5.2(c) or (d); and

(6) a pro se filing in an action brought under 28 U.S.C. §§ 2241, 2254, cr 2255.

(c) LIMITATIONS ON REMOTE ACCESS TO ELECTRONIC FILES; SOCIAL-SECURITY APPEALS AND IMMIGRATION CASES. Unless the court orders otherwise, in an action for benefits under the Social Security Act, and in an action or proceeding relating to an order of removal, to relief from removal, or to immigration benefits or detention, access to an electronic file is authorized as follows:

(1) the parties and their attorneys may have remote electronic access to any part of the case file, including the administrative record;

(2) any other person may have electronic access to the full record at the courthouse, but may have remote access only to :

(A) the docket maintained by the court; and

(B) an opinion, order, judgment, or other disposition of the court, but not any other part of the case file or the administrative record.

(d) FILINGS MADE UNDER SEAL. The court may order that a filing he made under seal without redaction. The court may later unseal the filing or order the person who made the filing to file a redacted version for the public record.

(e) PROTECTIVE ORDERS. For good cause, the court may by order in a case:

(1) require redaction of additional information; or

(2) limit or prohibit a nonparty's remote electronic access to a document filed with the court.

(f) OPTION FOR ADDITIONAL UNREDACTED FILING UNDER SEAL. A person making a redacted filing may also file an unredacted copy under seal. The court must retain the unredacted copy as part of the record.

(g) OPTION FOR FILING A REFERENCE LIST. A filing that contains information may be filed together with a reference list that identifies each item of redacted information and specifies an appropriate identifier that uniquely corresponds to each item listed. The list must be filed under seal and may be amended as of right. Any reference in the case to a listed identifier will be construed to refer to the corresponding item of information.

(h) WAIVER OF PROTECTION OF IDENTIFIERS. A person waives the protection of Rule 5.2(a) as to the person's own information by filing it without redaction and not under seal.

Rule 6. Computing and Extending Time; Time for Motion Papers

(a) COMPUTING TIME. The following rules apply in computing any time period specified in these rules, in any local rule or court order, or in any statute that does not specify a method of computing time.

(1) *Period Stated in Days or a Longer Unit.* When the period is stated in days or a longer unit of time:

(A) exclude the day of the event that triggers the period;

(B) count every day, including intermediate Saturdays, Sundays, and legal holidays; and

(C) include the last day of the period, but if the last day is a Saturday, Sunday, or legal holiday, the period continues to run until the end of the next day that is not a Saturday, Sunday, or legal holiday.

(2) *Period Stated in Hours.* When the period is stated in hours:

(A) begin counting immediately on the occurrence of the event that triggers the period;

(B) count every hour, including hours on intermediate Saturdays, Sundays, and legal holidays; and

(C) if the period would end on a Saturday, Sunday, or legal holiday, the period continues to run until the same time on the next day that is not a Saturday, Sunday, or legal holiday.

(3) *Inaccessibility of the Clerk's Office.* Unless the court orders otherwise, if the clerk's office is inaccessible:

(A) on the last day for filing under Rule 6(a)(1), then the time for filing is extended to the first day that is not a Saturday, Sunday, or legal holiday; or

(B) during the last hour of filing under Rule 6(a)(2), then the time for filing is extended to the same time on the first accessible day that is not a Saturday, Sunday, cr legal holiday.

(4) "LAST DAY" DEFINED. Unless a different time is set by a statute, local rule, or court order, the last day ends:

(A) for electronic filing, at midnight in the court's time zone; and

(B) for filing by other means, when the clerk's office is scheduled to close.

(5) *"Next Day" Defined.* The "next day" is determined by continuing to count forward when the period is measured after an event and backward when measured before an event.

(6) *"Legal holiday" Defined.* "Legal holiday" means:

(A) the day set aside by statute for observing New Year's Day, Martin Luther King Jr.'s Birthday, Washington's Birthday, Memorial Day, Independence Day, Labor Day, Columbus Day, Veterans' Day, Thanksgiving Day, or Christmas Day;

(B) any day declared a holiday by the President or Congress; and

(C) for periods that are measured after an event, any other day declared a holiday by the state where the district court is located.

(b) EXTENDING TIME.

(1) *In General.* When an act may or must be done within a specified time, the court may, for good cause, extend the time:

(A) with or without motion or notice if the court acts, or if a request is made, before the original time or its extension expires; or

(B) on motion made after the time has expired if the party failed to act because of excusable neglect.

(2) *Exceptions.* A court must not extend the time to act under Rules 50(b) and (d), 52(b), 59(b), (d), and (e), and 60(b).

(c) MOTIONS, NOTICES OF HEARING, AND AFFIDAVITS.

(1) *In General.* A written motion and notice of the hearing must be served at least 14 days before the time specified for the hearing, with the following exceptions:

(A) when the motion may be heard ex parte;

(B) when these rules set a different time; or

(C) when a court order – which a party may, for good cause, apply for ex parte – sets a different time.

(2) *Supporting Affidavit.* Any affidavit supporting a motion must be served with the motion. Except as Rule 59(c) provides otherwise, any opposing affidavit must be served at least 7 days before the hearing, unless the court permits service at another time.

(d) ADDITIONAL TIME AFTER CERTAIN KINDS OF SERVICE. When a party may or must act within a specified time after being served and service is made under Rule 5(b)(2)(C) (mail), (D) (leaving with the clerk), or (F) (other means consented to), 3 days are added after the period would otherwise expire under Rule 6(a).

Rule 7. Pleadings Allowed; Form of Motions and Other Papers

(a) PLEADINGS. Only these pleadings are allowed:

(1) a complaint;

(2) an answer to a complaint;

(3) an answer to a counterclaim designated as a counterclaim;

(4) an answer to a crossclaim;

(5) a third-party complaint;

(6) an answer to a third-party complaint; and

(7) if the court orders one, a reply to an answer.

(b) MOTIONS AND OTHER PAPERS.

(1) *In General*. A request for a court order must be made by motion. The motion must:

(A) be in writing unless made during a hearing or trial;

(B) state with particularity the grounds for seeking the order; and

(C) state the relief sought.

(2) *Form.* The rules governing captions and other matters of form in pleadings apply to motions and other papers.

Rule 7.1. Disclosure Statement

(a) WHO MUST FILE: CONTENTS. A nongovernmental corporate party must file 2 copies of a disclosure statement that:

(1) identifies any parent corporation and any publicly held corporation owning 10% or more of its stock; or

(2) states that there is no such corporation.

(b) TIME TO FILE: SUPPLEMENTAL FILING. A party must:

(1) file the disclosure statement with its first appearance, pleading, petition, motion, response, or other request addressed to the court; and

(2) promptly file a supplemental statement if any required information changes.

Rule 8. General Rules of Pleading

(a) CLAIM FOR RELIEF. A pleading that states a claim for relief must contain:

(1) a short and plain statement of the grounds for the court's jurisdiction, unless the court already has jurisdiction and the claim needs no new jurisdictional support;

(2) a short and plain statement of the claim needs showing that the pleader is entitled to relief; and

(3) a demand for the relief sought, which may Include relief in the alternative or different types of relief.

(b) DEFENSES; ADMISSIONS AND DENIALS.

(1) *In General*. In responding to a pleading, a party must:

(A) state in short and plain terms its defenses to each claim asserted against it; and

(B) admit or deny the allegations asserts against it by an opposing party.

(2) *Denials – Responding to the Substance*. A denial must fairly respond to the substance of the allegation.

(3) *General and Specific Denials*. A   party that intends in good faith to deny all the allegations must either specifically deny designated allegations generally deny all except those specifically admitted.

(4) *Denying Part of an Allegation*. A party that intends in good faith to deny only part of an allegation must admit the part that is true and deny the rest.

(5) *Lacking Knowledge or Information*. A party that lacks knowledge or information sufficient to form a belief about the truth of an allegation must so state, and the statement has the effect of a denial.

(6) *Effect of Failing to Deny.* An allegation – other than one relating to the amount of damages – is admitted if a responsive pleading is required and the allegation is not denied. If a responsive pleading is not required, an allegation is considered denied or avoided.

(c) AFFIRMATIVE DEFENSES.

   (1) *In General.* In responding to a pleading, a party must affirmatively state any avoidance or affirmative defense, including:

   - accord and satisfaction;
   - arbitration and award;
   - assumption of risk;
   - contributory negligence;
   - duress;
   - estoppel;
   - failure of consideration;
   - fraud;
   - illegality;
   - injury by fellow servant;
   - laches;
   - license;
   - payment;
   - release;
   - res judicata;
   - statute of frauds;
   - statute of limitations; and
   - waiver.

   (2) *Mistaken Designation.* If a party mistakenly designates a defense as a counterclaim, or a counterclaim as a defense, the court must, if justice requires, treat the pleading as though it was correctly designated, and may impose terms for doing so.

(d) PLEADING TO BE CONCISE AND DIRECT; ALTERNATIVE STATEMENTS; INCONSISTENCY.

   (1) *In General.* Each allegation must be simple, concise, and direct. No technical form is required.

   (2) *Alternative Statements of a Claim or Defense.* A party may set out two or more statements of a claim or defense alternatively or hypothetically, either in a single count or defense or in separate ones. If a party makes alternative statements, the pleading is sufficient if any one of them is sufficient.

   (3) *Inconsistent Claims or Defenses.* A party may state as many separate claims or defenses as it has, regardless of consistency.

(e) CONSTRUING PLEADINGS. Pleadings must be construed so as to do justice.

Rule 9. Pleading Special Matters

(a) CAPACITY OR AUTHORITY TO SUE; LEGAL EXISTENCE.

   (1) *In General.* Except when required to show that the court has jurisdiction, a pleading need not allege:

   (A) a party's capacity to sue or be sued;

   (B) a party's authority to sue or be sued in a representative capacity; or

   (C) the legal existence of an organized association of persons that is made a party.

   (2) *Raising Those Issues.* To raise any of those issues, a party must do so by a specific denial, which must state any supporting facts that are peculiarly within the party's knowledge.

(b) FRAUD OR MISTAKE; CONDITIONS OF MIND. In alleging fraud or mistake, a party must state with particularity the circumstances constituting fraud or mistake. Malice, intent, knowledge, and other conditions of a person's mind may be alleged generally.

(c) CONDITIONS PRECEDENT. In pleading conditions precedent, it suffices to allege generally that all conditions precedent has occurred or been performed. But when denying that a condition precedent has occurred or been performed, a party must do so with particularity.

(d) OFFICIAL DOCUMENT OR ACT. In pleading an official document or official act, it suffices to allege that the document was legally issued, or the act legally done.

(e) JUDGMENT. In pleading a judgment or decision of a domestic or foreign court, a judicial or quasi-judicial tribunal, or a board or officer, it suffices to plead the judgment or decision without showing jurisdiction to render it.

(f) TIME AND PLACE. An allegation of time or place is material when testing the sufficiency of a pleading.

(g) SPECIAL DAMAGES. If an item of special damage is claimed, it must be specifically stated.

(h) ADMIRALTY OR MARITIME CLAIM.

   (1) *How Designated.* If a claim for relief is within the admiralty or maritime jurisdiction and also within the court's subject-matter jurisdiction on some other ground, the pleading may designate the claim as an admiralty or maritime claim for purposes of Rules 14(c), 38(e), and 82 and the Supplemental Rules for Admiralty and Maritime Claims and Asset Forfeiture Actions. A claim cognizable only in the admiralty or maritime jurisdiction is an admiralty or maritime claim for those purposes, whether or not so designated.

   (2) *Designation for Appeal.* A case that includes an admiralty or maritime claim within this subdivision (h) is an admiralty case within 28 U.S.C. § 1292(a)(3).

Rule 10. Form of Pleadings

(a) CAPTION; NAMES OF PARTIES. Every pleading must have a caption with the court's name, a title, a file number, and a Rule 7(a) designation. The title of the complaint must name all the parties; the title of other pleadings, after naming the first party on each side, ma/ refer generally to other parties.

(b) PARAGRAPHS; SEPARATE STATEMENTS. A party must state its claims or defenses in numbered paragraphs, each limited as far as practicable to a single set of circumstances. A later pleading may refer by number to a paragraph in an earlier pleading. If doing so would promote clarity, each claim founded on a separate transaction or occurrence – and each defense other than a denial – must be stated in a separate count or defense.

(c) ADOPTION BY REFERENCE; EXHIBITS. A statement in a pleading may be adopted by reference elsewhere in the same pleading or in any other pleading or motion. A copy of a written instrument that is an exhibit to a pleading is a part of the pleading for all purposes.

Rule 11. Signing Pleadings, Motions, and Other Papers; Representations to the Court; Sanctions

(a) SIGNATURE. Every pleading, written motion, and other paper must be signed by at least one attorney of record in the attorney's name, or by a party personally if the party is unrepresented. The paper must state the signer's address, e-mail address, and telephone number. Unless a rule or statute specifically states otherwise, a pleading need not be verified or accompanied by an affidavit. The court must strike an unsigned paper unless the omission is promptly corrected after being called to the attorney's or party's attention.

(b) Representations to the Court. By presenting to the court a pleading, written motion, or other paper – whether by signing, filing, submitting, or later advocating it – an attorney or unrepresented party certifies that to the best of the person's knowledge, information, and belief, formed after an inquiry reasonable under the circumstances:

(1) it is not being presented for any improper purpose, such as to harass, cause unnecessary delay, or needlessly increase the cost of litigation;

(2) the claims, defenses, and other legal contentions are warranted by existing law or by a non-frivolous argument for extending, modifying, or reversing existing law or for establishing new law;

(3) the factual contentions have evidentiary support or, if specifically, so identified, will likely have evidentiary support after a reasonable opportunity for further investigation or discovery; and

(4) the denials of factual contentions are warranted on the evidence or, if specifically, so identified, are reasonably based on belief or a lack of information.

(c) SANCTIONS.

(1) *In General.* If, after notice and a reasonable opportunity to respond, the court determines that Rule 11(b) has been violated, the court may impose an appropriate sanction on any attorney, law firm, or party that violated the rule or is responsible for the violation. Absent exceptional circumstances, a law firm must be held jointly responsible for a violation committed by its partner, associate, or employee.

(2) *Motion for Sanctions.* A motion for sanctions must be made separately from any other motion and must describe the specific conduct that violates Rule 11(b). The motion must be served under Rule 5, but it must not be filed or be presented to the court if the challenged paper, claim, defense, contention, or denial is withdrawn or appropriately corrected within 21 days after service or within another time the court sets. If warranted, the court may award to the prevailing party the reasonable expenses, including attorney's fees, incurred for the motion.

(3) *On the Court's Initiative.* On its own, the court may order an attorney, law firm, or party to show cause why conduct specifically described in the order has not violated Rule 11(b).

(4) *Nature of a Sanction.* A sanction imposed under this rule must be limited to what suffices to deter repetition of the conduct or comparable conduct by others similarly situated. The sanction may include nonmonetary directives; an order to pay a penalty into court; or, if imposed on motion and warranted for effective deterrence, an order directing payment to the movant of part or all of the reasonable attorney's fees and other expenses directly resulting from the violation.

(5) *Limitations on Monetary Sanctions.* The court must not impose a monetary sanction:

(A) against a represented party for violating Rule 11(b)(2); or

(B) on its own, unless it issued the show-cause order under Rule 11(c)(3) before voluntary dismissal or settlement of the claims made by or against the party that is, or whose attorneys are, to be sanctioned.

(6) *Requirements for an Order.* An order imposing a sanction must describe the sanctioned conduct and explain the basis for the sanction.

(d) INAPPLICABILITY TO DISCOVERY. This rule does not apply to disclosures and discovery requests, responses, objections, and motions under Rules 26 through 37.

Rule 12. Defenses and Objections: When and How Presented; Motion for Judgment on the Pleadings; Consolidating Motions; Waiving Defenses; Pretrial Hearing

(a) TIME TO SERVE A RESPONSIVE PLEADING.

(1) *In General.* Unless another time is specified by this rule or a federal statute, the time for serving a responsive pleading is as follows:

(A) A defendant must serve an answer:

(i) within 21 days after being served with the summons and complaint; or

(ii) if it has timely waived service under Rule 4(d), within 60 days after the request for a waiver was sent to the defendant outside any judicial district of the United States.

(B) A party must serve an answer to a counterclaim or crossclaim within 21 days after being served with the pleading that states the counterclaim or crossclaim.

(C) A party must serve a reply to an answer within 21 days after being served with an order to reply, unless the order specifies a different time.

(2) *United States and Its Agencies, Officers, or Employees Sued in an Official Capacity.* The United States, a United States agency, or a United States officer or employee sued only in an official capacity must serve an answer to a complaint, counterclaim, or crossclaim within 60 days after service on the United States attorney.

(3) *United States Officers or Employees Sued in an Individual Capacity.* A United States officer or employee sued in an individual capacity for an act or omission occurring in connection with duties performed on the United States' behalf must serve an answer to a complaint, counterclaim, or crossclaim within 60 days after service on the officer or employee or service on the United States attorney, whichever is later.

(4) *Effect of a Motion.* Unless the court sets a different time, serving a motion under this rule alters these periods as follows:

(A) if the court denies the motion or postpones its disposition until trial, the responsive pleading must be served within 14 days after notice of the court's action; or

(B) if the court grants a motion for a more definite statement, the responsive pleading must be served within 14 days after the more definite statement is served.

(b) HOW TO PRESENT DEFENSES. Every defense to a claim of relief in any pleading must be asserted in the responsive pleading if one is required. But a party may assert the following defenses by motion:

(1) lack of subject-matter jurisdiction;

(2) lack of personal jurisdiction;

(3) improper venue;

(4) insufficient process;

(5) insufficient service of process;

(6) failure to state a claim upon which relief can be granted; and

(7) failure to join a party under Rule 19.

A motion asserting any of these defenses must be made before pleading if a responsive pleading is allowed. If a pleading sets out a claim for relief that does not require a responsive pleading, an opposing party may assert at trial any defense to that claim. No defense or objection is waived by joining it with one or more other defenses or objections in a responsive pleading or in a motion.

(c) MOTION FOR JUDGMENT ON THE PLEADINGS. After the pleadings are closed – but early enough not to delay a trial – a party may move for judgment of the pleadings.

(d) RESULT OF PRESENTING MATTERS OUTSIDE THE PLEADINGS. If, on a motion under Rule 12(b)(6) or 12(c), matters outside the pleadings are presented to and not excluded by the court, the motion must be treated as one for summary judgment under Rule 56. All parties must be given a reasonable opportunity to present all the material that is pertinent to the motion.

(e) MOTION FOR A MORE DEFINITE STATEMENT. A party may move for a more definite statement of a pleading to which a responsive pleading is allowed but which is so vague or ambiguous that the party cannot reasonable prepare a response. The motion must be made before filing a responsive pleading and it must point out the defects complained of and the details desired. If the court orders a more definite statement and the order is not obeyed within 14 days after notice of the order or within the time the court sets, the court may strike the pleading or issue any other appropriate order.

(f) Motion to Strike. The court may strike from a pleading an insufficient defense or any redundant, immaterial, impertinent, or scandalous matter. The court may act:

    (1) on its own; or

    (2) on motion made by a party either before responding to the pleading or, if a response is not allowed, within 21 days after being served with the pleading.

(g) JOINING MOTIONS.

    (1) *Right to Join.* A motion under this rule may be joined with any other motion allowed by this rule.

    (2) *Limitations on Further Motions.* Except as provided in Rule 12(h)(2) or (3), a party that makes a motion under this rule must not make another motion under this rule raising a defense or objection that was available to the party but omitted from its earlier motion.

(h) WAIVING AND PRESERVING CERTAIN DEFENSES.

    (1) *When Some Are Waived.* A party waives any defense listed in Rule 12(b)(2)-(5) by:

        (A) omitting it from a motion in the circumstances described in Rule 12(g)(2); or

        (B) failing to either:

            (i) make it by motion under this rule; or

            (ii) include it in a responsive pleading or in an amendment allowed by Rule 15(a)(1) as a matter of course.

    (2) *When to Raise Others.* Failure to state a claim upon which relief can be granted, to join a person required by Rule 19(b), or to state a legal defense to a claim may be raised:

        (A) in any pleading allowed or ordered under Rule 7(a);

        (B) by a motion under Rule 12(c); or

        (C) at trial.

    (3) *Lack of Subject-Matter Jurisdiction.* If the court determines at any time that it lacks subject-matter jurisdiction, the court must dismiss the action.

(i) HEARING BEFORE TRIAL. If a party so moves, any defense listed under Rule 12(b)(1)-(7) – whether made in a pleading or by motion – and a motion under Rule 12(c) must be heard and decided before trial unless the court orders a deferral until trial.

Rule 13. Counterclaim and Crossclaim

(a) COMPULSORY COUNTERCLAIM.

    (1) *In General.* A pleading must state as a counterclaim any claim that – at the time if its service – the pleader has against the opposing party if the claim:

        (A) arises out of the transaction or occurrence that is the subject matter of the opposing party's claim; and

        (B) does not require adding another party over whom the court cannot acquire jurisdiction.

    (2) *Exceptions.* The pleader need not state the claim if: when the action was commenced, the claim was the subject of another pending action; or the opposing party sued on its claim by attachment or other process that did not establish personal jurisdiction over the pleader in that claim, and the pleader does not assert any counterclaims under this rule.

(b) PERMISSIVE COUNTERCLAIM. A pleading may state as a counterclaim against an opposing party any claim that is not compulsory.

(c) RELIEF SOUGHT IN A COUNTERCLAIM. A counterclaim need not diminish or defeat the recovery sought by the opposing party. It may request relief that exceeds in amount or differs in kind from the relief sought by the opposing party.

(d) COUNTERCLAIM AGAINST THE UNITED STATES. These rules do not expand the right to assert a counterclaim – or to claim a credit – against the United States or a United States officer or agency.

(e) COUNTERCLAIM MATURING OR ACQUIRED AFTER PLEADING. The court may permit a party to file a supplemental pleading asserting a counterclaim that matured or was acquired by the party after serving an earlier pleading.

(f) [Abrogated]

(g) CROSSCLAIM AGAINST A COPARTY. A pleading may state as a crossclaim any claim by one party against a co-party if the claim arises out of the transaction or occurrence that is the subject matter of the original action or of a counterclaim, or if the claim relates to any property that is the subject matter of the original action. The crossclaim may include a claim that the co-party is or may be liable to the cross claimant for all or part of a claim asserted in the action against the cross claimant.

(h) JOINING ADDITIONAL PARTIES. Rules 19 and 20 govern the addition of a person as a party to a counterclaim or crossclaim.

(i) SEPARATE TRIALS; SEPARATE JUDGMENTS. If the court orders separate trials under Rule 42(b), it may enter judgment on a counterclaim or crossclaim under Rule 54(b) when it has jurisdiction to do so, even if the opposing party's claims have been dismissed or otherwise resolved.

Rule 14. Third-Party Practice

(a) WHEN A DEFENDING PARTY MAY BRING IN A THIRD PARTY.

(1) *Timing of the Summons and Complaint.* A defending party may, as third – party plaintiff, serve a summons and complaint on a nonparty who is or may be liable to it for all or part of the claim against it. But the third-party plaintiff must, by motion, obtain the court's leave if it files the third – party complaint more than 14 days after receiving its original answer.

(2) *Third-party Defendant's Claims and Defenses.* The person served with the summons and third-party complaint – the "third-party-defendant":

(A) must assert any defense against the third-party plaintiff's claim under rule 12.

(B) must assert any counterclaim against the third-party plaintiff under Rule 13(a), and may assert any counterclaim against the third-party plaintiff under Rule 13(b) or any crossclaim   against another third-party defendant under Rule 13(g);

(C) may assert against the plaintiff any defense that the third-party plaintiff has to the plaintiff's claim; and

(D) may also assert against the plaintiff any claim arising out of the transaction or occurrence that is the subject matter of the plaintiff's claim against the third-party plaintiff.

(3) *Plaintiff's Claims Against a Third-Party Defendant.* The plaintiff may assert against the third-party defendant any claim arising out of the transition or occurrence that is the subject matter of the plaintiff's claim against the third-party plaintiff. The third-party defendant must then assert any defense under Rule 12 and any counterclaim under Rule 13(a), and may assert any counterclaim under Rule 13(b) or any crossclaim under Rule 13(g).

(4) *Motion to Strike, Server, or Try Separately.* Any party may move to strike the third-party claim, to server it, or to try it separately.

(5) *Third-Party Defendant's Claim Against a Nonparty.* A third-party defendant may proceed under this rule against a defendant who is or may be liable and may proceed under this rule against a defendant who is or may be liable to the third-party defendant for all or part of any claim against it.

(6) *Third-Party Claim in Rem.* If it is within the admiralty or maritime jurisdiction, a third-party claim may be in rem. In that event, a reference in this rule to the "summons" includes the warrant of arrest, and a reference in this rule to the "summons" includes the warrant of arrest, and

a reference to the defendant or third-party plaintiff includes, when appropriate, a person who asserts a right under Supplemental rule C(6)(a)(i) in the property arrested.

(b) WHEN A PLAINTIFF MAY BRING IN A THIRD PARTY. When a claim is asserted against a plaintiff, the plaintiff may bring in a third party if this rule would allow a defendant to do so.

(c) ADMIRALTY OR MARITIME CLAIM.

(1) *Scope of Impleader.* If a plaintiff asserts an admiralty or maritime claim under Rule 9(h), the defendant or a person who asserts a right under Supplemental Rule C(96)(a)(i) may, as a third-party plaintiff, bring in a third-party defendant who may be wholly or partly liable – either to the plaintiff or to the third-party plaintiff—for remedy over, contribution, or otherwise on account of the same transaction, occurrence, or series of transactions or occurrences.

(2) *Defending Against a Demand for Judgment for the Plaintiff.* The third-party plaintiff may demand judgment in the plaintiff's favor against the third-party defendant. In that event, the third-party defendant must defend under Rule 12 against the plaintiff's claim as well as the third-party plaintiff's claim; and the action proceeds as if the plaintiff had sued both the third-party defendant and the third-party plaintiff.

Rule 15. Amended and Supplemental Pleadings

(a) AMENDMENTS BEFORE TRIAL.

(1) *Amending as a Matter of Course.* A party may amend its pleading once as a matter of course within:

(A) 21 days after serving it, or

(B) if the pleading is one to which a responsive pleading is required, 21 days after service of a responsive pleading or 21 days after service of a motion under Rule 12(b), (e), or (f), whichever is earlier.

(2) Other Amendments. In all other cases, a party may amend its pleading only with the opposing party's written consent or the court's leave. The court should freely give leave when justice so requires.

(3) Time to Respond. Unless the court orders otherwise, any required response to an amended pleading must be made within the time remaining to respond to the original pleading or within 14 days after service of the amended pleading, whichever is later.

(b) AMENDMENTS DURING AND AFTER TRIAL.

(1) *Based on an Objection at Trial.* If, at trial, a party objects that evidence is not within the issues raised in the pleadings, the court may permit the pleadings to be amended. The court should freely permit an amendment when doing so will aid in presenting the merits and the objecting party fails to satisfy the court that the evidence would prejudice that party's action or defense on the merits. The court may grant a continuance to enable the objecting party to meet the evidence.

(2) *For Issues Tried by Consent.* When an issue not raised by the pleadings is tried by the parties' express or implied consent, it must be treated in all respects as if raised in the pleadings. A party may move – at any time, even after judgment – to amend the pleadings to conform them to the evidence and to raise an unpleaded issue. But failure to amend does not affect the result of the trial of that issue.

(c) RELATION BACK OF AMENDMENTS.

(1) When an Amendment Relates Back. An amendment to a proceeding relates back to the date of the original proceeding when:

(A) the law that provides the applicable statute of limitations allows relation back;

(B) the amendment asserts a claim or defense that arose out of the conduct, transaction, or occurrence set out – or attempted to be set out – in the original pleading; or

(C) the amendment changes the party or naming of the party against whom a claim is asserted, if Rule 15(c)(1)(B) is satisfied and if, within the period provided by Rule 4(m) for serving the summons and complaint, the party to be brought in by amendment:

    (i) received such notice of the action that it will not be prejudiced in defending on the merits; and

    (ii) knew or should have known that the action would have been brought against it, but for a mistake concerning the proper party's identity.

(2) *Notice to the United States.* When the United States or a United States officer or agency is added as a defendant by amendment, the notice requirements of Rule 15(c)(l)(C)(i) and (ii) are satisfied if, during the stated period, process was delivered or mailed to the United States attorney or the United States attorney's designee, to the Attorney general of the United States, or to the officer or agency.

(d) SUPPLEMENTAL PLEADINGS. On motion and reasonable notice, the court may, on just terms, permit a party to serve a supplemental pleading setting out any transaction, occurrence, or event that happened after the date of the pleading to be supplemented. The court may permit supplementation even though the original pleading is defective in stating a claim or defense. The court may order that the opposing party plead to the supplemental pleading within a specified time.

Rule 16. Pretrial Conferences; Scheduling; Management

(a) PURPOSE OF A PRETRIAL CONFERENCE. In any action, the court may order the attorneys and any unrepresented parties to appear for one or more pretrial conferences for such purposes as:

    (1) expediting disposition of the action;

    (2) establishing early and continuing control so that the case will not be protracted because of lack of management;

    (3) discouraging wasteful pretrial activities;

    (4) improving the quality of the trial through more thorough preparation; and

    (5) facilitating settlement.

(b) SCHEDULING.

    (1) *Scheduling Order.* Except in categories of actions exempted by local rule, the district judge I or a magistrate judge when authorized by local rule – must issue a scheduling order:

        (A) after receiving the parties' report under Rule 26(f); or

        (B) after consulting with the parties' attorneys and any unrepresented parties at a scheduling conference or by telephone, mail, or other means.

    (2) *Time to Issue.* The judge must issue the scheduling order as soon as practicable, but in any event within the earlier of 120 days after any defend ant has been served with the complaint or 90 days after any defendant has app eared.

    (3) *Contents of the Order.*

        (A) *Required Contents.* The scheduling order must limit the time to join other parties, amend the pleadings, complete discovery, and file motions.

        (B) *Permitted Contents.* The scheduling order may:

            (i) modify the timing of disclosure under Rules 26(a) and 26(e)(1);

            (ii) modify the extent of discovery;

            (iii) provide for disclosure or discovery of electronically stored information;

            (iv) include any agreements the parties reach for asserting claims of privilege or of protection as trial-preparation material after information is produced;

            (v) set dates for pretrial conferences and for trial; and

            (vi) include other appropriate matters.

(4) Modifying a Schedule. A schedule may be modified only for good cause and with the judge's consent.

(c) ATTENDANCE AND MATTERS FOR CONSIDERATION AT A PRETRIAL CONFERENCE.

    (1) *Attendance*. A represented party must authorize as at least one of its attorneys to make stipulations and admissions about all matters that can reasonably be anticipated for discussion at a pretrial conference. If appropriate, the court may require that a party or its representative be present or reasonably available by other means to consider possible settlement.

    (2) *Matters for Consideration*. At any pretrial conference, the court may consider and take appropriate action on the following matters:

        (A) formulating and simplifying the issues, and eliminating frivolous claims or defenses;

        (B) amending the pleadings if necessary or desirable;

        (C) obtaining admissions and stipulations about facts and documents to avoid unnecessary proof, and ruling in advance on the admissibility of evidence;

        (D) avoiding unnecessary proof and cumulative evidence, and limiting the use of testimony under Federal Rule of Evidence 702;

        (E) determining the appropriateness and timing of summary adjudication under Rule 56;

        (F) controlling and scheduling discovery, including orders affecting disclosures and discovery under Rule 26 and Rules 29 through 37;

        (G) identifying witnesses and documents, scheduling the filing and exchange of any pretrial briefs, and setting dates for further conferences and for trial;

        (H) referring matters to a magistrate judge or master;

        (I) setting the case and using special procedures to assist in resolving the dispute when authorized by statute or local rule;

        (J) determining the form and content of the pretrial order;

        (K) disposing of pending motions;

        (L) adopting special procedures for managing potentially difficult or protracted actions that may involve complex issues, multiple parties, difficult legal questions, or unusual proof problems;

        (M) ordering a separate trial under Rule 42(b) of a claim, counterclaim, crossclaim, third-party claim, or particular issue;

        (N) ordering the presentation of evidence early in the trial on a manageable issue that might, on the evidence, be the basis for a judgment as a matter of law under Rule 50(a) or a judgment on partial findings under Rule 52(c);

        (O) establishing a reasonable limit on the time allowed to present evidence; and

        (P) facilitating in other ways the just, speedy, and inexpensive disposition of the action.

(d) PRETRIAL ORDERS. After any conference under this rule, the court should order an issue reciting the action taken, this order controls the course of the action unless the court modifies it.

(e) FINAL PRETRIAL CONFERENCE AND ORDERS. The court may hold a final pretrial conference to formulate a trial plan, including a plan to facilitate the admission of evidence. The conference must he held as close as possible to the start of trial as reasonable and must be attended by at least one attorney who will conduct the trial for each party and by an unrepresented party. The court may modify an order issued after a final pretrial conference only to prevent manifest injustice.

(f) SANCTIONS.

    (1) *In General*. On motion or on its own, the court may |Issue any just orders, including those authorized by Rule 37(b)(2)(A)(ii)-(vii), if a party or its attorney:

        (A) fails to appear at a scheduling or other pretrial conference;

        (B) is substantially unprepared to participate or does not participate in good faith – in the conference; or

(C) fails to obey a scheduling or other pretrial order.

(2) *Imposing Fees and Costs.* Instead of or in addition to any other sanction, the court must order the party, its attorney, or both to pay the reasonable expenses including attorney's fees – incurred because of any noncompliance with this rule, unless the noncompliance was substantially justified or other circumstances make an award of expenses unjust.

Rule 17. Plaintiff and Defendant; Capacity; Public Officers

(a) REAL PARTY IN INTEREST.

(1) *Designation in General.* An action must be prosecuted in the name of the real party in interest. The following may sue in their own names without joining the person for whose benefit the action is brought:

(A) an executor;

(B) an administrator;

(C) a guardian;

(D) a bailee;

(E) a trustee of an express trust;

(F) a party with whom or in whose name a contract has been made for another's benefit; and

(G) a party authorized by statute.

(2) *Action in the Name of the United States for Another's Use or Benefit.* When a federal statute so provides, an action for another's use or benefit must be brought in the name of the United States.

(3) *Joinder of the Real Party in Interest.* The court may not dismiss an action for failure to prosecute in the name of the real party in interest until, after an objection, a reasonable time has been allowed for the real party in interest to ratify, join, or be substituted into the action. After ratification, joinder, or substitution, the action proceeds as if it had been originally commenced by the real party in interest.

(b) CAPACITY TO SUE OR BE SUED. Capacity to sue or be sued is determined as follows:

(1) for an individual who is not acting in a representative capacity, by the law of the individual's domicile;

(2) for a corporation, by the law under which it was organized; and

(3) for all other parties, by the law of the state where the court is located, except that:

(A) a partnership or other unincorporated association with no such capacity under that state's law may sue or be sued in its common name to enforce a substantive right existing under the United States Constitution or laws; and

(B) 28 U.S.C. §§ 754 and 959(a) govern the capacity of a receiver appointed by a United States court to sue or be sued in a United States court.

(c) MINOR OR INCOMPETENT PERSON.

(1) *With a Representative.* The following representatives may sue or defend on behalf of a minor or an incompetent person:

(A) a general guardian;

(B) a committee;

(C) a conservator; or

(D) a like fiduciary.

(2) *Without a Representative.* A minor or incompetent person who does not have a duly appointed representative may sue by a next friend or guardian ad litem. The court must appoint guardian ad litem – or issue another appropriate order – to protect a minor or incompetent person who is unrepresented in an action.

(d) PUBLIC OFFICER'S TITLE AND NAME. A public officer who sues or is sued in an official capacity may be designated by official title rather than by name, but the court may order that the officer's name be added.

Rule 18. Joinder of Claims

(a) *In General*. A party asserting a claim, counterclaim, crossclaim, or third – party claim may join, as independent or alternative claims, as many claims as it has against an opposing party.

(b) *Joinder of Contingent Claims*. A party may join two claims even though one of them is contingent on the disposition of the other; but the court may grant relief only in accordance with the parties' substantive rights. In particular, a plaintiff may state a claim for money and a claim to set aside a conveyance that is fraudulent as to that plaintiff, without first obtaining a judgment for the money.

Rule 19. Required Joinder of Parties

(a) PERSONS REQUIRED TO BE JOINED IF FEASIBLE.

    (1) *Required Party*. A person who is subject to service of process and whose joinder will not deprive the court of subject-matter jurisdiction must be joined as a party if:

        (A) in that person's absence, the court cannot accord complete relief among existing parties; or

        (B) that person claims an interest relating to the subject of the action and is so situated that disposing of the action in the person's absence may:

            (i) as a practical matter impair or impede the person's ability to protect the interest; or

            (ii) leave an existing party subject to a substantial risk of incurring double, multiple, or otherwise inconsistent obligations because of the interest.

    (2) *Joinder by Court Order*. If a person has not been joined as required, the court must order that the person be made a party. A person who refuses to join as a plaintiff may be made either a defendant or, in a proper case, an involuntary plaintiff.

    (3) *Venue*. If a joined party objects to venue, and the joinder would make venue improper, the court must dismiss that party.

(b) WHEN JOINDER IS NOT FEASIBLE. If a person who is required to be joined if feasible cannot be joined, the court must determine whether, in equity and good conscience, the action should proceed among the existing parties or be dismissed. The factors for the court to consider include:

    (1) the extent to which a judgment rendered in the person's absence might prejudice that person or the existing parties;

    (2) the extent to which and prejudice could be lessened or avoided by:

        (A) protective provisions in the judgment;

        (B) shaping the relief; or

        (C) other measures;

    (3) whether a judgment rendered in the person's absence would be adequate; and

    (4) whether the plaintiff would have an adequate remedy if the action were dismissed for non-joinder.

(c) PLEADING THE REASONS FOR NONJOINDER. When asserting a claim for relief, a party must state:

    (1) the name, if known, of any person who is required to be joined if feasible but is not joined; and

    (2) the reasons for not joining that person.

(d) EXCEPTIONS FOR CLASS ACTIONS. This rule is subject to Rule 23.

Rule 20. Permissive Joinder of Parties

(a) PERSONS WHO MAY JOIN OR BE JOINED.

    (1) *Plaintiffs*. Persons may join in one action as plaintiffs if:

(A) they assert any right to relief jointly, severally, or in the alternative with respect to or arising out of the same transaction, occurrence, or series of transactions or occurrences; and

(B) any question of law or fact common to all plaintiff s will arise in the action.

(2) *Defendants.* Persons – as well as a vessel, cargo, or other property subject to admiralty process in rem – may be joined in one action as defendants if:

(A) any right to relief is asserted against them jointly, severally, or in the alternative with respect to or arising out of the same transaction, occurrence, or series of transactions or occurrences; and

(B) any question of law or fact common to all defendants will arise in the action.

(3) *Extent of Relief.* Neither a plaintiff nor a defendant need be interested in obtaining or defending against all the relief demanded. The court may grant judgment to one or more plaintiffs according to their rights, and against one or more defendants according to their liabilities.

(b) PROTECTIVE MEASURES. The court may issue orders – including an order for separate trials – to protect a party against embarrassment, delay, expense, or other prejudice that arises from including a person against whom the party asserts no claim and who asserts no claim against the party.

Rule 21. Misjoinder and Nonjoinder of Parties

Misjoinder of parties is not a ground for dismissing an action. On motion or on its own, the court may at any time, on just terms, add or drop a party. The court may also sever any claim against a party.

Rule 22. Interpleader

(a) GROUNDS.

(1) *By a Plaintiff.* Persons with claims that may expose a plaintiff to double or multiple liability may be joined as defendants and required to interplead. Joinder for interpleader is proper even though:

(A) the claims of several claimants, or the titles on which their claims depend, lack a common origin or are adverse and independent rather than identical; or

(B) the plaintiff denies liability in whole or in part to any or all of the claimants.

(2) *By a Defendant.* A defendant exposed to similar liability may seek interpleader through a crossclaim or counterclaim.

(b) Relation to Other Rules and Statutes. This rule supplements – and does not limit – the joinder of parties allowed by Rule 20. The remedy it provides is in addition to – and does not supersede or limit – the remedy provided by 28 U.S.C. §§ 1335, 1397, and 2361. An action under those statutes must be conducted under those rules.

Rule 23. Class Actions

(a) PREREQUISITES. One or more members of a class may sue or be sued as representative parties on behalf of all members only if:

(1) the class is so numerous that the joinder of all members is impracticable;

(2) there are questions of law or fact common to the class;

(3) the claims or defenses of the representative parties are typical of the claims or defenses of the class; and

(4) the representative parties will fairly and adequately protect the interests of the class.

(b) Types of Class Actions. A class action may be maintained if Rule 23(a) is satisfied and if:

(1) prosecuting separate actions by or against individual class members would create a risk of:

(A) inconsistent or varying adjudications with respect to individual class members that would establish incompatible standards of conduct for the party of the opposing class; or

(B) adjudications with respect to individual class members that, as a practical matter, would be dispositive of the interests of the other members not parties to the individual adjudications or would substantially impair or impede their ability to protect their interests;

(2) the party opposing the class has acted or refused to act on grounds that apply generally to the class, so that final injunctive relief or corresponding declaratory relief is appropriate respecting the class as a whole; or

(3) the court finds that the questions of law or fact common to class members predominate over any questions affecting only individual members, and that a class action is superior to other available methods for fairly and efficiently adjudicating the controversy. The matters pertinent to these findings include:

(A) the class members' interests in individually controlling the prosecution or defense of separate actions;

(B) the extent and nature of any litigation concerning the controversy already begun by or against class members;

(C) the desirability or undesirability of concentrating the litigation of the claims in the particular forum; and

(D) the likely difficulties in managing a class action.

(c) CERTIFICATION ORDER; NOTICE TO CLASS MEMBERS; JUDGMENT; ISSUES CLASSES; SUB-CLASSES.

(1) *Certification Order.*

(A) *Time to Issue.* At an early practicable time after a person sues or is sued as a class representative, the court must determine by order whether to certify the action as a class action.

(B) *Defining the Class; Appointing Class Counsel.* An order that certifies a class action must define the class and the class claims, issues, or defenses, and must appoint class counsel under Rule 23(g).

(C) *Altering or Amending the Order.* An order that grants or denies class certification may be altered or amended before final judgment.

(2) *Notice.*

(A) *For (b)(1) or (b)(2) Classes.* For any class certified under Rule 23(b)(1) or (b)(2), the court may direct appropriate notice to the class.

(B) *For (b)(3) Classes.* For any class certified under Rule 23(b)(3), the court must direct to class members the best notice that is practicable under the circumstances, including individual notice to all members who can be identified through reasonable effort. The notice must clearly and concisely state in plain, easily understood language:

(i) the nature of the action

(ii) the definition of the class certified;

(iii) the class claims, issues, or defenses;

(iv) that a class member may enter an appearance through an attorney if the member so desires;

(v) that the court will exclude from the class any member who requests exclusion;

(vi) the time and manner for requesting exclusion; and

(vii) the binding effect of a class judgment on members under Rule 23(c)(3).

(3) *Judgment.* Whether or not favorable to the class, the judgment in a class action must:

(A) for any class certified under Rule 23(b)(1) or (b)(2), include and describe those whom the court finds to be class members; and

(B) for any class certified under Rule 23(b)(3), include and specify or describe those to whom the Rule 23(c)(2) notice was directed, who have not requested exclusion, and whom the court finds to be class members.

(4) *Particular Issues.* When appropriate, an action may be maintained as a class action with respect to particular issues.

(5) *Subclasses.* When appropriate, a class may be divided into subclasses that are each treated as a class under this rule.

(d) CONDUCTING THE ACTION.

(1) *In General.* In conducting an action under this rule, the court may issue orders that:

(A) determine the course of proceedings or prescribe measures to prevent undue repetition or complication in presenting evidence or argument;

(B) require – to protect class members and fairly conduct the action giving notice to some or all class members of:

(i) any step in the action;

(ii) the proposed extent of the judgment; or

(iii) the members' opportunity to signify whether they consider the representation fair and adequate, to intervene and present claims or defenses, or to otherwise come into the action;

(C) impose conditions on the representative parties or on intervenors;

(D) require that the pleadings be amended to eliminate allegations about representation of absent persons and that the action proceed accordingly; or

(E) deal with similar procedural matters.

(2) *Combining and Amending Orders.* An order under Rule 23(d)(1) may be altered or amended from time to time and may be combined with an order under Rule 16.

(e) SETTLEMENT, VOLUNTARY DISMISSAL, OR COMPROMISE. The claims, issues, or defenses of a certified class may be settled, voluntarily dismissed, or compromised only with the court's approval. The following procedures apply to a proposed settlement, voluntary dismissal, or compromise:

(1) *Notice to the Class.*

(A) *Information That Parties Must Provide to the Court.* The parties must provide the court with information sufficient to enable it to determine whether to give notice of the proposal to the class.

(B) *Grounds for a Decision to Give Notice.* The court must direct notice in a reasonable manner to all class members who would be bound by the proposal if giving notice is justified by the parties' showing that the court will likely be able to:

(i) approve the proposal under Rule 23(e)(2); and

(ii) certify the class for purposes of judgment on the proposal.

(2) *Approval of the Proposal.* If the proposal would bind class members, the court may approve it only after a hearing and only on finding that it is fair, reasonable, and adequate after considering whether:

(A) the class representatives and class counsel have adequately represented the class;

(B) the proposal was negotiated at arm's length;

(C) the relief provided for the class is adequate, taking into account:

(i) the costs, risks, and delay of trial and appeal;

(ii) the effectiveness of any proposed method of distributing relief to the class, including the method of processing class-member claims;

        (iii) the terms of any proposed award of attorney's fees, including timing of payment; and

        (iv) any agreement required to be identified under Rule 23(e)(3); and

    (D) the proposal treats class members equitably relative to each other.

(3) *Identifying Agreements.* The parties seeking approval must file a statement identifying any agreement made in connection with the proposal.

(4) *New Opportunity to Be Excluded.* If the class action was previously certified under Rule 23(b)(3), the court may refuse to approve a settlement unless it affords a new opportunity to request exclusion to individual class members who had an earlier opportunity to request exclusion but did not do so.

(5) *Class-Member Objections.*

    (A) *In General.* Any class member may object to the proposal if it requires court approval under this subdivision (e). The objection must state whether it applies only to the objector, to a specific subset of the class, or to the entire class, and also state with specificity the grounds for the objection.

    (B) *Court Approval Required for Payment in Connection with an Objection.* Unless approved by the court after a hearing, no payment or other consideration may be provided in connection with:

        (i) forgoing or withdrawing an objection, or

        (ii) forgoing, dismissing, or abandoning an appeal from a judgment approving the proposal.

    (C) *Procedure for Approval After an Appeal.* If approval under Rule 23(e)(5)(B) has not been obtained before an appeal is docketed in the court of appeals, the procedure of Rule 62.1 applies while the appeal remains pending.

(f) Appeals. A court of appeals may permit an appeal from an order granting or denying class-action certification under this rule if a petition for permission to appeal is filed with the circuit clerk within 14 days after the order is entered. An appeal does not stay proceedings in the district court unless the district judge or the court of appeals so orders.

(g) CLASS COUNSEL.

(1) *Appointing Class Counsel.* Unless a statute provides otherwise, a court that certifies a class must appoint class counsel. In appointing class counsel, the court:

    (A) must consider:

        (i) the work the counsel has done in identifying potential claims in the action;

        (ii) counsel's experience in handling class actions, other complex litigation, and the types of claims asserted in the action;

        (iii) counsel's knowledge of the applicable law; and

        (iv) the resources that counsel will commit to representing the class;

    (B) may consider any other matter pertinent to counsel's ability to fairly and adequately represent the interests of the class;

    (C) may order potential class counsel to provide information on any subject pertinent to the appointment and to propose terms for attorney's fees and nontaxable costs;

    (D) may include in the appointing order provisions about the award of attorney's fees or nontaxable costs under Rule 23(h); and

    (E) may make further orders in connection with the appointment.

(2) *Standard for Appointing Class Counsel.* When one applicant seeks appointment as class counsel, the court may appoint that applicant only if the applicant is adequate under Rule 23(g)(1) and (4). If more than one adequate applicant seeks appointment, the court must appoint the applicant I lest able to represent the interests of the class.

(3) *Interim Counsel.* the court may designate interim counsel to act on behalf of a putative class before determining whether to certify the action as a class action.

(4) *Duty of Class Counsel.* Class counsel must fairly and adequately represent the interests of the class.

(h) ATTORNEY'S FEES AND NONTAXABLE COSTS. In a certified class action, the court may award reasonable attorney's I lees and nontaxable costs that are authorized by law or by the parties' agreement. The following procedures apply:

(1) A claim for an award must lie made by motion under Rule 54(d)(2), subject to the provisions of this subdivision (h), at a time the court sets. Notice of the motion must be served on all parties and, for motions by class counsel, directed to class members in a reasonable manner.

(2) A class member, or a party from whom payment is sought, may object to the motion.

(3) The court may hold a hearing and must find the facts and state its legal conclusions under Rule 52(a).

(4) The court may refer issues related to the amount of the award to a special master or a magistrate judge, as provided in Rule 54(d)(2)(D).

Rule 23.1 Derivative Actions

(a) PREREQUISITES. This rule applies when one or more shareholders or members of a corporation or an unincorporated association bring a derivative action to enforce a right that the corporation or association may properly assert but has failed to enforce. The derivative action may not be maintained if it appears that the plaintiff does not fairly and adequately represent the interests of shareholders or members who are similarly situated in enforcing the right of the corporation or association.

(b) PLEADING REQUIREMENTS. The complaint must be verified and must:

(1) allege that the plaintiff was a shareholder or member at the time of the transaction complained of, or that the plaintiff's share or membership later devolved on it by operation of law;

(2) allege that the action is not a collusive one to confer jurisdiction that the court would otherwise lack; and

(3) state with particularity:

(A) any effort by the plaintiff to obtain the desired action from the directors or comparable authority and, if necessary, from the shareholders or members; and

(B) the reasons for not obtaining the action or not making the effort.

(c) SETTLEMENT, DISMISSAL, AND COMPROMISE. A derivative action may be settled, voluntarily dismissed, or compromised only with the court's approval. Notice of a proposed settlement, voluntary dismissal, or compromise must be given to shareholders or members in the manner that the court orders.

Rule 23.2. Actions Relating to Unincorporated Associations

This rule applies to an action brought by or against the members of an unincorporated association as a class by naming certain members as representative parties. The action may be maintained only if it appears that those parties will fairly and adequately protect the interests of the association and its members. In conducting the action, the court may issue any appropriate orders corresponding with those in Rule 23(d), and the procedure for settlement, voluntary dismissal, or compromise must correspond with the procedure in Rule 23(e).

Rule 24. Intervention

(a) INTERVENTION OF RIGHT. On timely motion, the court must permit anyone to intervene who:

(1) is given an unconditional right to intervene by a federal statute; or

(2) claims an interest relating to the property or transaction that is the subject of the action and is so situated that disposing of the action may as a practical matter impair or impede the movant's ability to protect its interest, unless existing parties adequately represent that interest.

(b) PERMISSIVE INTERVENTION.

    (1) *In General*. On timely motion, the court may permit anyone to intervene who:

        (A) is given a conditional right to intervene by a federal statute; or

        (B) has a claim or defense that shares with the main action a common question of law or fact.

    (2) *By a Government Officer or Agency*. On timely motion, the court may permit a federal or state officer or agency to intervene if a party's claim or defense is based on:

        (A) a statute or executive order administered by the officer or agency; or

        (B) any regulation, order, requirement, or agreement issued or made under the statute or executive order.

    (3) *Delay or Prejudice*. In exercising its discretion, the court must consider whether the intervention will unduly delay or prejudice the adjudication of the original parties' rights.

(c) NOTICE AND PLEADING REQUIRED. A motion to intervene must be served on the parties as provided in Rule 5. the motion must state the grounds for intervention and be accompanied by a pleading that sets out the claim or defense for which the intervention is sought.

Rule 25. Substitution of Parties

(a) DEATH.

    (1) *Substitution if the Claim is Not Extinguished*. If a party dies and the claim is not extinguished, the court may order substitution of the proper party. A motion for substitution may be made by any party or by the decedent's successor or representative. If the motion is not made within 90 days after service of a statement noting the death, the action by or against the decedent must be dismissed.

    (2) *Continuation among the Remaining Parties*. After a parties' death, if the right sought to be enforced survives only to or against the remaining parties, the action does not abate, but proceeds in favor of or against the remaining parties. The death should be noted on the record.

    (3) *Service*. A motion to substitute, together with a notice of hearing, must be served on the parties as provided in Rule 5 and on nonparties as provided in Rule 4. A statement noting death must be served in the same manner. Service may be made in any judicial district.

(b) INCOMPETENCY. If a party becomes incompetent, the court may, on motion, permit the action to be continued by or against the parties' representative. The motion must lie served as Provided in Rule 25(a)(3).

(c) TRANSFER OF INTEREST. If an interest is transferred, the action may be continued by or against the original party unless the court, on motion, orders the transferee to be substituted in the action or joined with the original party. The motion must be served as provided in Rule 25(a)(3).

(d) PUBLIC OFFICERS; DEATH OR SEPARATION FROM OFFICE. An action does not abate when a public officer who is a party in an official capacity dies, resigns, or otherwise ceases to hold office while an action is pending. The officer's successor is automatically substituted as a party. Later proceedings should be in the substituted party's name, but any misnomer not affecting the parties' substantial rights must be disregarded. The court may order substitution at any time, but the absence of such an order does not affect the substitution.

Rule 26. Duty to Disclose; General Provisions Governing Discovery

(a) REQUIRED DISCLOSURES.

(1) *Initial Disclosure.*

    (A) *In General.* Except as exempted by Rule 26(a)(1)(B) or as otherwise stipulated or ordered by the court, a party must, without awaiting a discovery request, provide the other parties:

        (i) the name and, if known, the address and telephone number of each individual likely to have discoverable information – along with the subjects of that information – that the disclosing party may use to support its claims or defenses, unless the use would be solely for impeachment;

        (ii) a copy or a description by category and location – of all documents, electronically stored information, and tangible things that the disclosing party has in its possession, custody, or control and may use to support its claims or defenses, unless the use would be solely for impeachment;

        (iii) a computation of each category of damages claimed by the disclosing party – who must also make available for inspection and copying as under Rule 34 the documents or other evidentiary material, unless privileged or protected from disclosure, on which each computation is based, including materials bearing on the nature and extent of injuries suffered; and

        (iv) for inspection and copying as under Rule 34, any insurance agreement under which an insurance business may be liable to satisfy all or part of a possible judgment in the action or to indemnify or reimburse for payments made to satisfy the judgment.

    (B) Proceedings Exempt from Initial Disclosure. The following proceedings are exempt from initial disclosure:

        (i) an action for review on an administrative record;

        (ii) a forfeiture action in rem arising from a federal statute;

        (iii) a petition for habeas corpus or any other proceeding to challenge a criminal conviction or sentence;

        (iv) an action brought without an attorney by a person in the custody of the United States, a state, or a state subdivision;

        (v) an action to enforce or quash an administrative summons or subpoena;

        (vi) an action by the United States to recover benefit payments;

        (vii) an action by the United States to collect on a student loan guaranteed by the United States;

        (viii) a proceeding ancillary to a proceeding in another court; and

        (ix) an action to enforce an arbitration award.

    (C) *Time for Initial Disclosures – In General.* A party must make the initial disclosures at or within 14 days after the parties' Rule 26(f) conference unless a different time is set by stipulation or court order, or unless a party objects during the conference that initial disclosures are not appropriate in this action and states the objection in the proposed discovery plan. In ruling on the objection, the court must determine what disclosures, if any, are to be made and must set the time for disclosure.

    (D) *Time for Initial Disclosures – For Parties Served or Joined Later.* A party that is first served or otherwise joined after the Rule 26(f) conference must make the initial disclosures within 30 days after being served or joined, unless a different time is set by stipulation or court order.

    (E) *Basis for Initial Disclosure; Unacceptable Excuses.* A party must make its initial disclosures based on the information then reasonably available to it. A party is not excused from making its disclosures because it has not fully investigated the case or because it challenges the sufficiency of another party's disclosures or because another party has not made its disclosures.

(2) *Disclosure of Expert Testimony.*

    (A) *In General.* In addition to the disclosures required by Rule 26(a)(1), a party must disclose to the other parties the identity of any witness it may use at trial to present evidence under Federal Rule of Evidence 702,703, ac 705.

    (B) Witnesses Who Mist Provide a. Written Report. Unless otherwise stipulated or ordered by the court, this disclosure must be accompanied by a written report – prepared and signed by the witness – if the witness is one retained or specially employed to provide expert testimony in the case or one whose duties as the party's employee regularly involve giving expert testimony, the report must contain:

        (i) a complete statement of all opinions the witness will express and the basis and reasons for them;

        (ii) the facts or data considered by the witness in forming them;

        (iii) any exhibits that will be used to summarize or support them;

        (iv) the witness's qualifications, including a list of all publications authored in the previous 10 years;

        (v) a list of all other cases in which, during the previous 4 years, the witness testified as an expert at trial or by deposition; and

        (vi) a statement of the compensation to be paid for the study and testimony in the case.

    (C) Witnesses Who Do Not Provide a Written Report. Unless otherwise stipulated or ordered by the court, if the witness is not required to provide a written report, this disclosure must state:

        (i) the subject matter on which the witness is expected to present evidence under Federal Rule of Evidence 702, 703, or 705; and

        (ii) a summary of the facts and opinions to which the witness is expected to testify.

    (D) *Time to Disclose Expert Testimony.* A party must make these disclosures at the times and in the sequence that the court orders. Absent a stipulation or a court order, the disclosures must be made:

        (i) at least 90 days before the date set for trial or for the case to be ready for trial; or

        (ii) if the evidence is intended solely to contradict or rebut evidence on the same subject matter identified by another party under Rule 26 (a)(2)(B) or (C), within 30 days after the other party's disclosure.

    (E) *Supplementing the Disclosure.* The parties must supplement these disclosures when required under Rule 26(e).

(3) *Pretrial Disclosures.*

    (A) *In General.* In addition to the disclosures required by Rule 26(a)(1) and (2), a party must provide to the other parties and promptly file the following information about the evidence that it may present at trial other than solely for impeachment:

        (i) the name and, if not previously provided, the address and telephone number of each witness – separately identifying those the party expects to present and those it may call if the need arises;

        (ii) the designation of those witnesses whose testimony the party expects to present deposition and, if not taken stenographically, a transcript of the pertinent parts of the deposition; and

        (iii) an identification of each document or other exhibit, including summaries of other evidence – separately identifying those items the party expects to offer and those it may offer if the need arises.

(B) *Time for pretrial Disclosures; Objections.* Unless the court orders otherwise, these disclosures must be made at least 30 days before trial. Within 14 days after they are made, unless the court sets a different time, a party may serve and promptly file a list of the following objections: any objections to the use under Rule 32(a) of a deposition designated by another party under Rule 26(a)(3)(A)(ii); and any objection, together with the grounds for it, that may be made to the admissibility of materials identified under Rule 26(l)(3)(A)(iii). An objection not so made – except for one under Federal Rule of Evidence 402 or 403 – is waived unless excused by the court for good cause.

(4) *Form of Disclosures.* Unless the court orders otherwise, all disclosures under Rule 26(a) must be in writing, signed, and served.

(b) DISCOVERY SCOPE AND LIMITS.

(1) *Scope in General.* Unless otherwise limited by court order, the scope of discovery is as follows: Parties may obtain discovery regarding any unprivileged matter that is relevant to any party's claim or defense,, including the existence, description, nature, custody, condition, and location of any documents or other tangible things and the identity and location of persons who know of any discoverable matter. For good cause, the court may order discovery of any matter relevant to the subject matter involved in the action. Relevant information need not be admissible at the trial if the discovery appears reasonably calculated to lead to the discovery of admissible evidence. All discovery is subject to the limitations imposed by Rule 26(b)(2)(C).

(2) *Limitations on Frequency and Extent.*

(A) *When Permitted,* by order, the court may alter the limits in these rules on the number of depositions and interrogatories or on the length of depositions under Rule 30. By order or local rule, the court may also limit the number of requests under Rule 36.

(B) *Specific Limitations on Electronically Stored Information.* A party need not provide discovery of electronically stored information from sources that the party identifies as not reasonably accessible because of undue burden or cost. On motion to compel discovery or for a protective order, the party from whom discovery is sought must show that the information is not reasonably accessible because of undue burden or cost. If that showing is made, the court may nonetheless order discovery from such sources if the requesting party shows good cause, considering the limitations of Rule 26(b)(2)(C). The court may specify conditions for the discovery.

(C) *When Required.* On motion or on its own, the court must limit the frequency or extent of discovery otherwise allowed by these rules or by local rule if it determines that:
  (i) the discovery sought is unreasonably cumulative or duplicative, or can be obtained from some other source that is more convenient, less burdensome, or less expensive;
  (ii) the party seeking discovery has had ample opportunity to obtain the information by discovery in the action; or
  (iii) the proposed discovery is outside the scope permitted by Rule 26(b)(1).

(3) *Trial Preparation: Materials.*

(A) *Documents and Tangible Things.* Ordinarily, a party may not discover documents and tangible things that are prepared in anticipation of litigation or for trial by or for another party or its representative (including another party's attorney, consultant, surety, indemnitor, insurer, or agent). But, subject to Rule 26(b)(4), those materials may be discovered if:
  (i) they are otherwise discoverable under Rule 26(b)(1); and
  (ii) the party shows that it has substantial need for the materials to prepare its case and cannot, without undue hardship, obtain their substantial equivalent by other means.

(B) *Protection Against Disclosure.* If the court orders discovery of those materials, it must protect against disclosure of the mental impressions, conclusions, opinions, or legal theories of a party's attorney or other representative concerning the litigation.

(C) *Previous Statement.* Any party or other person may, on request and without the required showing, obtain the person's own previous statement about the action or its subject matter. If the request is refused, the person may move for a court order, and Rule 37(a)(5) applies to the award of expenses. A previous statement is either:

(i) a written statement that the person has signed or otherwise adopted or approved; or

(ii) a contemporaneous stenographic, mechanical, electrical, or other recording – or a transcription of it – that recites substantially verbatim the person's oral statement.

(4) *Trial Preparation: Experts.*

(A) *Deposition of an Expert Who May Testify.* A party may depose any person , who has been identified as an expert whose opinions may be presented at trial. If Rule 26(a)(2)(B) requires a report from the expert, the deposition may be conducted only after the report is provided.

(B) *Trial-Preparation Protection for Draft Reports or Disclosures.* Rules 26(b)(3)(A) and (B) protect drafts of any report or disclosure required under Rule 26(a)(2), regardless of the form in which the draft is recorded.

(C) *Trial-Preparation Protection for Communications Between a Party's Attorney and Expert Witnesses.* Rules 26(b)(3)(A) and (B) protect communications between the party's attorney and any witness required to provide a report under rule 26(a)(2)(B), regardless of the form of the communications, except to the extent that communications:

(i) relate to compensation for the expert's study or testimony;

(ii) identify facts or data that the party's attorney provided and that the expert considered in forming the opinions to be expressed; or

(iii) identify assumptions that the party's attorney provided and that the expert relied on in forming the opinions to be expressed.

(D) *Expert Employed Only for Trial Preparation.* Ordinarily, a party may not, by interrogatories or deposition, discover facts known or opinions held by an expert who has been retained or specially employed by another party in anticipation of litigation or to prepare for trial and who is not expected to be called as a witness at trial. But a party may do so only:

(i) as provided in Rule 35(b); or

(ii) on showing exceptional circumstances under which, it is impracticable for the party to obtain facts or opinions on the same subject by other means.

(E) *Payment.* Unless manifest injustice would result, the court must require that the party seeking discovery:

(i) pay the expert a reasonable fee for time spent in responding to discovery under Rule 26(b)(4)(A) or (D); and

(ii) for discovery under (D), also pay the other party a fair portion of the fees and expenses it reasonably incurred in obtaining the expert's facts and opinions.

(5) *Claiming Privilege or Protecting Trial-Preparation Materials.*

(A) *Information Withheld.* When a party withholds information otherwise discoverable by claiming that the information is privileged or subject to protection as trial-preparation material, the party must:

(i) expressly make the claim; and

(ii) describe the nature of the documents, communications, or tangible things not produced or disclosed – and do so in a manner that, without revealing information itself privileged or protected, will enable other parties to assess the claim.

(B) *Information Produced.* If information produced in discovery is subject to a claim of privilege or of protection as trial-preparation material, the party making the claim may notify any party that received the information of the claim and the basis for it. After being notified, a party must promptly return, sequester, or destroy the specified information and any copies it has; must not use or disclose the information until the claim is resolved; must take reasonable steps to retrieve the information if the party disclosed it before notified; and may promptly present the information to the court under seal for a determination of the claim. The producing party must preserve the information until the claim is resolved.

(c) PROTECTIVE ORDERS.

(1) *In General.* A party or any person from whom discovery is sought may move for a protective order in the court where the action is pending – or as an alternative on matters relating to a deposition, in the court for the district where the deposition will be taken. The motion must include a certification that the movant has in good faith conferred or attempted to confer with other affected parties in an effort to resolve the dispute without court action. The court may, for good cause, issue an order to protect a person or party from annoyance, embarrassment, oppression, or undue burden or expense, including one or more of the following:

(A) forbidding the disclosure or discovery;

(B) specifying terms, including time and place, for the disclosure or discovery;

(C) prescribing a discovery method other than the one selected by the party seeking discovery;

(D) forbidding inquiry into certain matters, or limiting the scope of disclosure or discovery to certain matters;

(E) designating the persons who may be present while the discovery is conducted;

(F) requiring that a deposition be sealed and opened only on court order;

(G) requiring that a trade secret or other confidential research, development, or commercial information not be revealed or be revealed only in a specified way; and

(H) requiring that the parties simultaneously file specified documents or information in sealed envelopes, to be opened as the court directs.

(2) *Ordering Discovery.* If a motion for a protective order is wholly or partly denied, the court may, on just terms, order that any person provide or permit discovery.

(3) *Awarding Expenses.* Rule 37(a)(5) applies to the award of expenses.

(d) TIMING AND SEQUENCE OF DISCOVERY.

(1) *Timing.* A party may not seek discovery from any source before the parties have conferred as required by Rule 26(f), except in a proceeding exempted from initial disclosure under Rule 26(a)(1)(B), or when authorized by these rules, by stipulation, or by court order.

(2) *Early Rule 34 Requests.*

(A) *Time to Deliver.* More than 21 days after the summons and complaint are served on a party, a request under Rule 34 may be delivered:

(i) to that party by any other party, and

(ii) by that party to any plaintiff or to any other party that has been served.

(B) When Considered Served. The request is considered to have been served at the first Rule 26(f) conference.

(3) *Sequence.* Unless, on motion, the court orders otherwise for the parties' and witnesses' convenience and in the interests of justice:

(A) methods of discovery may be used in any sequence; and

(B) discovery by one party does not require any other party to delay its discovery.

(e) SUPPLEMENTING DISCLOSURES AND RESPONSES.
  (1) *In General.* A party who has made a disclosure under Rule 26(a) – or who has responded to an interrogatory, request for production, or request for admission – must supplement or correct its disclosure or response:
    (A) in a timely manner if the party learns that in some material respect the disclosure or response is incomplete or incorrect, and if the additional or corrective information has not otherwise been made known to the other parties during the discovery process in writing; or
    (B) as ordered by the court.
  (2) *Expert Witness.* For an expert whose report must be disclosed under Rule 26(a)(2)(B), the party's duty to supplement extends both to information included in the report and to information given during the expert's deposition. Any additions or changes to this information must be disclosed by the time the party's pretrial disclosures under Rule 26(a)(3) are due.
(f) CONFERENCE OF THE PARTIES; PLANNING FOR DISCOVERY.
  (1) *Conference Timing.* Except .in a proceeding exempted from initial disclosure under Rule 26(a)(1)(B) or when the court orders otherwise, the parties must confer as soon as practicable, and in any event at least 21 days before a scheduling conference is held or a scheduling order is due under Rule 16(b).
  (2) *Conference Content; Parties' Responsibilities.* In conferring, the parties must consider the nature and basis of their claims and defenses and the possibilities for promptly settling or resolving the case; make or arrange for the disclosures required by Rule 26(a)(1); discuss any issues about preserving discoverable information; and develop a proposed discovery plan. The attorneys of record and all unrepresented parties that have appeared in the case are jointly responsible for arranging the conference, for attempting in good faith to agree on the proposed discovery plan, and for submitting to the court within 14 days after the conference a written report outlining the plan. The court may order the parties or attorneys to attend the conference in person.
  (3) *Discovery Plan.* A discovery plan must state the parties' views and proposals on:
    (A) what changes should be made in the timing, form, or requirement for disclosures under Rule 26(a), including a statement of when initial disclosures were made or will be made;
    (B) the subjects on which discovery may be needed, when discovery should be completed, and whether discovery should be conducted in phases or be limited to or focused on particular issues;
    (C) any issues about disclosure or discovery of electronically stored information, including the form or forms in which it should be produced;
    (D) any issues about claims of privilege or of protection as trial-preparation materials, including – if the parties agree on a procedure to assert these claims after production – whether to ask the court to include their agreement in an order;
    (E) what changes should be made in the limitations on discovery imposed under these rules or by local rule, and what other limitations should be imposed; and
    (F) any other orders that the court should issue under Rule 26(c) or under Rule 16(b) and (c).
  (4) *Expedited Schedule.* If necessary, to comply with its expedited schedule for Rule 16(b) conferences, a court my by local rule:
    (A) require the parties' conference to occur less than 21 days before the scheduling conference is held or a scheduling order is due under Rule 16(b); and
    (B) require the written report outlining the discovery plan to be filed less than 14 days after the parties' conference or excuse the parties from submitting a written report and permit them to report orally on their discovery plan at the Rule 16(b) conference.

(g) Signing Disclosures and Discovery Requests, Responses, and Objections.

    (1) *Signature Required; Effect of Signature.* Every disclosure under Rule 26(a)(1) or (a)(3) and every discovery request, response, or objection must be signed by at least one attorney of record in the attorney's own name – or by the party personally, if unrepresented – and must state the signer's address, e-mail address, and telephone number. By signing, an attorney or party certifies that to the best of the person's knowledge, information, and belief, formed after a reasonable inquiry:

    (A) with respect to a disclosure, it is complete and correct as of the time it is made; and

    (B) with respect to a discovery request, response, or objection, it is:

        (i) consistent with these rules and warranted by existing law or by a non-frivolous argument for extending, modifying, or reversing existing law, or for establishing new law;

        (ii) not interposed for any improper purpose, such as to harass, cause unnecessary delay, or needlessly increase the cost of litigation; and

        (iii) neither unreasonable nor unduly burdensome or expensive, considering the needs of the case, prior discovery for the case, the amount in controversy and the importance of the issues at stake in the action.

    (2) *Failure to Sign.* Other parties have no duty to act on an unsigned disclosure, request, response, or objection until it is signed, and the court must strike it unless a signature is promptly supplied after the omission is called to the attorney's or party's attention.

    (3) *Sanction for Improper Certification.* If a certification violates this rule without substantial justification, the court, on motion or on its own, must impose an appropriate sanction on the signer, the party on whose behalf the signer was acting, or both. The sanction may include an order to pay the reasonable expenses, including attorney's fees, caused by the violation.

Rule 27. Depositions to Perpetuate Testimony

(a) Before an Action Is Filed.

    (1) *Petition.* A person who wants to perpetuate testimony about any matter cognizable in a United States court may file a verified petition in the district court for the district where any expected adverse party resides. The petition must ask for an order authorizing the petitioner to depose the named persons in order to perpetuate their testimony. The petition must be titled in the petitioner's name and must show:

    (A) that the petitioner expects to be a party to an action cognizable in a United States court but cannot presently bring it or cause it to be brought;

    (B) the subject matter of the expected action and the petitioner's interest;

    (C) the facts that the petitioner wants to establish by the proposed testimony and the reasons to perpetuate it;

    (D) the names or a description of the persons whom the petitioner expects to be adverse parties and their addresses, so far as known; and

    (E) the name, address, and expected substance of the testimony of each deponent.

    (2) *Notice and Service.* At least 21 days before the hearing date, the petitioner must serve each expected adverse party with a copy of the petition and a notice stating the time and place of the hearing. The notice may be served either inside or outside the district or state in the manner provided in Rule 4. If that service cannot be made with reasonable diligence on an adverse party, the court may order service by publication or otherwise. The court must appoint an attorney to represent persons not served in the manner provided in Rule 4 and to cross-examine the deponent if an unserved person is not otherwise represented. If any expected adverse party is a minor or is incompetent, Rule 1.7(c) applies.

(3) *Order and Examination.* If satisfied that perpetuating the testimony may prevent a failure or delay of justice, the court must issue an order that designates or describes the persons whose depositions may be taken, specifies the subject matter of the examinations, and states whether the depositions will be taken orally or by written interrogatories. The depositions may then be taken under these rules, and the court may issue orders like those authorized by Rules 34 and35. A reference in these rules to the court where an action is pending means, for purposes of this rule, the court where the petition for the deposition was filed.

(4) *Using the Deposition.* A deposition to perpetrate testimony may be used under Rule 32(a) in any later-filed district-court action involving the same subject matter if the deposition either was taken under these rules or, although not so taken, would be admissible in evidence in the courts of the state where it was taken.

(b) PENDING APPEAL.

(1) *In General.* The court where a judgment has been rendered may, if an appeal has been taken or may still be taken, permit a party to depose witnesses to perpetuate their testimony for use | In the event of further proceedings in that court.

(2) *Motion.* The party who wants to perpetuate testimony may move for leave to take the depositions, on the same notice and service as if the action were pending in the district court, the motion must show:

(A) the name, address, and expected substance of the testimony of each deponent; and

(B) the reasons for perpetuating the testimony.

(3) *Court Order.* If the court finds that perpetuating the testimony may prevent a failure or delay of justice, the court may permit the depositions to be taken and may issue orders like those authorized by Rules 34 and 35. The depositions may be taken and used like any other deposition taken in a pending district-court action.

(c) PERPETUATION BY AN ACTION. This rule does not limit a court's power to entertain an action to perpetuate testimony.

Rule 28. Persons before Whom Depositions May Be Taken

(a) WITHIN THE UNITED STATES.

(1) *In General.* Within the United States or a territory or insular possession subject to United States jurisdiction, a deposition must be taken before:

(A) an officer authorized to administer oaths either by federal law or by the law in the place of examination; or

(B) a person appointed by the court where action is pending to administer oaths and take testimony.

(C) *Definition of "Officer."* The term "officer" in Rules 30, 31, and 32 includes a person appointed by the court under this rule or designated by the parties under Rule 29(a).

(b) IN A FOREIGN COUNTRY.

(1) *In General.* A deposition may be taken in a foreign country:

(A) under an applicable treaty or convention;

(B) under a letter of request, whether or not captioned a "letter rogatory"

(C) on notice, before a person authorized to administer oaths either by federal law or by the law in the place of examination; or

(D) before a person commissioned by the court to administer any necessary oath and take testimony.

(2) *Issuing a Letter of Request or a Commission.* A letter of request, a commission, or both may be issued:

(A) on appropriate terms after an application and notice of it; and

(B) without a showing that taking the deposition in another manner is impracticable or inconvenient.

(3) *Form of a Request, Notice, or Commission.* When a letter of request or any other device is used according to a treaty or convention, it must be captioned in the form prescribed by that treaty or convention. A letter of request may be addressed "To the Appropriate Authority in [name of country]." A deposition or notice or a commission must designate by name or descriptive title the person before whom the deposition is to be taken.

(4) *Letter of Request – Admitting Evidence.* Evidence obtained in response to a letter of request need not be excluded merely because it is not a verbatim transcript, because the testimony was not taken under oath, or because of any similar departure from the requirements for depositions taken within the United States.

(c) DISQUALIFICATION. A deposition must not be taken before a person who is any party's relative, employee, or attorney; who is related to or employed by any party's attorney; or who is financially interested in the action.

Rule 29. Stipulations About Discovery Procedure

Unless the court orders otherwise, the parties may stipulate that:

(a) a deposition may be taken before any person, at any time or place, on any notice, and in the manner specified – in which event it may be used in the same way as any other deposition; and

(b) other procedures governing or limiting discovery be modified – but a stipulation extending the time for any form of discovery must have court approval if it would interfere with the time set for completing discovery, for hearing a motion, or for trial.

Rule 30. Depositions by Oral Examination

(a) WHEN A DEPOSITION MAY BE TAKEN.

(1) *Without Leave.* A party may, by oral questions, depose any person, including a party, without leave of court except as provided in Rule 30 (a)(2). The deponent's attendance may be compelled by subpoena under Rule 45.

(2) *With Leave.* A party must obtain leave of court, and the court must grant leave to the extent consistent with Rule 26(b)(2):

(A) if the parties have not stipulated to the deposition and:

(i) the deposition would result in more than 10 depositions being taken under this rule or Rule 31 by the plaintiffs, or by the defendants, or by the third-party defendants;

(ii) the deponent has already been deposed in the case; or

(iii) the party seeks to take the deposition before the time specified in Rule 26(d), unless the party certifies in the notice, with supporting facts, that the deponent is expected to leave the United States and be unavailable for examination in this country after that time; or

(B) if the deponent is confined in prison.

(b) NOTICE OF THE DEPOSITION; OTHER FORMAL REQUIREMENTS.

(1) *Notice in General.* A party who wants to depose a person by oral questions must give reasonable written notice to every other party. The notice must state the time and place of the deposition and, if known, the deponent's name and address. If the name is unknown, the notice must provide a general description sufficient to identify the person or the particular class or group to which the person belongs.

(2) *Producing Documents.* If a subpoena duces tecum is to be served on the deponent, the materials designated for production, as set out in the subpoena, must be listed in the notice or

in an attachment. The notice to a party deponent may be accompanied by a request complying with Rule 34 to produce documents and tangible things at the deposition.

(3) *Method of Recording.*

    (A) *Method Stated in the Notice.* The party who notices the deposition must state in the notice the method for recording the testimony. Unless the court orders otherwise, testimony may be recorded by audio, audiovisual, or stenographic means. The noticing party bears the recording costs. Any party may arrange to transcribe a deposition.

    (B) *Additional Method.* With prior notice to the deponent and other parties, any party may designate another method for recording the testimony in addition to that specified in the original notice. That party bears the expense of the additional record or transcript unless the court orders otherwise.

(4) *By Remote Means.* The parties may stipulate – or the court may on motion order – that a deposition be taken by telephone or other remote means, for the purpose of this rule and Rule 28(a), 37(a)(2), and 37(b)(1), the deposition takes place where the deponent answers questions.

(5) *Officer's Duties.*

    (A) *Before the Deposition.* Unless the parties stipulate otherwise, a deposition must be conducted before an officer appointed or designated under Rule 28. The officer must begin the deposition with an on-the-record statement that includes:

        (i) the officer's name and business address;

        (ii) the date, time, and place of the deposition;

        (iii) the deponent's name;

        (iv) the officer's administration of the oath or affirmation to the deponent; and

        (v) the identity of all persons present.

    (B) *Conducting the Deposition; Avoiding Distortion.* If the deposition is recorded non-stenographically, the officer must repeat the items in Rule 30(b)(5)(A)(di)-(iii) at the beginning of each unit of the recording medium. The deponent's and attorney's appearance or demeanor must not be distorted through recording techniques.

    (C) *After the Deposition.* At the end of a deposition, the officer must state on the record that the deposition is complete and must set out any stipulations made by the attorneys about custody of the transcript or recording and of the exhibits, or about any other pertinent matters.

(6) *Notice or Subpoena Directed to an Organization.* In its notice or subpoena, a party may name as the deponent a public or private corporation, a partnership, an association, a governmental agency, or other entity and must describe with reasonable particularity he matters for examination. The named organization must then designate one or more officers, directors, or managing agents, or designate other persons who consent to testify on its behalf; and it may set out the matters on which each person designated will testify. A subpoena must ad visa a nonparty organization of its duty to make this designation. The persons designated must testify about information known or reasonable available to the organization. This paragraph (60 does not preclude a deposition by any other procedure allowed by these rules.

(c) EXAMINATION AND CROSS-EXAMINATION; RECORD OF THE EXAMINATION; OBJECTIONS; WRITTEN QUESTIONS.

(1) *Examination and Cross-Examination.* The examination and cross-examination of a deponent proceed as they would at trial under the federal Rules of Evidence, except Rules 103 and 615. After putting the deponent under oath or affirmation, the officer must record the testimony by the method designated under Rule 30(b)(3)(A). The testimony must be recorded by the officer personally or by a person acting in the presence and under the direction of the officer.

(2) *Objections.* An objection at the time of examination – whether to evidence, to a party's conduct, to the officer's qualifications, to the manner of taking the deposition, or to any aspect of the deposition – must be noted on the record, but the examination still proceeds; the testimony is subject to any objection. An objection must be stated concisely in a nonargumentative and nonsuggestive manner. A person may instruct a deponent not to answer only when necessary to protect a privilege, to enforce a limitation ordered by the court, or to present a motion under Rule 30(d'X3).

(3) *Participating Thorough Written Questions.* Instead of participating in the oral examination, a party may serve written questions in a sealed envelope on the party noticing the deposition, who must deliver them to the officer. The officer must ask the deponent those questions and record the answers verbatim.

(d) DURATION; SANCTION; MOTION TO TERMINATE OR LIMIT.

(1) *Duration.* Unless other vise stipulated or ordered by the court, a deposition is limited to 1 day of 7 hours. The court must allow additional time consistent with Rule 26(b)(2) if needed to fairly examine the deponent or if the deponent, another person, or any other circumstances impedes or delays the examination.

(2) *Sanction.* The court may impose an appropriate sanction – including the reasonable expenses and attorney's fees incurred by any party – on a person who impedes, delays, or frustrates the fair examination of the deponent.

(3) *Motion to Terminate or Limit.*

(A) *Grounds.* At any time during a deposition, the deponent or a party may move to terminate it or limit it on the ground that it is being conducted in bad faith or in a manner that unreasonably annoys, embarrasses, or oppresses the deponent or party. The motion may be filed in the court where the action is pending, or the deposition is being taken. If the objecting deponent or party so demands, the deposition must be suspended for the time necessary to obtain an order.

(B) *Order.* The court may order that the deposition be terminated or may limit its scope and manner as provided in Rule 26,(c). If terminated, the deposition may be resumed only by order of the court where the action is pending.

(C) *Award of Expenses.* Rule 37(a)(5) applies to the award of expenses.

(e) REVIEW BY THE WITNESS; CHANGES.

(1) Review; Statement of Changes. On request by the deponent or a party before the deposition is completed, the deponent must be allowed 30 days after being notified by the officer that the transcript recording is available in which:

(A) to review the transcript or recording; and

(B) if there are changes in form or substance, to sign a statement listing the changes and the reasons for making them.

(2) *Changes Indicated in the Officer's Certificate.* The officer must note in the certificate prescribed by Rule 30(f)(1) whether a review was requested and, if so, must attach any changes the deponent makes during the 30-day period.

(f) CERTIFICATE AND DELIVERY; EXHIBITS; COPIES OF THE TRANSCRIPT OR RECORDING; FILING.

(1) *Certification and Delivery.* The officer must certify in writing that the witness was duly sworn, and that the deposition accurately records the witness's testimony. The certificate must accompany the record of the deposition. Unless the court orders otherwise, the officer must seal the deposition in an envelope or package bearing the title of the action and marked 'Imposition of [witness's name]" and must promptly send it to the attorney who arranged for the transcript or recording. The attorney must store it under conditions that will protect it against loss, destruction, tampering, or deterioration.

(2) *Document s and Tangible Things*.
(A) *Originals and Copies*. Documents and tangible things produced for inspection during a deposition must, on a party's request, be marked for identification and attached to the deposition. Any party may inspect and copy them. But if the person who produced them wants to keep the originals, the person may:
(i) offer copies to be marked, attached to the deposition, and then used as originals – after giving all parties a fair opportunity to verify the copies by comparing them with the originals; or
(ii) give all parties a fair opportunity to inspect and copy the originals after they are marked – in which event the originals may be used as if attached to the deposition.
(B) *Order regarding the Originals*. Any party may move for an order that the originals be attached to the deposition pending final, disposition of the case.
(3) *Copies of the Transcript or Recording*. Unless otherwise stipulated or ordered by the court, the officer must retain the stenographic notes of a deposition taken stenographically or a copy of the recording of the deposition taken by another method. When paid reasonable charges, the officer must furnish a copy of the transcript or recording to any party or the deponent.
(4) Notice of Filing. A party who files the deposition must promptly notify all other parties of the filing.
(g) Failure to Attend a Deposition or Serve a Subpoena; Expenses. A party who, expecting a deposition to be taken, attends in person or by an attorney may recover reasonable expenses for attending, including attorney's fees, if the noticing party failed to:
(1) attend and proceed with the deposition; or
(2) serve a subpoena on a nonparty deponent, who consequently did not attend.

Rule 31. Depositions by Written Questions

(a) When a Deposition May Be Taken.
(1) *Without Leave*. A party may, by written questions, depose any person, including a party, without leave of court except as provided in Rule 31(a)(2). The deponent's attendance m^ be compelled by subpoena under Rule 45**.;**
(2) *With Leave*. A party must obtain leave of court, and the court must grant leave to the extent consistent with Rule 26(b)(1) and (2):
(A) if the parties have not stipulated to the deposition and:
(i) the deposition would result in more than 10 depositions being taken under this rule or Rule 30 by the plaintiffs, or by the defendants, or by the third-party defendant's;
(ii) the deponent has already been deposed in the case; or
(iii) the party seeks to take a deposition before the time specified in Rule 26(d); or
(B) if the deponent is confined in prison.
(3) *Service; Required Notice*. A party who wants to depose a person by written questions must serve them on every other party, with a notice stating, if known, the deponent's name and address. If the name is unknown, the notice must provide a general description sufficient to identify the person or the particular class or group to which the person belongs. The notice must also state the name or descriptive title and the address of the officer before whom the deposition will be taken.
(4) *Questions Directed to an Organization*. A public or private corporation, a partnership, an association, or a governmental agency may be deposed by written questions in accordance with Rule 30(b)(6).
(5) *Questions from Other Parties*. Any questions to the deponent from other parties must be served on all parties as follows: cross-questions, within 14 days after being served with the

notice and direct questions; redirect questions, within 7 days after being served with cross-questions; and recross-questions, within 7 days of being served with redirect questions. The court may, for good cause, extend or shorten these times.

(b) DELIVERY TO THE OFFICER; OFFICER'S DUTIES. The party who noticed the deposition must deliver/to the office: a copy of all the questions served and of the notice. The officer must promptly proceed in the manner provided in Rule 30(c),(e), and (f) to:

(1) take the deponent's testimony in response to the questions;

(2) prepare and certify the deposition; and

(3) send it to the party, attaching a copy of the questions and of the notice.

(c) NOTICE OF COMPLETION OR FILING.

(1) *Completion*. The party who noticed the deposition must notify all other parties when it is completed.

(2) *Filing*. A party who files the deposition must promptly notify all other parties of the filing.

Rule 32. Using Depositions in Court Proceedings

(a) USING DEPOSITIONS.

(1) *In General*. At a hearing or trial, all or part of a deposition m^ be used against a party on these conditions:

(A) the party was present ore represented at the taking of the deposition or had reasonable notice of it;

(B) it is used to the extent it would be admissible under the Federal Rules of Evidence if the deponent were present and testifying; and

(C) the use is allowed by Rule 32(a)(2) through (8).

(2) *Impeachment and Other Uses*. Any party may use a deposition to contradict or impeach the testimony given by the deponent as a witness, or for any other purpose allowed by the Federal Rules of Evidence.

(3) *Depositions of Party, Agent, or Designee*. An adverse party may use for any purpose the deposition of a party or anyone who, when deposed, was the party's officer, director, managing agent, or designee under Rule 30(b)(6) or 31(a)(4).

(4) *Unavailable Witnesses*. A party may use for any purpose the deposition of a witness, whether or not a party, if the court finds:

(A) that the witness is dead;

(B) that the witness is more than 100 miles from the place of hearing or trial or is outside the United States, unless it appears that the witness's absence was procured by the party offering the deposition;

(C) that the witness cannot attend or testify because of age, illness, infirmity, or imprisonment;

(D) that the party offering the deposition could not procure the witness's attendance by subpoena; or

(E) on motion and notice, that exceptional circumstances make it desirable – in the interest of justice and with due regard to the importance of live testimony in open court – to permit the deposition to be used.

(5) *Limitations on Use*.

(A) *Deposition Taken on Short Notice*. A deposition must not lie used against a party who, having received less than 14 days' notice of the deposition, promptly moved for a protective order under Rule 26(c)(1)(B) requesting that it not be taken or taken at a different time or place – and this motion was still pending when the deposition was taken.

(B) *Unavailable Deponent; Party Could not Obtain an Attorney*. A deposition taken without leave of court under the unavailability provision of Rule 30(a)(2)(A)(iii) must not be used against a party who shows that, when served with the notice, it could not, despite diligent efforts, obtain an attorney to represent it at the deposition.

(6) *Using Part of a Deposition*. If a party offers in evidence only part of a deposition, an adverse party may require the offeror to introduce other parts that in fairness should be considered with the part introduced, and any party may itself introduce any other parts.

(7) *Substituting a Party*. Substituting a party under Rule 25 does not affect the right to use a deposition previously taken.

(8) *Deposition taken in an Earlier Action*. A deposition lawfully taken and, if required, filed in any federal – or state-court action may be used in a later action involving the same subject matter between the same parties, or their representatives or successors in interest, to the same extent as if taken in the later action. A deposition previously taken may also be used as allowed by the Federal rules of Evidence.

(b) OBJECTIONS TO ADMISSIBILITY. Subject to Rules 28(b) and 32(d)(3), an objection may be made at a hearing or trial to the admission of any deposition testimony that would be inadmissible if the witness were present and testifying.

(c) FORM OF PRESENTATION. Unless the court orders otherwise, a party must provide a transcript of any deposition testimony the party offers, but may provide the court with the testimony in nontranscript form as well. On any party's request, deposition testimony offered in a jury trial for any purpose other than impeachment must be presented in nontranscript form, if available, unless the court for good cause orders otherwise.

(d) WAIVER OF OBJECTIONS.

(1) *To the Notice*. An objection to an error or irregularity in a deposition notice is waived unless promptly served in writing on the party giving the notice.

(2) *To the Officer's Qualification*. An objection based on disqualification of the officer before whom a deposition is to be taken is waived if not made:

(A) before the deposition begins; or

(B) promptly after the basis for disqualification becomes known or, with reasonable diligence, could have been known.

(3) *To the Taking of the Deposition*.

(A) *Objection to Competence, Relevance, or Materiality*. An objection to a deponent's competence – or to the competence, relevance, or materiality of testimony – is not waived by a failure to make the objection before or during the deposition, unless the ground for it might have been corrected at that time.

(B) *Objection to an Error or Irregularity*. An objection to an error or irregularity at an oral examination is waived if:

(i) it relates to the manner of taking the deposition, the form of a question or answer, the oath or affirmation, a party's conduct, or other matters that might have been corrected at that time; and

(ii) it is not timely made during the deposition.

(C) *Objections to a Written Question*. An objection to the form of a written question under Rule 31 is waived if not served in writing on the party submitting the question within the time for serving responsive questions or, if the question is a recross-question, within 7 days after being served with it.

(4) *To Completing and Returning the Deposition*. An objection to how the officer transcribed the testimony – or prepared, signed, certified, sealed, endorsed, sent, or otherwise dealt with the

deposition – is waived unless a motion to suppress is made promptly after the error or irregularity becomes known or, with reasonable diligence, could have been known.

Rule 33. Interrogatories to Parties

(a) IN GENERAL.

(1) *Number.* Unless otherwise stipulated or ordered by the court, a party may serve on any other party no more than 25 written interrogatories, including all discrete subparts. Leave to serve additional interrogatories may be granted to the extent consistent with Rule 26(b)(2).

(2) *Scope.* An interrogatory may relate to any matter that may be inquired into under Rule 26(b). An interrogatory is not objectionable merely because it asks for an opinion or contention that relates to fact or the application of law to fact, but the court may order that the interrogatory need not be answered until designated discovery is complete, or until a pretrial conference or some other time.

(b) Answers and Objections.

(1) *Responding Party.* The interrogatories must be answered:

(A) by the party to whom they are directed; or

(B) if that party is a public or private corporation, a partnership, an association, or a governmental agency, by any officer or agent, who must furnish the information available to the party.

(2) *Time to Respond.* The responding party must serve its answers and any objections within 30 days after being served with the interrogatories. A shorter or longer time may be stipulated to under Rule 29 or be ordered by the court.

(3) *Answering Each Interrogatory.* Each interrogatory must, to the extent it is not objected to, be answered separately and fully In writing under oath.

(4) *Objections.* The grounds for objecting to an interrogatory must be stated with specificity. Any ground not stated in a timely objection is waived unless the court, for good cause, excuses the failure.

(5) *Signature.* The person who makes the answers must sign them, and the attorney who objects must sign any objections.

(c) USE. An answer to an interrogatory may be used to the extent allowed by the Federal Rules of Evidence.

(d) OPTION TO PRODUCE BUSINESS RECORDS. If the answer to an interrogatory may be determined by examining, auditing, compiling, abstracting, or summarizing a party's business records(including electronically stored information), and if the burden of deriving or ascertaining the answer will be substantially the same for either party, the responding party may answer by:

(1) specifying the records that must be reviewed, in sufficient detail to enable the interrogating party to locate and identify them as readily as the responding party could; and

(2) giving the interrogating party a reasonable opportunity to examine and audit the records and to make copies, compilations, abstracts, and summaries.

Rule 34. Producing Documents, Electronically Stored Information, and Tangible Things, or Entering onto land, for Inspection and Other Purposes

(a) IN GENERAL. A party may serve on any other party a request within the scope of Rule 26(b):

(1) to produce and permit the requesting party or its representative to inspect, copy, test, or sample the following item's in the responding party's possession, custody, or control:

(A) any designated documents or electronically stored information – including writings, drawings, graphs, charts, photographs, sound recordings, images, and other data or data compilations – stored in any medium from which information can be obtained either directly or, if necessary, after translation by the responding party into a reasonably usable form; or

(B) any designated tangible things; or

(2) to permit entry onto designated land or other property possessed or controlled by the responding party, so that the requesting party may inspect, measure, survey, photograph, test, or sample the property or any designated object or operation on it.

(b) PROCEDURE.

(1) *Contents of the Request.* The request:

(A) must describe with reasonable particularity each item or category of items to be inspected;

(B) must specify a reasonable time, place, and manner for the inspection and for performing the related acts; and

(C) may specify the form or forms in which electronically stored information is to be produced.

(2) RESPONSES AND OBJECTIONS.

(A) *Time to Respond.* The party to whom the request is directed must respond in writing within 30 days after being served. A shorter or longer time may be stipulated to under Rule 29 or be ordered by the court.

(B) *Responding to Each Item.* For each item of category, the response must either state that inspection and related activities will be permitted as requested or state an objection to the request, including the reasons.

(C) *Objections.* An objection to part of a request must specify the part and permit inspection of the rest.

(D) *Responding to a Request for Production of Electronically Stored Information.* The response may state an objection to a requested form for producing electronically stored information. If the responding party objects to a request form – or if no form was specified in the request – the party must state the form or forms it intends to use.

(E) *Producing the Documents or Electronically Stored Information.* Unless otherwise stipulated or ordered by the court, these procedures apply to producing documents or electronically stored information:

(i) A party must produce documents as they are kept in the usual course of business or must organize and label them to correspond to the categories in the request;

(ii) If a request does not specify a form for producing electronically stored information, a party must produce it in a form or forms which is ordinarily maintained or in a reasonably usable form or forms; and

(iii) A party need not produce the same electronically stored information in more than one form.

(c) NONPARTIES. As provided in Rule 45, a nonparty may be compelled to produce documents and tangible things or to permit an inspection.

Rule 35. Physical and Mental Examinations

(a) ORDER FOR AN EXAMINATION.

    (1) *In General*. The court where the action is pending may order a party whose mental or physical condition – including blood group is in controversy to submit to a physical or mental examination by a suitably licensed or certified examiner. The court has the same authority to order a party to produce for examination a person who is in its custody or under its legal control.

    (2) *Motion and Notice; Contents of the Order*. The order:

        (A) may be made only on motion for good cause and on notice to all parties and the person to be examined; and

        (B) must specify the time, place, manner, conditions, and scope of the examination, as well as the person or persons who will perform it.

(b) EXAMINER'S REPORT.

    (1) *Request by the Party or Person Examined*. The party who moved for the examination must, on request, deliver to the requester a copy of the examiner's report, together with like reports of all earlier examinations of the same condition. The request may be made by the party against whom the examination order was issued or by the person examined.

    (2) *Contents*. The examiner's report must be in writing and must set out in detail the examiner's findings, including diagnoses, conclusions, and the results of any tests.

    (3) *Request by the Moving Party*. After delivering the reports, the party who moved for the examination may request – and is entitled to receive – from the party against whom the examination order was issued like reports of all earlier or later examinations of the same condition. But those reports need not be delivered by the party with custody or control of the person examined if the party shows that it could not obtain them.

    (4) *Waiver of Privilege*. By requesting and obtaining the examiner's report, or by deposing the examiner, the party examined waives any privilege it may have – in that action or any other action involving the same controversy – concerning testimony about all examinations of the same condition.

    (5) *Failure to Deliver a Report*. The court on motion may order – on just terms – that a party deliver the report of an examination. If the report is not provided, the court may exclude the examiner's testimony at trial.

    (6) *Scope*. This subdivision (b) applies also to an examination made by the parties' agreement, unless the agreement states otherwise. This subdivision does not preclude obtaining an examiner's report or deposing an examiner under other rules.

Rule 36. Requests for Admission

(a) SCOPE AND PROCEDURE.

    (1) *Scope*. A party may serve on any other party a written request to admit, for purposes of the pending action only, the truth of any matters within the scope of Rule 26(b)(1) relating to:

        (A) facts, the application of law to fact, or opinions about either; and

        (B) the genuineness of any described documents.

    (2) *Form; Copy of a Document*. Each matter must be separately stated. A request to admit the genuineness of a document must be accompanied by a copy of the document unless it is, or has been, otherwise furnished or made available for inspection and copying.

    (3) *Time to Respond; Effect of Not Responding*. A matter is admitted unless, within 30 days after being served, the party to whom the request is directed serves on the requesting party a written answer or objection addressed .to the matter and signed by the party or its attorney. A shorter or longer time for responding may be stipulated to under Rule 29 or be ordered by the court.

(4) *Answer.* If a matter is not admitted, the answer must specifically deny it or state in detail why the answering party cannot truthfully admit or deny it. A denial must fairly respond to the substance of the matter; and when good faith requires that a party qualify an answer or deny only part of a matter, the answer must specify the part admitted and qualify or deny the rest. The answering party may assert lack of knowledge or information as a reason for failing to admit or deny only if the party states that is has made reasonable inquiry and that the information it knows or can readily obtain is insufficient to enable it to admit or deny.

(5) *Objections.* The grounds for objecting to a request must be stated. A party must not object solely on the ground that it presents a genuine issue for trial.

(6) *Motion Regarding the Sufficiency of an Answer or Objection.* The requesting party may move to determine the sufficiency of an answer or objection. Unless the court finds an objection justified, it must order that an answer be served. On finding that an answer does not comply with this rule, the court may order either that the matter is admitted or that an amended answer be served. The court may defer its final decision until a pretrial conference or a specified time before trial. Rule 37(a)(5) applies to an award of expenses.

(b) EFFECT OF AN ADMISSION; WITHDRAWING OR AMENDING IT. A matter admitted under this rule is conclusively established unless the court, on motion, permits the admission to be withdrawn or amended. Subject to Rule 16(e), the court may permit the withdrawal or amendment if it would promote the presentation of the merits of the action and if the court is not persuaded that it would prejudice the requesting party in maintaining or defending the action on the merits. An admission under this rule is not an admission for any other purpose and cannot be used against the party in any other proceeding.

Rule 37. Failure to Make Disclosures or to Cooperate in Discovery; Sanctions

(a) MOTION FOR AN ORDER COMPELLING DISCLOSURE OR DISCOVERY.

(1) *In General.* On notice to other parties and all affected persons, a party may move for an order compelling disclosure or discovery. The motion must include a certification that the movant has in good faith conferred or attempted to confer with the person or party failing to make disclosure or discovery I In an effort to obtain it without court action.

(2) *Appropriate Court.* A motion for an order to a party must life made in the court where the action is pending. A motion for an order to a nonparty must be made in the court where the discovery is or will be taken.

(3) *Specific Motions.*

(A) *To Compel Disclosure.* If a party fails to make a disclosure required by Rule 26(a), any other party may move to compel disclosure and for appropriate sanctions.

(B) *To Compel a Discovery Response.* A party seeking discovery may move for an order compelling an answer, designation, production, or inspection. This motion may be made if:

(i) a deponent fails to answer a question asked under Rule 30 or 31;

(ii) a corporation or other entity fails to make a designation under Rule 30(b)(6) or 31(a)(4);

(iii) a party fails to answer an interrogatory submitted under Rule 33; or

(iv) a party fails to respond that inspection will be permitted – or fails to permit inspection – as requested under Rule 34.

(C) *Related to a Deposition.* When taking an oral deposition, the party asking a question may complete or adjourn the examination before moving for an order.

(4) *Evasive or Incomplete Disclosure, Answer, or Response*. For purposes of this subdivision (a), an evasive or incomplete disclosure, answer, or response must be treated as a failure to disclose, answer, or respond.

(5) *Payment of Expenses; Protective Orders.*

    (A) *If the Motion Is Granted (Or Disclosure or Discovery Is Provided After Filing).* If the motion is granted – or if the disclosure or requested discovery is provided after the motion was filed – the court must, after giving an opportunity to be heard, require the party or deponent whose conduct necessitated the motion, the party or attorney advising that conduct, or both to pay the movant's reasonable expenses incurred in making the motion, including attorney's fees. But the court must not order this payment if:

        (i) the movant filed the motion before attempting in good faith to obi lain the disclosure or discovery without court action;

        (ii) the opposing party's nondisclosure, response or objection was substantially justified; or

        (iii) other circumstances make an award of expenses unjust.

    (B) *If the Motion Is Denied.* If the motion is denied, the court may issue any protective order authorized under Rule 26(c) and must, after giving an opportunity to be heard, require the movant, the attorney filing the motion, or both to pay the party or deponent who opposed the motion its reasonable expenses incurred in opposing the motion, including attorney's fees. But the court must not order this payment if the motion was substantially justified or other circumstances make an award of expenses unjust.

    (C) *If the Motion Is Granted In Part and Denied In Part.* If the motion is granted in part and denied in part, the court may issue any protective order authorized under Rule 26(c) and may, after giving an opportunity to be heard, apportion the reasonable expenses for the motion.

(b) FAILURE TO COMPLY WITH A COURT ORDER.

    (1) *Sanctions Sought in the District Where the Deposition is Taken*. If the court where the discovery is taken orders a deponent to be sworn or to answer a question and the deponent fails to obey, the failure may be treated as contempt of court. If a deposition-related motion is transferred to the court where the action is pending, and that court orders a deponent to be sworn or to answer a question and the deponent fails to obey, the failure may be treated as contempt of either the court where the discovery is taken or the court where the action is pending.

    (2) *Sanctions Sought in the District Where the Action is Pending.*

        (A) *For Not Obeying a Discovery Order.* If a party or a party's officer, director, or managing agent – or a witness designated under Rule 30(b)(6) or 31(a)(4) – fails to obey an order to provide or permit discovery, including an order under Rule 26(f), 35, or 37(a), the court where the action is pending ,ay issue further just orders. They may include the following:

            (i) directing that matters embraced in the order or other designated facts be taken as established for purposes of the action, as the prevailing party claims;

            (ii) prohibiting the disobedient party from supporting or opposing designated claims or defenses, or from introducing designated miters in evidence;

            (iii) striking pleadings in whole or in part;

            (iv) staying further proceedings until the order is obeyed;

            (v) dismissing the action or proceeding in whole or in part;

            (vi) rendering a default judgment against the disobedient party; or

            (vii) treating as contempt of court the failure to obey any order except an order to submit to a physical or mental examination.

(B) *For not producing a Person for Examination.* If a party fails to comply with an order under Rule 35(a) requiring it to produce another person for examination, the court may I Issue any of the orders listed in Rule 37(b)(2)(A)(i)-(vi), unless the disobedient party shows that it cannot produce the other person.

(C) *Payment of Expenses.* Instead of or in addition to the orders listed above, the court must order the disobedient party, the attorney advising that party, or both to pay the reasonable expenses, including attorney's fees, caused by the failure, unless the failure was substantially justified or other circumstances make an award of expenses unjust.

(c) FAILURE TO DISCLOSE, TO SUPPLEMENT AN EARLIER RESPONSE, OR TO ADMIT.

(1) *Failure to Disclose or Supplement.* If a party fails to provide information or identify a witness as required by Rule 26(a) or (e), the party is not allowed to use that information or witness to supply evidence on a motion, at a hearing, or at a trial, unless the failure was substantially justified or is harmless. In addition to or instead of this sanction, the court, on motion and after giving an opportunity to be heard:

(A) may order payment of the reasonable expenses, including attorney's fees, caused by the failure;

(B) may inform the jury of the party's failure; and

(C) may impose other appropriate sanctions, including any of the orders listed in Rule 37(b)(2)(A)(i)-(vi).

(2) *Failure to Admit.* If a party fails to admit what is requested under Rule 36 and if the requesting party later proves a document to be genuine or the matter true, the requesting party may move that the party who failed to admit pay the reasonable expenses, including attorney's fees, incurred in making that proof. The court must so order unless:

(A) the request was held objectionable under Rule 36(a);

(B) the admission sough t was of no substantial importance;

(C) the party failing to admit had a reasonable ground to believe that it might prevail on the matter; or

(D) there was other good reason for the failure to admit.

(d) PARTY'S FAILURE TO ATTEND ITS OWN DEPOSITION, SERVE ANSWERS TO INTERROGATORIES, OR RESPOND TO A REQUEST FOR INSPECTION.

(1) *In General.*

(A) *Motion; Grounds for Sanctions.* The court where the action is pending may, on motion, order sanctions if:

(i) a party or party's officer, director, or managing agent – or a person designated under Rule 30(b)(6) or 31(a)(4) – fail§, after being served with proper notice, to appear for that person's deposition; or

(ii) a party, after being properly served with interrogatories under Rule 33 or a request for inspection under Rule 34, fails to serve its answers, objections, or written response.

(B) *Certification.* A motion for sanctions for failing to answer or respond must include a certification that the movant has in good faith conferred or attempted to confer with the party failing to act in an effort to obtain the answer or response without court action.

(2) *Unacceptable Excuse for Failing to Act.* A failure described in Rule 37(d)(1)(A) is not excused on the ground that the discovery sought was objectionable, unless the party failing to act has a pending motion for a protective order under Rule 26(c).

(3) *Types of Sanctions.* Sanctions may include any of the orders listed in Rule 37(b)(2)(A)(i)-(vi). Instead of or in addition to these sanctions, the court must require the party failing to act, the attorney advising that party, or both to pay the reasonable expenses, including attorney's fees,

caused by the failure, unless the failure was substantially justified or other circumstances make an award of expenses unjust.

(e) FAILURE TO PROVIDE ELECTRONICALLY STORED INFORMATION. If electronically stored information that should have been preserved in the anticipation or conduct of litigation is lost because a party failed to take reasonable steps to preserve it, and it cannot be restored or replaced through additional discovery, the court:

(1) upon finding prejudice to another party from loss of the information, may order measures no greater than necessary to cure the prejudice; or

(2) only upon finding that the party acted with the intent to deprive another party of the information's use in the litigation may:

(A) presume that the lost information was unfavorable to the party;

(B) instruct the jury that it may or must presume the information was unfavorable to the party; or

(C) dismiss the action or enter a default judgment.

(f) FAILURE TO PARTICIPATE IN FRAMING A DISCOVERY PLAN. If a party or its attorney fails to participate in good faith in developing and submitting a proposed discovery plan as required by Rule 26(f), the court may, after giving an opportunity to be heard, require that party or attorney to pay to any other party the reasonable expenses, including attorney's fees, caused by the failure.

Rule 38. Right to a Jury Trial; Demand

(a) RIGHT PRESERVED. The right of trial by jury as declared by the Seventh Amendment to the Constitution – or as provided by a federal statute – is preserved to the parties inviolate.

(b) DEMAND. On any issue triable of right by a jury, a party may demand a jury trial by:

(1) serving the other parties with a written demand – which may be included in a pleading – no later than 14 days after the last pleading directed to the issue is served; and

(2) filing the demand in accordance with Rule 5(d).

(c) SPECIFYING ISSUES. In its demand, a party may specify the issues that it wishes to have tried by a jury; otherwise, it is considered to have demanded a jury trial on all the issues so triable. If the party has demanded a jury trial on only some issues, any other party may-within 14 days after being served with the demand or within a shorter time ordered by the court – serve a demand for a jury trial on any other or all factual issues triable by jury.

(d) WAIVER; WITHDRAWAL. A party waives a jury trial unless its demand is properly served and filed. A proper demand may be withdrawn only if the parties consent.

(e) ADMIRALTY AND MARITIME CLAIMS. These rules do not create a right to a jury trial on issues in a claim designated as an admiralty or maritime claim under Rule 9(h).

Rule 39. Trial by Jury or by the Court

(a) WHEN A DEMAND IS MADE. When a jury trial has been demanded under Rule 38, the action must be designated on the docket as a jury action. The trial on all issues so demanded must be by jury unless:

(1) the parties or their attorneys file a stipulation to a nonjury trial or so stipulate on the record; or

(2) the court, on motion or on its own, finds that on some or all of those issues there is no federal right to a jury trial.

(b) WHEN NO DEMAND IS MADE. Issues on which a jury trial is not properly demanded are to be tried by the court. But the court may, on motion, order a jury trial on any issue for which a jury might have been demanded.

(c) ADVISORY JURY; JURY TRIAL BY CONSENT. In an action not triable by a jury, the court, on motion or on its own:

(1) may try any Issue with an advisory jury; or

(2) may, with the parties' consent, try any issue by a jury whose verdict has the same effect as if a jury trial had been a matter of right, unless the action is against the United States and a federal statute provides for a nonjury trial.

Rule 40. Scheduling Cases for Trial

Each court may provide by rule for scheduling trials. The court must give priority to actions entitled to priority by a federal statute.

Rule 41. Dismissal of Actions

(a) VOLUNTARY DISMISSAL.

    (1) *By the Plaintiff.*

        (A) *Without a Court Order.* Subject to Rules 23(e), 23.1(c), 23.2, and 66 and any applicable federal statute, the plaintiff may dismiss as action without a court order by filing:

            (i) a notice of dismissal before the opposing party serves either an answer or a motion for summary judgment; or

            (ii) a stipulation of dismissal signed by all parties who have appeared.

        (B) *Effect.* Unless the notice or stipulation states otherwise, the dismissal is without prejudice. But if the plaintiff previously dismissed any federal – or state-court action based on or including the same claim, a notice of dismissal operates as an adjudication on the merits.

    (2) *By Court Order; Effect.* Except as provided in Rule 41(a)(1), an action may be dismissed at the plaintiff's request only by court order, on terms that the court considers proper. If a defendant has pleaded a counterclaim before being served with the plaintiff's motion to dismiss, the action may be dismissed over the defendant's objection only if the counterclaim can remain pending for independent adjudication. Unless the order states otherwise, a dismissal under this paragraph (2) is without prejudice.

(b) INVOLUNTARY DISMISSAL; EFFECT, if the plaintiff fails to prosecute or comply with these rules or a court order, a defendant may move to dismiss the action or any claim against it. Unless the dismissal order states otherwise, a dismissal under this subdivision (b) and any dismissal not under this rule – except one for lack of jurisdiction, improper venue, or failure to join a party under Rule 19 – operates as an adjudication on the merits.

(c) DISMISSING A COUNTERCLAIM, CROSSCLAIM, OR THIRD-PARTY CLAIM. This rule applies to a dismissal of any counterclaim, crossclaim, or third-party claim. A claimant's voluntary dismissal under Rule 4(l)(a)(l)(A)(i) must be made:

    (1) before a responsive pleading is served; or

    (2) if there is no responsive pleading, before evidence is introduced at a hearing or trial.

(d) COSTS OF A PREVIOUSLY DISMISSED ACTION. If a plaintiff who previously dismissed an action in any court files an action based on or including the same claim against the same defendant, the court:

    (1) may order the plaintiff to pay all or part of the costs of that previous action; and

    (2) may stay the proceedings until the plaintiff has complied.

Rule 42. Consolidation; Separate Trials

(a) CONSOLIDATION. If actions before the court involve a common question of law or fact, the court may:

    (1) join for hearing or trial any or all matters at issue in the actions;

    (2) consolidate the actions; or

    (3) issue any other orders to avoid unnecessary cost or delay.

(b) SEPARATE TRIALS. For convenience, to avoid prejudice, or to expedite and economize, the court may order a separate trial of one or more separate issues, claims, crossclaims, counterclaims, or third-party claims. When ordering a separate trial, the court must preserve any federal right to a jury trial.

Rule 43. Taking Testimony

(a) IN OPEN COURT. At trial, the witnesses' testimony must be taken in open court unless a federal statute, the Federal Rules of Evidence, these rules, or other rules adopted by the Supreme court provide otherwise. For good cause in compelling circumstances and with appropriate safeguards, the court may permit testimony in open court by contemporaneous transmission from a different location.

(b) AFFIRMATION INSTEAD OF AN OATH. When these rules require an oath, a solemn affirmation suffices.

(c) EVIDENCE ON A MOTION. When a motion relies on facts outside the record, the court may hear the matter on affidavits or may hear it wholly or partly on oral testimony or on deposition.

(d) INTERPRETER. The court may appoint an interpreter of its choosing; fix reasonable compensation to be paid from funds provided by law or by one or more parties; and tax the compensation as costs.

Rule 44. Proving an Official Record

(a) MEANS OF PROVING.

(1) *Domestic Record.* Each of the following evidences an official record – or an entry in it – that is otherwise admissible and is kept within the United States, any state, district, or commonwealth, or any territory subject to the administrative or judicial jurisdiction of the United States:

(A) an official publication of the record; or

(B) a copy attested by the officer with legal custody of the record – or by the officer's deputy – and accompanied by a certificate that the officer has custody. The certificate must be made under seal:

(i) by a judge of a court of record in the district or political subdivision where the record is kept; or

(ii) by any public officer with a seal of office and with official duties in the district or political subdivision where the record is kept.

(2) *Foreign Record.*

(A) *In General.* Each of the following evidences a foreign official record – or an entry in it – that is otherwise admissible:

(i) an official publication of the record; or

(ii) the record – or a copy – that is attested by an authorized person and is accompanied either by a final certification of genuineness or by a certification under a treaty or convention to which the United States and the country where the record id located are parties.

(B) *Final Certification of Genuineness.* A final certification must certify the genuineness of the signature and official position of the attester or of any foreign official whose certificate of genuineness relates to the attestation or is in a chain of certificates of genuineness relating to the attestation. A final certification may be made by a secretary of a United States embassy or legation; by a consul general, vice consul, or consular agent of the United States; or by a diplomatic or consular official of the foreign country assigned or accredited to the United States.

(C) *Other Means of Proof.* If all parties have had a reasonable opportunity to investigate a foreign record's authenticity and accuracy, the court may, for good cause, either:
- (i) admit an attested copy without final certification; or
- (ii) permit the record to be evidenced by an attested summary with or without a final certification.

(b) LACK OF A RECORD. A written statement that a diligent search of designated records revealed no record or entry of a specified tenor is admissible as evidence that the records contain no such record or entry. For domestic records, the statement must be authenticated under Rule 44(a)(1). For foreign records, the statement must comply with (a)(2)(C)(ii).

(c) OTHER PROOF. A party may prove an official record – or an entry or lack c£ an entry an it – by any other method authorized by law.

Rule 44.1. Determining Foreign law

A party who intends to raise an issue about a foreign country's law must give notice by a pleading or in other writing. In determining foreign law, the court may consider any relevant material or course, including testimony, whether or not submitted by a party or admissible under the Federal Rules of Evidence. The court's determination must be treated as a ruling on a question of law.

Rule 45. Subpoena

(a) IN GENERAL.
- (1) *Forms and Contents.*
  - (A) *Requirements – In General.* Every subpoena must:
    - (i) state the court from which it issued;
    - (ii) state the title of the action and its civil-action number;
    - (iii) command each person to whom it is directed to do the following at a specified time and place: attend and testify; produce designated documents, electronically stored information, or tangible things in that person's possession, custody, or control; or permit the inspection of premises; and
    - (iv) set out the text of Rule 45(d) and (e).
  - (B) *Command to Attend a Deposition – Notice of the Recording Method.* A subpoena commanding attendance at a deposition must state the method for recording the testimony.
  - (C) *Combining or Separating a Command to Produce or Permit Inspection; Specifying the Form for Electronically Stored Information.* A command to produce documents, electronically stored information, or tangible things Or to permit the inspection of premises may be included in a subpoena commanding attendance at a deposition, hearing or trial, or may be set out in a separate subpoena. A subpoena may specify the form or forms in which electronically stored information is to be produced.
  - (D) *Command to Produce; Included Obligations.* A command in a subpoena to produce documents, electronically stored information, or tangible things requires the responding party to permit inspection, copying, testing, or sampling of the materials.
- (2) *Issuing Court.* A subpoena must issue from the court where the action is pending.
- (3) *Issued By Whom.* The clerk must issue a subpoena, signed but otherwise in blank, to a party who requests it. That party must complete it before service. An attorney also may issue and sign a subpoena if the attorney is authorized to practice in the issuing court.
- (4) *Notice to Other Parties before Service.* If the subpoena commands the production of documents, electronically stored information, or tangible things or the inspection of premises before trial, then before it is served on the person to whom it is directed, a notice and a copy of the subpoena must be served on each party.

(b) SERVICE.

(1) *By Whom and How; Tendering Fees.* Any person who is at least 18 years old and not a party may serve a subpoena. Serving a subpoena requires delivering a copy to the named person and, if the subpoena requires that person's attendance, tendering the fees for 1 day's attendance and mileage allowed by law. Fees and mileage need not be tendered when the subpoena issues on behalf of the United States or any of its officers or agencies.

(2) *Service in the United States.* A subpoena may be served at any place in the United States.

(3) *Service in a Foreign Country.* 28 U.S.C. § 1783 governs issuing and serving a subpoena directed to a United States national or resident who is in a foreign country.

(4) *Proof of Service.* Proving service, when necessary, requires filing with the issuing court a statement showing the date and manner of service and the names of the persons served. The statement must be certified by the server.

(c) PLACE OF COMPLIANCE.

(1) *For a Trial, Hearing, or Deposition.* A subpoena may command a person to attend a trial, hearing, or deposition only as follows:

(A) within 100 miles of where the person resides, is employed, or regularly transacts business in person; or

(B) within the state where the person resides, is employed, or regularly transacts business in person if the person

(i) is a party or a party's officer; or

(ii) is commanded to attend a trial and would not incur substantial expense.

(2) *For Other Discovery.* A subpoena may command:

(A) production of documents, electronically stored information, or tangible things at a place within 100 miles of where the person resides, is employed, or regularly transacts business in person; and

(B) inspection of premises at the premises to be inspected.

(d) PROTECTING A PERSON SUBJECT TO A SUBPOENA; ENFORCEMENT.

(1) *Avoiding Undue Burden or Expense; Sanctions.* A party or attorney responsible for issuing and serving a subpoena must take reasonable steps to avoid imposing undue burden or expense on a person subject to the subpoena. The court for the district where compliance is required must enforce this duty and impose an appropriate sanction – which may include lost earnings and reasonable attorney's fees on a party or attorney who fails to comply.

(2) *Command to Produce Materials or Permit Inspection.*

(A) *Appearance Not Required.* A person commanded to produce documents, electronically stored information, or tangible things, or to permit the inspection of premises, need not appear in person at the place of production or inspection unless also commanded to appear for a deposition, hearing, or trial.

(B) *Objections.* A person commanded to produce documents or tangible things or to permit inspection may serve on the party or attorney designated in the subpoena a written objection to inspecting, copying, testing, or sampling any or all of the materials or to inspecting the premises – or to producing electronically stored information in the form or forms requested. The objection must be served before the earlier of the time specified for compliance or 14 days after the subpoena is served. If an objection is made, the following rules apply:

(i) At any time, on notice to the commanded person, the serving party may move the court for the district where compliance is required for an order compelling production or inspection.

(ii) These acts may be required only as directed in the order, and the order must protect a person who is neither a party nor a party's officer from significant expense resulting from compliance.

(3) *Quashing or Modifying a Subpoena.*

    (A) *When Required.* On timely motion, the court for the district where compliance is required must quash or modify a subpoena that:

        (i) fails to allow a reasonable time to comply;

        (ii) requires a person to comply beyond the geographical limits specified in Rule 45(c);

        (iii) requires disclosure of privileged or other protected matter, if no exception or waiver applies; or

        (iv) subjects a person to undue burden.

    (B) *When permitted.* To protect a person subject to or affected by a subpoena, the court for the district where compliance is required may, on motion, quash or modify the subpoena if it requires:

        (i) disclosing a trade secret or other confidential research, development, or commercial information; or

        (ii) disclosing an unrestrained expert's opinion or information that does not describe specific occurrences in dispute and results from the expert's study that was not requested by a party.

    (C) *Specifying Conditions as an Alternative.* In the circumstances described in Rule 45(d)(3)(B), the court may, instead of quashing or modifying a subpoena, order appearance or production under specified conditions if the serving party:

        (i) shows a substantial need for the testimony or material that cannot be otherwise met without undue hardship; and

        (ii) ensures that the subpoenaed person will be reasonably compensated.

(e) DUTIES IN RESPONDING TO A SUBPOENA.

    (1) *Producing Documents or Electronically Stored Information.* These procedures apply to producing documents or electronically stored information.

        (A) *Documents.* A person responding to a subpoena to produce documents must produce them as they are kept in the ordinary course of business or must organize and label them to correspond to the categories in demand.

        (B) *Form for Producing Electronically Stored Information Not Specified.* If a subpoena does not specify a form for producing electronically stored information, the person responding must produce it in a form or forms in which it is ordinarily maintained or in a reasonably usable form or forms.

        (C) *Electronically Stored Information Produced in Only One Form.* The person responding need not produce the same electronically stored information in more than one form.

        (D) *Inaccessible Electronically Stored Information.* The person responding need not provide discovery of electronically stored information from sources that the person identifies as not reasonably accessible because of undue burden or cost. On motion to compel discovery or for a protective order, the person responding must show that the information is not reasonably accessible because of undue burden or cost. If that showing is made, the court may nonetheless order discovery from such sources if the requesting party shows good cause, considering the limitations of Rule 26(b)(2)(C). The court may specify conditions for the discovery.

    (2) *Claiming Privilege or Protection.*

        (A) Information Withheld. A person withholding subpoenaed information under a claim that it is privileged or subject to protection as trial-preparation material must:

      (i) expressly make the claim; and

      (ii) describe the nature of the withheld documents, communications, or tangible things in a manner that, without revealing information itself privileged or protected, will enable the parties to assess the claim.

    (B) *Information Produced.* If information produced in response to a subpoena is subject to a claim of privilege or of protection as trial – preparation material, the person making the claim may notify any party that received the information of the claim and the basis for it. After being notified, a party must promptly return, sequester, or destroy the specified information and any copies it has; must not use or disclose the information until the claim is resolved; must take reasonable steps to retrieve the information if the party disclosed it before being notified; and may promptly present the information under seal to the court for the district where compliance is required for a determination of the claim. The person who produced the information must preserve the information until the claim is resolved.

(f) TRANSFERRING A SUBPOENA-RELATED MOTION. When the court where compliance is required did not issue the subpoena, it may transfer a motion under this rule to the issuing court if the person subject to the subpoena consents or if the court finds exceptional circumstances. Then, if the attorney for a person subject to a subpoena is authorized to practice in the court where the motion was made, the attorney may file papers and appear on the motion as an officer of the issuing court. To enforce its order, the issuing court may transfer the order to the court where the motion was made.

(g) CONTEMPT. The court for the district where compliance is required and also, after a motion is transferred, the issuing court-may hold in contempt a person who, having been served, fails without adequate excuse to obey the subpoena or an order related to it.

Rule 46. Objecting to a Ruling or Order

A formal exception to a ruling or order is unnecessary. When the ruling or order is requested or made, a party need only state the action that it wants the court to take or objects to, along with the grounds for the request or objection. Failing to object does not prejudice a party who had no opportunity to do so when the ruling or order was made.

Rule 47. Selecting Jurors

(a) EXAMINING JURORS. The court may permit the parties or their attorneys to examine prospective jurors or may I Itself do so. If the court examines the jurors, it must permit the parties or their attorneys to make any further inquiry lit considers proper or must itself ask any of their-additional questions it considers proper.

(b) PEREMPTORY CHALLENGES. The court must allow the number of peremptory challenges provided by 28 U.S.C. § 1870.

(c) Excusing a Juror. During trial or deliberation, the court may excuse a juror for good cause.

Rule 48 Number of Jurors; Verdict; Polling

(a) NUMBER OF JURORS. A jury must begin with at least 6 and no more than 12 members, and each juror must participate in the verdict unless excused under Rule 47(c).

(b) VERDICT. Unless the parties stipulate otherwise, the verdict must be unanimous and must be returned by a jury of at least 6 members.

(c) POLLING. After a verdict is returned but before the jury is discharged, the court must on a party's request, or may on its own, poll the jurors individually. If the poll reveals a lack of unanimity or lack of assent by the number of jurors that the parties stipulated to, the court may direct the jury to deliberate further or may order a new trial.

Rule 49. Special Verdict; General Verdict and Questions

(a) SPECIAL VERDICT.

    (1) *In General.* The court may require a jury to return only a special verdict in the form of a written finding on each issue of fact. The court may do so by:

        (A) submitting written questions susceptible of a categorical or other brief answer;

        (B) submitting written forms of the special findings that might properly be made under the pleadings and evidence; or

        (C) using any other method that the courts considers appropriate.

    (2) *Instructions.* The court must give the instructions and explanations necessary to enable the jury to make its findings on each submitted issue.

    (3) *Issues Not Submitted.* A party waives the right to a jury trial on any Issue of fact raised by the pleadings or evidence but not submitted to the jury unless, before the jury retires, the party demands its submission to the jury. If the party does not demand submission, the court may make a finding on the issue. If the court makes no finding, it is considered to have made a finding consistent with its judgment on the special verdict.

(b) GENERAL VERDICT WITH ANSWERS TO WRITTEN QUESTIONS.

    (1) *In General.* The court may submit to the jury forms for a general verdict, together with written questions on one or more issues of fact that the jury must decide, the court must give the instructions and explanations necessary to enable the jury to render a general verdict and answer the questions in writing, and must direct the jury to do both.

    (2) *Verdict and Answers Consistent.* When the general verdict and the answers are consistent, the court must approve, for entry under Rule 58, an appropriate judgment on the verdict and answers.

    (3) *Answers Inconsistent with the Verdict.* When the answers are consistent with each other but one or more is inconsistent with the general verdict, the court may:

        (A) approve, for entry under Rile 58, an appropriate judgment according to the answers, notwithstanding the general verdict;

        (B) direct the jury to further consider its answers and verdict; or

        (C) order a new trial.

    (4) *Answers Inconsistent with Each Other and the Verdict.* When the answers are inconsistent with each other and one or more is also inconsistent with the general verdict, judgment must not be entered; instead, the court must direct the jury to further consider its answers and verdict or must order a new trial.

Rule 50. Judgment as a Matter of Law in a Jury Trial; Related Motion for a New Trial; Conditional Ruling

(a) JUDGMENT AS A MATTER OF LAW.

    (1) *In General.* If a party has been fully heard on an issue during a jury trial and the court finds that a reasonable jury would not have a legally sufficient evidentiary basis to find for the party on that issue, the court may:

        (A) resolve the issue against the party; and

        (B) grant a motion for judgment as a matter of law against the party on a claim or defense that, under the controlling law, can be maintained or defeated only with a favorable finding on that issue.

        (C) *Motion.* A motion for judgment as a matter of law may be made at any time before the case is submitted to the jury. The motion must specify the judgment sought and the law and facts that entitle the movant to the judgment.

(b) RENEWING THE MOTION AFTER TRIAL; ALTERNATIVE MOTION FOR A NEW TRIAL. If the court does not grant a motion for judgment as a matter of law made under Rule 50(a), the court is considered to have submitted the action to the jury subject to the court's later deciding the legal questions raised by the motion. No later than 28 days after the entry of judgment – or if the motion addresses a jury issue not decided by a verdict, no later than 28 days after the jury was discharged – the movant may file a renewed motion for judgment as a matter of law and may I Include an alternative or joint request for a new trial under Rule 59. In ruling on the renewed motion, the court may:

(1) allow judgment on the verdict, if the jury returned a verdict;

(2) order a new trial; or

(3) direct the entry of judgment as a matter of law.

(c) GRANTING THE RENEWED MOTION; CONDITIONAL RULING ON A MOTION FOR A NEW TRIAL.

(1) *In General.* If the court grants a renewed motion for judgment as a matter of law, it must also conditionally rule on any motion for a new trial by determining whether a new trial should be granted if the judgment is later vacated or reversed. The court must state the grounds for conditionally granting or denying the motion for a new trial.

(2) *Effect of a Conditional Ruling.* Conditionally granting the motion for a new trial does not affect the judgment's finality; if the judgment is reversed the new trial must proceed unless the appellate court orders otherwise. If the motion for a new trial is conditionally denied, the appellee may assert error in that denial; if the judgment is reversed, the case must proceed as the appellate court orders.

(d) TIME FOR A LOSING PARTY'S NEW-TRIAL MOTION. Any motion for a new trial under Rule 59 by a party against whom judgment as a matter of law is rendered must be filed no later than 28 days after the entry of the judgment.

(e) DENYING THE MOTION FOR JUDGMENT AS A MATTER OF LAW; REVERSAL ON APPEAL. If the court denies the motion for judgment as a matter of law, the prevailing party may, as appellee, assert grounds entitling it to a new trial should the appellate court conclude that the trial court erred in denying the motion. If the appellate court reverses the judgment, it may order a new trial, direct the trial court to determine whether a new trial should be granted, or direct the entry of judgment.

Rule 51. Instructions to the Jury; Objections; Preserving a Claim of Error

(a) REQUESTS.

(1) *Before the Close of the Evidence.* At the close of the evidence or at any earlier reasonable time that the court orders, a party may file and furnish to every other party written requests for the jury instructions it wants the court to give.

(2) *After the Close of Evidence.* After the close of evidence, a party may:

(A) file requests for instructions on issues that could not reasonably have been anticipated by an earlier time that the court set for requests; and

(B) with the court's permission, file untimely requests for instructions on any issue.

(b) INSTRUCTIONS. The court:

(1) must inform the parties of its proposed instructions and proposed action on the requests before instructing the jury and before final jury arguments;

(2) must give the parties an opportunity to object on the record and out of the jury's hearing before the instructions and arguments are delivered; and

(3) may instruct the jury at any time before the jury is discharged.

(c) OBJECTIONS.

(1) *How to Make.* A party who objects to an instruction or the failure to give an instruction must do so on the record, stating distinctly the matter objected to and the grounds for the objection.

(2) *When to Make.* An objection is timely if:

(A) a party objects at the opportunity provided under Rule 51(b)(2); or

(B) a party was not informed of an instruction or action on a request before that opportunity to object, and the party objects promptly after learning that the instruction or request will be, or has been, given or refused.

(d) ASSIGNING ERROR; PLAIN ERROR.

(1) *Assigning Error.* A party may assign as error:

(A) an error in an instruction actually given, if that party properly objected; or

(B) a failure to give an instruction, if that party properly requested it and – unless the court rejected the request in a definitive ruling on the record – also properly objected.

(2) *Plain Error.* A court may consider a plain error in the instructions that has not been preserved as required by Rule 51(d)(1) if the error affects substantial rights.

Rule 52. Findings and Conclusions by the Court; Judgment on Partial Findings

(a) FINDINGS AND CONCLUSIONS.

(1) *In General.* In an action tried on the facts without a jury or an advisory jury, the court must find the facts specially and state its conclusions of law separately. The findings and conclusions may be stated on the record after the close of the evidence or may appear in an opinion or memorandum of decision filed by the court. Judgment must be entered under Rule 58.

(2) *For an Interlocutory Injunction.* In granting or refusing an interlocutory injunction, the court must similarly state the findings and conclusions that support its action.

(3) *For a Motion.* The court is not required to state findings or conclusions when ruling on a motion under Rule 12 or 56 or, unless these rules provide otherwise, on any other motion.

(4) *Effect of a Master's Findings.* A master's findings, to the extent adopted by the court, must be considered the court's findings.

(5) *Questioning the Evidentiary Support.* A party may later question the sufficiency of the evidence supporting the findings, whether or not the party requested findings, objected to them, moved to amend them, or moved for partial findings.

(6) *Setting Aside the Findings.* Findings of fact, whether based on oral or other evidence, must not be set aside unless clearly erroneous, and the reviewing court must give due regard to the trial court's opportunity to judge the witnesses' credibility.

(b) AMENDED OR ADDITIONAL FINDINGS. On a party's motion filed no later than 28 days after the entry of judgment, the court may amend its findings – or make additional findings – and may amend the judgment accordingly. The motion may accompany a motion for a new trial under Rule 59.

(c) JUDGMENT ON PARTIAL FINDINGS. If a party has been fully heard on an issue during a nonjury trial and the court finds against the party on that issue, the court may enter judgment against the party on a claim or defense that, under the controlling law, can be maintained or defeated only with a favorable ruling on that issue. The court may, however, decline to render any judgment until the close of evidence. A judgment on partial findings must be supported by findings of fact and conclusions of law as required by Rule 52(a).

Rule 53. Masters

(a) APPOINTMENT.

(1) *Scope.* Unless a statute provides otherwise, a court may appoint a master only to:

    (A) perform duties consented to by the parties;

    (B) hold trial proceedings and make or recommend findings of fact on issues to be decided without a jury if appointment is warranted by:

        (i) some exceptional condition; or

        (ii) the need to perform an accounting or resolve a difficult computation of damages; or

    (C) address pretrial and post-trial matters that cannot be effectively and timely addressed by an available district judge or magistrate judge of the district.

  (2) *Disqualification.* A master must not have a relationship to the parties, attorneys, action, or court that would require disqualification of a judge under 28 U.S.C. § 455, unless the parties, with the court's approval, consent to the appointment after the master discloses any potential grounds for disqualification.

  (3) *Possible Expense or Delay.* In appointing a master, the court must consider the fairness of imposing the likely expenses on the parties and must protect against unreasonable expense or delay.

(b) ORDER APPOINTING A MASTER.

  (1) *Notice.* Before appointing a master, the court must give the parties notice and an opportunity to be heard. Any party may suggest candidates for appointment.

  (2) *Contents.* The appointing order must direct the master to proceed with all reasonable diligence and must state:

    (A) the master's duties, including any investigation or enforcement duties, and any limits on the master's authority under Rule 53(c);

    (B) the circumstances, if any, in which the master may communicate ex parte with the court or a party;

    (C) the nature of the materials to be preserved and filed as the record of the master's activities;

    (D) the time limits, method of filing the record, other procedures, and standards for reviewing the master's orders, findings, and recommendations; and

    (E) the basis, terms, and procedure for fixing the master's compensation under Rule 53(g).

  (3) *Issuing.* The court may issue the order only after:

    (A) the master files an affidavit disclosing whether there is any grounds for disqualification under 28 U.S.C. § 455; and

    (B) if a ground is disclosed, the parties, with the court's approval, waive the disqualification.

  (4) *Amending.* The order may be amended at any time after notice to the parties and an opportunity to be heard.

(c) MASTER'S AUTHORITY.

  (1) *In General.* Unless the appointing order directs otherwise, a master may:

    (A) regulate all proceedings;

    (B) take all appropriate measured to perform the assigned duties fairly and efficiently; and

    (C) if conducting an evidentiary hearing, exercise the appointing court's power to compel, take, and record evidence.

  (2) *Sanctions.* The master may by order impose on a party any noncontempt sanction provided by Rule 37 or 45 and may recommend a contempt sanction against a party and sanctions against a nonparty.

(d) MASTER'S ORDERS. A master who issues an order must file it and promptly serve a copy on each party; the clerk must enter the order on the docket.

(e) MASTER'S REPORTS. A master must report to the court as required by the appointing order. The master must file the report and promptly serve a copy on each party, unless the court orders otherwise.

(f) ACTION ON THE MASTER'S ORDER, REPORT, OR RECOMMENDATIONS.

(1) *Opportunity for a Hearing; Action in General.* In acting on a master's order, report, or recommendations, the court must give the parties notice and an opportunity to be heard; may receive evidence; and may adopt or affirm, modify, wholly or partly reject or reverse, or resubmit to the master with instructions.

(2) *Time to Object or Move to Adopt or Modify.* A party may file objections to – or a motion to adopt or modify – the master's order, report, or recommendations no later than 21 days after a copy is served, unless the court sets a different time.

(3) *Reviewing Factual Findings.* The court must decide de novo all objections to findings of fact made or recommended by a master, unless the parties, with the court's approval, stipulate that:

(A) the findings will be reviewed for clear error; or

(B) the findings of a master appointed under Rule 53(a)(1)(A) or (C) will be final.

(4) *Reviewing Legal Conclusions.* The court must decide the novo all objections to conclusions of law made or recommended by a master.

(5) *Reviewing Procedural Matters.* Unless the appointing order establishes a different standard of review, the court may set aside a master's ruling on a procedural matter only for an abuse of discretion.

(g) COMPENSATION.

(1) *Fixing Compensation.* Before or after judgment, the court must fix the master's compensation on the basis and terms stated in the appointing order, but the court may set a new basis and terms after giving notice and an opportunity to be heard.

(2) *Payment.* The compensation must be paid either:

(A) by a party or parties; or

(B) from a fund or subject matter of the action within the court's control.

(3) *Allocating Payment.* The court must allocate payment among the parties after considering the nature and amount of the controversy, the parties' means, and the extent to which any party is more responsible than other parties for the reference to a master. An interim allocation may be amended to reflect a decision on the merits.

(h) APPOINTING A MAGISTRATE JUDGE. A magistrate judge is subject to this rule only when the order referring a matter to the magistrate judge states that the reference is made under this rule.

Rule 54. Judgments; Costs

(a) DEFINITION; Form. "Judgment" as used in these rules includes a decree and any order from which an appeal lies. A judgment must not include recitals of pleadings, a master's report, or a record of prior proceedings.

(b) JUDGMENT ON MULTIPLE CLAIMS OR INVOLVING MULTIPLE PARTIES. When an action presents more than one claim for relief – whether as a claim, counterclaim, crossclaim, or third-party claim – or when multiple parties are involved, the court may direct entry of a final judgment as to one or more, but fewer than all, claims or parties only if the court expressly determines that there is no just reason for delay. Otherwise, any order or other decision, however designated, that adjudicates fewer than all the claims or the rights and liabilities of fewer than all the parties does not end the action as to any of the claims or parties and may be revised at any time before the entry of a judgment adjudicating all the claims and all the parties' rights and liabilities.

(c) DEMAND FOR JUDGMENT; RELIEF TO BE GRANTED. A default judgment must not differ in kind from, or exceed in amount, what is demanded in the pleadings. Every other final judgment should grant the relief to which each party is entitled, even if the party has not demanded that relief in its pleadings.

(d) COSTS; ATTORNEY'S FEES.

(1) *Costs Other Than Attorney's Fees.* Unless a federal statute, these rules, or a court order provides otherwise, costs – other than attorney's fees – should be allowed to the prevailing party. But costs against the United States, its officers, and its agencies may be imposed only to the extent allowed by law, the clerk may tax costs on 14 days' notice. On motion served within the next 7 days, the court may review the clerk's action.

(2) *Attorney's Fees.*

    (A) *Claim to Be by Motion.* A claim for attorney's fees and related nontax – able expenses must be made by motion unless the substantive law requires those fees be proved at trial as an element of damages.

    (B) *Timing and Contents of the Motion.* Unless a statute or a court order provides otherwise, the motion must:

        (i) be filed no later than 14 days after the entry of judgment;

        (ii) specify the judgment and the statute, rule, or other grounds entitling the movant to the award;

        (iii) state the amount sought or provide a fair estimate of it; and

        (iv) disclose, if the court so orders, the terms of any agreement about fees for the services for which claim is made.

    (C) *Proceedings.* Subject to Rule 23(h), the court must, on a party's request, give an opportunity for adversary submissions on the motion in accordance with Rule 43(c) or 78. The court may decide issues of liability for fees before receiving submissions on the value of services. The court must find the facts and state its conclusions of law as provided in Rule 52(a).

    (D) *Special Procedures by Local Rule; Reference to a Master or Magistrate Judge.* By local rule, the court may establish special procedures to resolve fee-related issues without extensive evidentiary hearings. Also, the court may refer issues concerning the value of services to a special master under Rule 53(a)(1) and may refer a motion for attorney's fees to a magistrate judge under Rule 72(b) as if it were a dispositive pretrial matter.

    (E) *Exceptions.* Subparagraphs (A)-(D) do not apply to claims for fees and expenses as sanctions for violating these rules or as sanctions under 28 U.S.C. § 1927.

Rule 55. Default; Default Judgment

(a) ENTERING A DEFAULT. When a party against whom a judgment for affirmative relief is sought has failed to plead or otherwise defend, and that failure is shown by affidavit or otherwise, the clerk must enter the party's default.

(b) ENTERING A DEFAULT JUDGMENT.

    (1) *By the Clerk.* If the plaintiff's claim is for a sum certain or a sum that can be made certain by computation, the clerk – on the plaintiff's request, with an affidavit showing the amount due – must enter judgment for that amount and costs against a defendant who has been defaulted for not appearing and who is neither a minor nor an incompetent person.

    (2) *By the Court.* In all other cases, the party must apply to the court for a default judgment. A default judgment may be entered against a minor or incompetent person only if represented by a general guardian, conservator, or other like fiduciary who has appeared. If the party against whom a default judgment is sought has appeared personally or by a representative, that party or its representative must be served with written notice of the application at least 7 days before the hearing. The court may conduct hearings or make referrals – preserving any federal statutory right to a jury trial – when, to enter or effectuate judgment, it needs to:

    (A) conduct an accounting;

(B) determine the amount of damages;

(C) establish the truth of any allegation by evidence; or

(D) investigate any other matter.

(c) SETTING ASIDE A DEFAULT OR DEFAULT JUDGMENT. The court may set aside an entry of default for good cause, and it may set aside a default judgment under Rule 60(b).

(d) JUDGMENT AGAINST THE UNITED STATES. A default judgment may be entered against the United States, its officers, or its agencies only if the claimant establishes a claim or right to relief by evidence that satisfies the court.

Rule 56. Summary Judgment

(a) MOTION FOR SUMMARY JUDGMENT OR PARTIAL SUMMARY JUDGMENT. A party may move for summary judgment, identifying each claim or defense – or the part of each claim or defense – on which summary judgment is sought. The court shall grant summary judgment if the movant shows that there is no genuine dispute as to any material fact and the movant is entitled to judgment as a matter of law. The court should state on the record the reasons for granting or denying the motion.

(b) TIME TO FILE A MOTION. Unless a different time is set by local rule or the court orders otherwise, a party may file a motion for summary judgment at any time until 30 days after the close of all discovery.

(c) PROCEDURES.

(1) *Supporting Factual Positions.* A party asserting that a fact cannot be or is genuinely disputed must support the assertion by:

(A) citing to particular parts of materials in the record, including depositions, documents, electronically stored information, affidavits or declarations, stipulations (including those made for purposes of the motion only), admissions, interrogatory answers, or other materials; or

(B) showing that the materials cited do not establish the absence or presence of a genuine dispute, or that an adverse party cannot produce admissible evidence to support the fact.

(2) *Objection That a Fact Is Not Supported by Admissible Evidence.* A party may object that the material cited to support or dispute a fact cannot be presented in a form that would be admissible in evidence.

(3) *Materials not Cited.* The court need consider only the cited materials, but it may consider other materials in the record.

(4) *Affidavits or Declarations.* An affidavit or declaration used to support or oppose a motion must be made on personal knowledge, set out facts that would be admissible in evidence, and show that the affiant or declarant is competent to testify on the matters stated.

(d) WHEN FACTS ARE UNAVAILABLE TO THE NONMOVANT. If a nonmovant shows by affidavit or declaration that, for specified reasons, it cannot present facts essential to justify its opposition, the court may:

(1) defer considering the motion or deny it;

(2) allow time to obtain affidavits or declarations or to take discovery; or

(3) issue any other appropriate order.

(e) FAILING TO PROPERLY SUPPORT OR ADDRESS A FACT. If a party fails to properly support an assertion of fact or fails to properly address another party 's assertion of fact as required by Rule 56(c), the court may:

(1) give an opportunity to properly support or address the fact;

(2) consider the fact undisputed for purposes of the motion;

(3) grant summary judgment if the motion and supporting materials – including the facts considered undisputed – show that the movant is entitled to it; or

(4) issue any other appropriate order.

(f) JUDGMENT INDEPENDENT OF THE MOTION. After giving notice and a reasonable time to respond, the court may:

(1) grant summary judgment for a nonmovant;

(2) grant the motion on grounds not raised by a party; or

(3) consider summary judgment on its own after identifying for the parties material facts that may not be genuinely in dispute.

(g) FAILING TO GRANT ALL THE REQUESTED RELIEF. If the court does not grant all the relief requested by the motion, it may enter an order stating any material fact – including an item of damages or other relief – that is not genuinely in dispute and treating the fact as established in the case.

(h) AFFIDAVIT OR DECLARATION SUBMITTED IN BAD FAITH. If satisfied that an affidavit or declaration under this rule is submitted in bad faith or solely for delay, the court – after notice and a reasonable time to respond – may order the submitting party to pay the other party the reasonable expenses, including attorney's fees, it incurred as a result. An offending party or attorney may also be held in contempt or subjected to other sanctions.

Rule 57. Declaratory Judgment

These rules govern the procedure for obtaining a declaratory judgment under 28 U.S.C. § 2201. Rules 38 and 39 govern a demand for a jury trial. The existence of another adequate remedy does not preclude a declaratory judgment that is otherwise appropriate. The court may order a speedy hearing of a declaratory – judgment action.

Rule 58. Entering Judgment

(a) SEPARATE DOCUMENT. Every judgment and amended judgment must be set out in a separate document, but a separate document is not required for an order disposing of a motion:

(1) for judgment under Rule 50(b);

(2) to amend or make additional findings of fact under Rule 52(b);

(3) for attorney's fees under Rule 54;

(4) for a new trial, or to alter or amend the judgment, under Rule 59; or

(5) for relief under Rule 60.

(b) ENTERING JUDGMENT.

(1) *Without the Court's Direction*. Subject to Rule 54(b) and unless the court orders otherwise, the clerk must, without awaiting the court's direction, promptly prepare, sign, and enter the judgment when:

(A) the jury returns a general verdict;

(B) the court awards only costs or a sum certain; or

(C) the court denies all relief.

(2) *Court's Approval Required*. Subject to Rule 54(b), the court must promptly approve the form of judgment, which the clerk must promptly enter, when:

(A) the jury returns a special verdict or a general verdict with answers to written questions; or

(B) the court grants other relief not described in this subdivision (b).

(c) TIME OF ENTRY. For purposes of these rules, judgment is entered at the following times:

(1) if a separate document is not required, when the judgment is entered on the civil docket under Rule 79(a); or

(2) if a separate document is required, when the judgment is entered in the civil docket under Rule 79(a) and the earlier of these events occurs:

(A) it is set out in a separate document; or

(B) 150 days have run from the entry in the civil docket.

(d) REQUEST FOR ENTRY. A party may request that judgment be set out in a separate document as required by Rule 58(a).

(e) COST OR FEE AWARDS. Ordinarily, the entry of judgment may not be delayed, nor the time for appeal extended, in order to tax costs or award fees. But if a timely motion for attorney's fees is made under Rule 54(d)(2), the court may act before a notice of appeal has been filed and become effective to order that the motion have the same effect under Federal Rule of Appellate Procedure 4(a)(4) as a timely motion under Rule

Rule 59. New Trial; Altering or Amending a Judgment

(a) IN GENERAL.

(1) *Grounds for New Trial.* The court may, on motion, grant a new trial on all or some of the issues – and to any party – as follows:

(A) after a jury trial, for any reason for which a new trial has heretofore been granted in an action at law in federal court; or

(B) after a nonjury trial, for any reason for which a rehearing has heretofore been granted in a suit in equity in federal court.

(2) *Further Action after a Nonjury Trial.* After a nonjury trial, the court may, on motion for a new trial, open the judgment if one has been entered, take additional testimony, amend findings of fact and conclusions of law or make new ones, and direct the entry of a new judgment.

(b) *Time to File a Motion for a New Trial.* A motion for a new trial must be filed no later than 28 days after the entry of the judgment.

(c) *Time to Serve Affidavits.* When a motion for a new trial is based on affidavits, they must be filed with the motion. The opposing party has 14 days after being served to file opposing affidavits. The court may permit reply affidavits.

(d) *New Trial on the Court's Initiative or for Reasons Not in the Motion.* No later than 28 days after the entry of the judgment, the court, on its own, may order a new trial for any reason that would justify granting one on a party's motion. After giving the parties notice and an opportunity to be heard, the court may grant a timely motion for a new trial for a reason not stated in the motion. In either event, the court must specify the reasons in the order.

(e) *Motion to Alter or Amend a Judgment.* A motion to alter or amend a judgment must be filed no later than 28 days after the entry of the judgment.

Rule 60. Relief from a Judgment or Order

(a) CORRECTIONS BASED ON CLERICAL MISTAKES; OVERSIGHTS AND OMISSIONS. The court may correct a clerical mistake or a mistake arising from an oversight or omission whenever one is found in a judgment, order, or other part of the record. The court may do so on motion or on its own, with or without notice. But after an appeal has been docketed in the appellate court and while it is still pending, such a mistake may be corrected only with the appellate court's leave.

(b) GROUNDS FOR RELIEF FROM A FINAL JUDGMENT, ORDER, OR PROCEEDING. On motion and just terms, the court may relieve a party or its legal representative from a final judgment, order, or proceeding for the following reasons:

(1) mistake, inadvertence, surprise, or excusable neglect;

(2) newly discovered evidence that, with reasonable diligence, could not have been discovered in time to move for a new trial under Rule 59(b);

(3) fraud (whether previously called intrinsic or extrinsic), misrepresentation, or misconduct by an opposing party;

(4) the judgment is void;

(5) the judgment has been satisfied, released, or discharged; it is based on an earlier judgment that has been reversed or vacated; or applying it prospectively is no longer equitable; or

(6) any other reason that justifies relief.

(c) TIMING AND EFFECT OF THE MOTION.

(1) *Timing.* A motion under Rule 60(b) must be made within a reasonable time – and for reasons (1), (2), and (3) no more than a year after the entry of the judgment or order or the date of the proceeding.

(2) *Effect on Finality.* The motion does not affect the judgment's finality or suspend its operation.

(d) OTHER POWERS TO GRANT RELIEF. This rule does not limit a court's power to:

(1) Entertain an independent action to relive a party from a Judgment, order, or proceeding;

(2) grant relief under 28 USC § 1655 to a defendant who was not personally notified of the action; or

(3) set aside a Judgment for fraud on the court.

(e) BILLS AND WRITS ABOLISHED. The following are abolished: bills of review, bills in the nature of bills of review, and writs of *coram nobis*, *coram vobis*, and *audita querela*.

Rule 61. Harmless Error

Unless justice requires otherwise, no error in admitting or excluding evidence – or any other error by the court or a party – is ground for granting a new trial, for setting aside a verdict, or for vacating, modifying, or otherwise disturbing a judgment or order. At every stage of the proceeding, the court must disregard all errors and defects that do not affect any party's substantial rights.

Rule 62. Stay of Proceedings to Enforce a Judgment

(a) AUTOMATIC STAY. Except as provided in Rule 62(c) and (d), execution on a judgment and proceedings to enforce it are stayed for 30 days after its entry, unless the court orders otherwise.

(b) STAY BY BOND OR OTHER SECURITY. At any time after judgment is entered, a party may obtain a stay by providing a bond or other security. The stay takes effect when the court approves the bond or other security and remains in effect for the time specified in the bond or other security.

(c) STAY OF AN INJUNCTION, RECEIVERSHIP, OR PATENT ACCOUNTING ORDER. Unless the court orders otherwise, the following are not stayed after being entered, even if an appeal is taken:

(1) an interlocutory or final judgment in an action for an injunction or receivership; or

(2) a judgment or order that directs an accounting in an action for patent infringement.

(d) INJUNCTION PENDING AN APPEAL. While an appeal is pending from an interlocutory order or final judgment that grants, dissolves, or denies an injunction, the court may suspend, modify, restore, or grant an injunction on terms for bond or other terms that secure the opposing party's rights. If the judgment appealed from is rendered by a statutory three-judge district court, the order must be made either:

(1) by that court sitting in open session; or

(2) by the assent of all its judges, as evidenced by their signatures.

(e) STAY WITHOUT BOND ON AN APPEAL BY THE UNITED STATES, ITS OFFICERS, OR ITS AGENCIES. The court must not require a bond, obligation, or other security from the appellant when granting a stay on an appeal by the United States, its officers, or its agencies or on an appeal directed by a department of the federal government.

(f) STAY IN FAVOR OF A JUDGMENT DEBTOR UNDER STATE LAW. If a judgment is a lien on the judgment debtor's property under the law of the state where the court is located, the judgment debtor is entitled to the same stay of execution the state court would give.

(g) APPELLATE COURT'S POWER NOT LIMITED. This rule does not limit the power of the appellate court or one of its judges or justices:

(1) to stay proceedings – or suspend, modify, restore, or grant an injunction – while an appeal is pending; or

(2) to issue an order to preserve the status quo or the effectiveness of the judgment to be entered.

(h) STAY WITH MULTIPLE CLAIMS OR PARTIES. A court may stay the enforcement of a final judgment entered under Rule 54(b) until it enters a later judgment or judgments, and may prescribe terms necessary to secure the benefit of the stayed judgment for the party in whose favor it was entered.

Rule 62.1. Indicative Ruling on a Motion for Relief That is Barred By a Pending Appeal

(a) RELIEF PENDING APPEAL. If a timely motion is made for relief that the court lacks authority to grant because of an appeal that has been docketed and is pending, the court may:

(1) defer considering the motion;

(2) deny the motion; or

(3) state either that it would grant the motion if the court of appeals remands for that purpose or that the motion raises a substantial issue.

(b) NOTICE TO THE COURT OF APPEALS. The movant must promptly notify the circuit clerk under Federal Rule of Appellate Procedure 12.1 if the district court states that it would grant the motion or that the motion raises a substantial issue.

(c) REMAND. The district court may decide the motion if the court of appeals remands for that purpose.

Rule 63. Judge's Inability to Proceed

If a judge conducting a hearing or trial is unable to proceed, any other judge may proceed upon certifying familiarity with the record and determining that the case may be completed without prejudice to the parties. In a hearing or a nonjury trial, the successor judge must, at a party's request, recall any witness whose testimony is material and disputed and who is available to testify again without undue burden. The successor judge may also recall any other witness.

Rule 64. Seizing a Person or Property

(a) REMEDIES UNDER STATE LAW – IN GENERAL. At the commencement of and throughout an action, every remedy is available that, under the law of the state where the court is located, provides for seizing a person or property to secure satisfaction of the potential judgment. But a federal statute governs to the extent it applies.

(b) SPECIFIC KINDS OF REMEDIES. The remedies available under this rule include the following – however designated and regardless of whether state procedure requires an independent action:

• arrest;

• attachment;

• garnishment;

• replevin;

• sequestration; and

• other corresponding or equivalent remedies.

Rule 65. Injunctions and Restraining Orders

(a) PRELIMINARY INJUNCTION.

(1) *Notice.* The court may issue a preliminary injunction only on notice to the adverse party.

(2) *Consolidating the Hearing with the Trial on the Merits.* Before or after beginning a hearing on a motion for a preliminary injunction, the court may advance the trial on the merits and consolidate it with the hearing. Even when consolidation is not ordered, evidence that is

received on the motion and that would be admissible at trial becomes part of the trial record and need not be repeated at trial. But the court must preserve any party's right to a jury trial.

(b) TEMPORARY RESTRAINING ORDER.

(1) *Issuing Without Notice.* The court may issue a temporary restraining order without written or oral notice to the adverse party or its attorney only if:

(A) specific facts in an affidavit or a verified complaint clearly show that immediate and irreparable injury, loss, or damage will result to the movant before the adverse party can be heard in opposition; and

(B) the movant's attorney certifies in writing any efforts made to give notice and the reasons why it should not be required.

(2) *Contents; Expiration.* Every temporary restraining order issued without notice must state the date and hour it was issued; describe the injury and state why it was irreparable; state why the order was issued without notice; and be promptly filed in the clerk's office and entered in the record. The order expires at the time after entry not to exceed 14 days – that the court sets, unless before that time the court, for good cause, extends it for a like period or the adverse party consents to a longer extension. The reasons for an extension must be entered in the record.

(3) *Expediting the Preliminary-Injunction Hearing.* If the order is issued without notice, the motion for a preliminary injunction must be set for hearing at the earliest possible time, taking precedence over all other matters except hearings on older matters of the same character. At the hearing, the party who obtained the order must proceed with the motion; if the party does not, the court must dissolve the order.

(4) *Motion to Dissolve.* On 2 days' notice to the party who obtained the order without notice – or on shorter notice set by the court – adverse party may appear and move to dissolve or modify the order, the court must then hear and decide the motion as promptly as justice requires.

(c) SECURITY. The court may issue a preliminary injunction or a temporary restraining order only if the movant gives security in an amount that the court considers proper to pay the costs and damages sustained by any party found to have been wrongfully enjoined or restrained. The United States, its officers, and its agencies are not required to give security.

(d) CONTENTS AND SCOPE OF EVERY INJUNCTION AND RESTRAINING ORDER.

(1) *Contents.* Every order granting an injunction and every restraining order must:

(A) state the reasons why it was issued;

(B) state the terms specifically; and

(C) describe in reasonable detail – and not by referring to the complaint or other document – the act or acts restrained or required.

(2) *Persons Bound.* The order binds only the following who receive actual notice of it by personal service or otherwise:

(A) the parties;

(B) the parties' officers, agents, servants, employees, and attorneys; and

(C) other persons who are in active concert or participation with anyone described in Rule 62(d)(2)(A) or (B).

(e) OTHER LAWS NOT MODIFIED. These rules do not modify the following:

(1) any federal statute relating to temporary restraining orders or preliminary injunctions in actions affecting employer and employee;

(2) 28 U.S.C. § 2361, which relates to preliminary injunctions in actions of interpleader or in the nature of interpleader;

(3) 28 U.S.C. § 2284, which relates to actions that must be heard and decided by a three-judge district court.

(f) COPYRIGHT IMPOUNDMENT. This rule applies to copyright – impoundment proceedings.

Rule 65.1. Proceedings Against a Security Provider

Whenever these rules (including the Supplemental Rules for Admiralty or Maritime Claims and Asset Forfeiture Actions) require or allow a party to give security, and security is given with one or more security providers, each provider submits to the court's jurisdiction and irrevocably appoints the court clerk as its agent for receiving service of any papers that affect its liability on the security. The security provider's liability may be enforced on motion without an independent action. The motion, and any notice that the court orders, may be served on the court clerk who must promptly send a copy of each to every security provider whose address is known.

Rule 66. Receivers

These rules govern an action in which the appointment of a receiver is sought or a receiver sues or is sued. But the practice in administering an estate by a receiver or a similar court-appointed officer must accord with the historical practice in federal courts or with a local rule. An action in which a receiver has been appointed may be dismissed only by court order.

Rule 67. Deposit into Court

(a) DEPOSITING PROPERTY. If any part of the relief sought is a money judgment or the disposition of a sum of money or some other deliverable thing, a party on notice to every other party and by leave of court – may deposit with the court all or part of the money or thing, whether or not that party claims any of it. The depositing party must deliver to the clerk a copy of the order permitting deposit.

(b) INVESTING AND WITHDRAWING FUNDS. Money paid into court under this rule must be deposited and withdrawn in accordance with 28 U.S.C. §§ 2041 and 2042 and any like statute. The money must be deposited in an interest-bearing account or invested in a court-approved, interest-bearing instrument.

Rule 68. Offer of Judgment

(a) MAKING AN OFFER; JUDGMENT ON AN ACCEPTED OFFER. At least 14 days before the date set for trial, a party defending against a claim may serve on an opposing party an offer to allow judgment on specified terms, with the costs then accrued. If, within 14 days after being served, the opposing party serves written notice accepting the offer, either party may then file the offer and notice of acceptance, plus proof of service. The clerk must then enter judgment.

(b) UNACCEPTED OFFER. An unaccepted offer is considered withdrawn, but does not preclude a later offer. Evidence of an unaccepted offer is not admissible except in a proceeding to determine costs.

(c) OFFER AFTER LIABILITY IS DETERMINED. When one party's liability to another has been determined but the extent of liability remains to be determined by further proceedings, the party held liable may make an offer of judgment. It must be served within a reasonable time – but at least 14 days – before the date set for a hearing to determine the extent of liability.

(d) PAYING COSTS AFTER AN UNACCEPTED OFFER. If the judgment that the offeree finally obtains is not more favorable than the unaccepted offer, the offeree must pay the costs incurred after the offer was made.

Rule 69. Execution

(a) IN GENERAL.

(1) *Money Judgment; Applicable Procedure*. A money judgment is enforced by a writ of execution, unless the court directs otherwise. The procedure on execution – and in proceedings

supplementary to and in aid of judgment or execution must accord with the procedure of the state where the court is located, but a federal statute governs to the extent it applies.

 (2) *Obtaining Discovery.* In aid of the judgment or execution, the judgment creditor or a successor in interest whose interest appears of record may obtain discovery from any person – including the judgment debtor as provided in these rules or by the procedure of the state where the court is located.

(b) AGAINST CERTAIN PUBLIC OFFICERS. When a judgment has been entered against a revenue officer in the circumstances stated in 28 U.S.C. § 2006, or against an officer of Congress in the circumstances stated in 2 U.S.C. § 118, the judgment must be satisfied as those statutes provide.

Rule 70. Enforcing a Judgment for a Specified Act

(a) PARTY'S FAILURE TO ACT; ORDERING ANOTHER TO ACT. If a judgment requires a party to convey land, to deliver a deed or other document, or to perform any other specific act and the party fails to comply within the time specified, the court may order the act to be done – at the disobedient party's expense – by another person appointed by the court. When done, the act has the same effect as if done by the party.

(b) VESTING TITLE. If the real or personal property is within the district, the court – instead of ordering a conveyance – may enter a judgment divesting any party's title and vesting it in others. That judgment has the effect of a legally executed conveyance.

(c) OBTAINING A WRIT OF ATTACHMENT OR SEQUESTRATION. On application by a party entitled to performance of an act, the clerk must issue a writ of attachment or sequestration against the disobedient party's property to compel obedience.

(d) OBTAINING A WRIT OF EXECUTION OR ASSISTANCE. On application by a party who obtains a judgment or order for possession, the clerk must issue a writ of execution or assistance.

(e) HOLDING IN CONTEMPT. The court may also hold the disobedient party in contempt.

Rule 71. Enforcing Relief for or Against a Nonparty.

When an order grants relief for a nonparty or may be enforced against a nonparty, the procedure for enforcing the order is the same as for a party.

Rule 71.1. Condemning Real or Personal Property

(a) APPLICABILITY OF OTHER RULES. These rules govern proceedings to condemn real and personal property by eminent domain, except as this rule provides otherwise.

(b) JOINDER OF PROPERTIES. The plaintiff may join separate pieces of property in a single action, no matter whether they are owned by the same persons or sought for the same use.

(c) COMPLAINT.

 (1) *Caption.* The complaint must contain a caption as provided in Rule 1.0(a). The plaintiff must, however, name as defendants both the property-designated generally by kind, quantity, and location – and at least one owner of some part of or interest in the property.

 (2) *Contents.* The complaint must contain a short and plain statement of the following:

  (A) the authority for the taking;

  (B) the uses for which the property is to be taken;

  (C) a description sufficient to identify the property;

  (D) the interests to be acquired; and

  (E) for each piece of property, a designation of each .defendant who has been joined as an owner or owner of an interest in it.

 (3) *Parties.* When the action commences, the plaintiff need join as defendants only those persons who have or claim an interest in the property and whose names are then known. But before any hearing on compensation, the plaintiff must add as defendants all those persons who have

or claim an interest and whose names have become known or can be found by a reasonably diligent search of the records, considering both the property's character and value and the interests to be acquired. All others may be made defendants under the designation "Unknown Owners."

(4) *Procedure.* Notice must be served on all defendants as provided in Rule 71.1(d), whether they were named as defendants when the action commenced or were added later. A defendant may answer as provided in Rule 71.1(e). The court, meanwhile, may order any distribution of a deposit that the facts warrant.

(5) *Filing; Additional Copies.* In addition to filing the complaint, the plaintiff must give the clerk at least one copy for the defendants' use and additional copies at the request of the clerk or a defendant.

(d) PROCESS.

(1) *Delivering Notice to the Clerk.* On filing a complaint, the plaintiff must promptly deliver to the clerk joint or several notices directed to the named defendants. When adding defendants, the plaintiff must deliver to the clerk additional notices directed to the new defendants.

(2) *Contents of the Notice.*

(A) *Main Contents.* Each notice must name the court, the title of the action, and the defendant to whom it is directed. It must describe the property sufficiently to identify it, but need not describe any property other than that to be taken from the named defendant. The notice must also state:

(i) that the action is to condemn property;

(ii) the interest to be taken;

(iii) the authority for the taking;

(iv) the uses for which the property is to be taken;

(v) that the defendant may serve an answer on the plaintiff's attorney within 21 days after being served with the notice;

(vi) that the failure to so serve an answer constitutes consent to the taking and to the court's authority to proceed with the action and fix the compensation; and

(vii) that a defendant who does not serve an answer-may file a notice of appearance.

(B) *Conclusion.* The notice must conclude with the name, telephone number, and e-mail address of the plaintiff's attorney and an address within the district in which the action is brought where the attorney may be served.

(3) *Serving the Notice.*

(A) *Personal Service.* When a defendant whose address is known resides within the United States or a territory subject to the administrative or judicial jurisdiction of the United States, personal service of the notice (without a copy of the complaint) must be made in accordance with Rule 4.

(B) *Service by Publication.*

(i) A defendant may be served by publication only when the plaintiff's attorney files a certificate stating that the attorney believes the defendant cannot be personally served, because after diligent inquiry within the state where the complaint is filed, the defendant's place of residence is still unknown or, if known, that it is beyond the territorial limits of personal service. Service is then made by publishing the notice – once a week for at least three successive weeks – in a newspaper published in the county where the property is located or, if there is no such newspaper, in a newspaper with general circulation where the property is located. Before the last publication, a copy of the notice must also be mailed to every defendant who cannot be personally served but whose place of residence is then known. Unknown owners may be served by publication in the same manner by a notice addressed to "Unknown Owners."

(ii) Service by publication is complete on the date of the last publication. The plaintiff's attorney must prove publication and mailing by a certificate, attach a printed copy of the published notice, and mark on the copy the newspaper's name and the dates of publication.

(4) *Effect of Delivery and Service*. Delivering the notice to the clerk and serving it have the same effect as serving a summons under Rule 4.

(5) *Amending the Notice; Proof of Service and Amending the Proof*. Rule 4(a)(2) governs amending the notice. Rule 4(1) governs proof of service and amending it.

(e) APPEARANCE OR ANSWER.

(1) *Notice of Appearance*. A defendant that has no objection or defense to the taking of his property may serve a notice of appearance designating the property in which it claims an interest. The defendant must then be given notice of all later proceedings affecting the defendant.

(2) *Answer*. A defendant that has an objection or defense to the taking must serve an answer within 21 days after being served with the notice. The answer must:

(A) identify the property in which defendant claims an interest;

(B) state the nature and extent of the interest; and

(C) state all the defendant's objections and defenses to the taking.

(3) *Waiver of Other Objections and Defenses; Evidence on Compensation*. A defendant waives all objections and defenses not stated in its answer. No other pleading or motion asserting an additional objection or defense is allowed. But at the trial on compensation, a defendant – whether or not it has previously appeared or answered – may present evidence on the amount of compensation to be paid and may share in the award.

(f) AMENDING PLEADINGS. Without leave of court, the plaintiff may – as often as it wants – amend the complaint at any time before the trial on compensation. But no amendment may be made if it would result in a dismissal inconsistent with Rule 71.1(i)(l) or (2). The plaintiff need not serve a copy of an amendment, but must serve notice of the filing, as provided in Rule 5(b), on every affected party who has appeared and, as provided in Rule 71.1(d), on every affected party who has not appeared. In addition, the plaintiff must give the clerk at least one copy of each amendment for the defendants' use, and additional copies at the request of the clerk or a defendant. A defendant may appear or answer in the time and manner and with the same effect as provided in Rule 71.1(e).

(g) SUBSTITUTING PARTIES. If a defendant dies, becomes incompetent, or transfers an interest after being joined, the court may, on motion and notice of hearing, order that the proper party be substituted. Service of the motion and notice on a nonparty must be made as provided in Rule 71.1(d)(3).

(h) TRIAL OF THE ISSUES.

(1) *Issues Other Than Compensation; Compensation*. In an action involving eminent domain under federal law, the court tries all issues, including compensation, except when compensation must be determined:

(A) by any tribunal specially constituted by a federal statute to determine compensation; or

(B) if there is no such tribunal, by a jury when a party demands one within the time to answer or within any additional time the court sets, unless the court appoints a commission.

(2) *Appointing a Commission; Commission's Power's and Report*.

(A) Reasons for Appointing, if a party has demanded a jury, the court may instead appoint a three-person commission to determine compensation because of the character, location, or quantity of the property to be condemned or for other just reasons.

(B) *Alternate Commissioners.* The court may appoint up to two additional persons to serve as alternate commissioners to hear the case and replace commissioners who, before a decision is filed, the court finds unable or disqualified to perform their duties. Once the commission renders its final decision, the court must discharge any alternate who has not replaced a commissioner.

(C) *Examining the Prospective Commissioners.* Before making its appointments, the court must advise the parties of the identity and qualifications of each prospective commissioner and alternate and may permit the parties to examine them. The parties may not suggest appointees, but for good cause may object to a prospective commissioner or alternate.

(D) *Commission's Power and Report.* A commission has the powers of a master under Rule 53(c). Its action and report are determined by a majority. Rule 53(d), (e), and (f) apply to its action and report.

(i) DISMISSAL OF THE ACTION OR A DEFENDANT.

  (1) *Dismissing the Action.*

    (A) *By the Plaintiff.* If no compensation hearing on a piece of property has begun, and if the plaintiff has not acquired title or a lesser interest or taken possession, the plaintiff may, without a court order, dismiss the action as to that property by filing a notice of dismissal briefly describing the property.

    (B) *By Stipulation.* Before a judgment is entered vesting the plaintiff with title or a lesser interest in or possession of the property, the plaintiff and affected defendants may, without a court order, dismiss the action in whole or in ‖art by filing a stipulation of dismissal. And if the parties so stipulate, the court may vacate a judgment already entered.

    (C) *By Court Order.* At any time before compensation has been determined and paid, the court may, after a motion and hearing, dismiss the action as to a piece of property. But if the plaintiff has already taken title, a lesser interest, or possession as to any part of it, the court must award compensation for title, lesser interest, or possession taken.

  (2) *Dismissing a Defendant.* The court may at any time dismiss a defendant who was unnecessarily or improperly joined.

  (3) *Effect.* A dismissal is without prejudice unless otherwise stated in the notice, stipulation, or court order.

(j) DEPOSIT AND ITS DISTRIBUTION.

  (1) *Deposit.* The plaintiff must deposit with the court any money required by law as a condition to the exercise of eminent domain and may make a deposit when allowed by statute.

  (2) *Distribution; Adjusting Distribution.* After a deposit, the court and attorneys must expedite the proceedings so as to distribute the deposit and to determine and pay compensation. If the compensation finally awarded to a defendant is less than the amount distributed to that defendant, the court must enter judgment against that defendant for the overpayment.

(k) CONDEMNATION UNDER A STATE'S POWER OF EMINENT DOMAIN. This rule governs an action involving eminent domain under state law. But if gate law provides for trying an issue by jury – or for trying the issue of compensation by jury or commission or both – that law governs.

(l) COSTS. Costs are not subject to Rule 54(d).

Rule 72. Magistrate Judges: Pretrial Order

(a) NONDISPOSITIVE MATTERS. When a pretrial matter not dispositive of a party's claim or defense is referred to a magistrate judge to hear and decide, the magistrate judge must promptly conduct the required proceedings and, when appropriate, issue a written order stating the decision. A party may serve and file objections to the order within 14 days after being served with a copy. A party may not assign as error a defect in the order not timely objected to. The district judge in the case must consider timely objections and modify or set aside any part of the order that is clearly erroneous or is contrary to law.

(b) DISPOSITIVE MOTIONS AND PRISONER PETITIONS.

    (1) *Findings and Recommendations.* A magistrate judge must promptly conduct the required proceedings when assigned, without the parties' consent, to hear a pretrial matter dispositive of a claim or defense or a prisoner petition challenging the conditions of confinement. A record must be made of all evidentiary proceedings and may, at the magistrate judge's discretion, be made of any other proceedings. The magistrate judge must enter a recommended disposition, including, if appropriate, proposed findings of fact. The clerk must mail a copy to each party.

    (2) *Objections.* Within 14 days after being served with a copy of the recommended disposition, a party may serve and file specific written objections to the proposed findings and recommendations. A party may respond to another party's objections within 14 days after being served with a copy. Unless the district judge orders otherwise, the objecting party must promptly arrange for transcribing the record, or whatever portions of it the parties agree to or the magistrate judge considers sufficient.

    (3) *Resolving Objections.* The district judge must determine de novo any part of the magistrate judge's disposition that has been properly objected to. The district judge may accept, reject, or modify the recommended disposition; receive further evidence; or return the matter to the magistrate judge with instructions.

Rule 73. Magistrate Judges: Trial by Consent; Appeal

(a) TRIAL BY CONSENT. When authorized under 28 U.S.C. § 636(c), a magistrate judge may, if all parties consent, conduct a civil action or proceeding, including a jury or nonjury trial. A record must be made in accordance with 28 U.S.C. § 636(c)(5).

(b) CONSENT PROCEDURE.

    (1) *In General.* When a magistrate judge has been designated to conduct civil actions or proceedings, the clerk must give the parties written notice of their opportunity to consent under 28 U.S.C. § 636(c). To signify their consent, the parties must jointly or separately file a statement consenting to the referral. A district judge or magistrate judge may be informed of a party's response to the clerk's notice only if all parties have consented to the referral.

    (2) *Reminding the Parties About Consenting.* A district judge, magistrate judge, or other court official may remind the parties of the magistrate judge's availability but must also advise them that they are free to withhold consent without adverse substantive consequences.

    (3) *Vacating a Referral.* On its own for good cause – or when a party shows extraordinary circumstances – the district judge may vacate a referral to a magistrate judge under this rule.

(c) APPEALING A JUDGMENT. In accordance with 28 U.S.C. § 636(c)(3), an appeal from a judgment entered at a magistrate judge's direction may be taken to the court of appeals as would any other appeal from a district-court judgment.

Rule 74. – 76 [Abrogated]

Rule 77. Conducting Business; Clerk's Authority; Notice of an Order or Judgment

(a) WHEN COURT IS OPEN. Every district court is considered always open for filing any paper, issuing and returning process, making a motion, or entering an order.

(b) PLACE FOR TRIAL AND OTHER PROCEEDINGS. Every trial on the merits must be conducted in open court and, so far as convenient, in a regular courtroom. Any other act or proceeding may be done or conducted by a judge in chambers, without the attendance of the clerk or other court official, and anywhere inside or outside the district. But no hearing – other than one ex parte – may be conducted outside the district unless all parties consent.

(c) CLERK'S OFFICE HOURS; CLERK'S ORDERS.

    (1) *Hours.* The clerk's office – with a clerk or deputy on duty – must be open during business hours every day except Saturdays, Sundays, and legal holidays. But a court may, by local rule or order, require that the office be open for specified hours on Saturday or a particular legal holiday other than one listed in Rule 6(a)(6)(A).

    (2) *Orders.* Subject to the court's power to suspend, alter, or rescind the clerk's action for good cause, the clerk may:

        (A) issue process;

        (B) enter a default;

        (C) enter a default judgment under Rule 55(b)(1); and

        (D) act on any other matter that does not require the court's attention.

(d) SERVING NOTICE OF AN ORDER OR JUDGMENT.

    (1) *Service.* Immediately after entering an order or judgment, the clerk must serve notice of the entry, as provided in Rule 5(b), on each party who is not in default for failure to appear. The clerk must record the service on the docket. A party also may serve notice of the entry as provided in Rule 5(b).

    (2) *Time to Appeal Not Affected by Lack of Notice.* Lack of notice of the entry does not affect the time for appeal or relieve – or authorize the court to relieve a party for failing to appeal within the time allowed, except as allowed by Federal Rule of Appellate Procedure (4)(a).

Rule 78. Hearing Motions; Submissions on Briefs

(a) PROVIDING A REGULAR SCHEDULE FOR ORAL HEARINGS. A court may establish regular times and places for oral hearings on motions.

(b) PROVIDING FOR SUBMISSIONS ON BRIEFS. By rule or order, the court may provide for submitting and determining motions on briefs, without oral hearings.

Rule 79. Records Kept by the Clerk

(a) CIVIL DOCKET.

    (1) *In General.* The clerk must keep a record known as the "civil docket" in the form and manner prescribed by the Director of the Administrative Office of the United States Courts with the approval of the Judicial Conference of the United States. The clerk must enter each civil action in the docket. Actions must be assigned consecutive file numbers, which must be noted in the docket where the first entry of the action is made.

    (2) *Items to be Entered.* The following items must be marked with the file number and entered chronologically in the docket:

        (A) papers filed with the clerk;

        (B) process issued, and proofs of service or other returns showing execution; and

        (C) appearances, orders, verdicts, and judgments.

    (3) *Contents of Entries; Jury Trial Demanded.* Each entry must briefly show the nature of the paper filed or writ issued, the substance of each proof of service or other return, and the substance and date of entry of each order and judgment. When a jury trial has been properly demanded or ordered, the clerk must enter the word "jury" in the docket.

(b) CIVIL JUDGMENTS AND ORDERS. The clerk must keep a copy of every final judgment and appealable order; of every order affecting title to or a lien on real or personal property; and of any other order that the court directs to be kept. The clerk must keep these in the form and manner prescribed by the Director of the Administrative Office of the United States Courts with the approval of the Judicial Conference of the United States.

(c) INDEXES; CALENDARS. Under the court's direction, the clerk must:

(1) keep indexes of the docket and of the judgments and orders described in Rule 79(b); and

(2) prepare calendars of all actions ready for trial, distinguishing jury trials from nonjury trials.

(d) OTHER RECORDS. The clerk must keep any other records required by the Director of the Administrative Office of the United States Courts with the approval of the Judicial Conference of the United States.

Rule 80. Stenographic Transcript as Evidence

If stenographically reported testimony at a hearing or trial is admissible in evidence at a later trial, the testimony may be proved by a transcript certified by the person who recorded it.

Rule 81. Applicability of the Rules in General; Removed Actions

(a) APPLICABILITY TO PARTICULAR PROCEEDINGS.

(1) *Prize Proceedings.* These rules do not apply to prize proceedings in admiralty governed by 10 U.S.C. §§ 7651-7681.

(2) *Bankruptcy.* These rules apply to bankruptcy proceedings to the extent provided by the Federal Rules of bankruptcy Procedure.

(3) *Citizenship.* These rules apply to proceedings for admission to citizenship to the extent that the practice in those proceedings is not specified in federal statutes and has previously conformed to the practice in civil actions. The provisions of 8 U.S.C. § 1451 for service by publication and for answers apply in proceedings to cancel citizenship certificates.

(4) *Special Writs.* These rules apply to proceedings for habeas corpus and for quo warrantor to the extent that the practice in those proceedings:

(A) is not specified in a federal statute, the Rules Governing Section 2254 Cases, cr the Rules Governing Section 2255 Cases; and

(B) has previously conformed to the practice in civil actions.

(5) *Proceedings Involving a Subpoena.* These rules apply to proceedings to compel testimony or the production of documents through subpoena issued by a United States officer or agency under a federal statute, except as otherwise provided by statute, by local rule, or by court order in the proceedings.

(6) *Other Proceedings.* These rules, to the extent applicable, govern proceedings under the following laws, except as these laws provide other procedures:

(A) 7 U.S.C. §§ 292, 499g(c), for reviewing an order of the Secretary of Agriculture;

(B) 9 U.S.C., relating to arbitration;

(C) 15 U.S.C. § 522, for reviewing an order of the Secretary of the Interior;

(D) 15 U.S.C. § 715d(c), for reviewing an order denying a certificate of clearance;

(E) 29 U.S.C. §§ 159, 160, for enforcing an order of the National Labor Relations Board;

(F) 33 U.S.C. §§ 918, 921, for enforcing or reviewing a compensation order under the Longshore and Harbor Worker's Compensation Act; and

(G) 45 U.S.C. § 159, for reviewing an arbitration award in a railway-labor dispute.

(b) SCIRE FACIAS AND MANDIXNUS. The writs of scire facias and mandamus are abolished. Relief previously available through them may be obtained by appropriate action or motion under these rules.

(c) REMOVED ACTIONS.

(1) *Applicability.* These rules apply to a civil action after it is removed from a state court.

(2) *Further Pleading.* After removal, repleading is unnecessary unless the court orders it. A defendant who did not answer before removal must answer or present other defenses or objections under these rules within the longest of these periods:

(A) 21 days after receiving – through service or otherwise – a copy of the initial pleading stating the claim for relief;

(B) 21 days after being served with the summons for an initial pleading on file at the time of service; or

(C) 7 days after the notice of removal is filed.

(3) *Demand for a Jury Trial.*

(A) *As Affected by State Law.* A party who, before removal, expressly demanded a jury trial in accordance with state law need not renew the demand after removal. If the state law did not require an express demand for a jury trial, a party need not make one after removal unless the court orders the parties to do so within a specified time. The court must so order at a party's request and may so order on its own. A party who fails to make a demand when so ordered waives a jury trial.

(B) *Under Rule 38.* If all necessary pleadings have been served at the time of removal, a party entitled to a jury trial under Rule 38 must be given one if the party serves a demand within 14 days after:

(i) it files a notice of removal; or

(ii) it is served with a notice of removal filed by another party.

(d) LAW APPLICABLE.

(1) "State law" Defined. When these rules refer to state law, the term "law" includes the state's statutes and the state's judicial decisions.

(2) "State" Defined. The term "state" includes, where appropriate, the District of Columbia and any United States commonwealth or territory.

(3) "Federal Statute" Defined in the District of Columbia. In the United States District Court for the District of Columbia, the term "federal statute" includes any Act of Congress that applies locally to the District.

Rule 82. Jurisdiction and Venue Unaffected

These rules do not extend or limit the jurisdiction of the district courts or the venue of actions in those courts. An admiralty or maritime claim under Rule 9(h) is governed by 28 U.S.C. § 1390

Rule 83. Rules by District Courts; Judge's Directives

(a) LOCAL RULES.

(1) *In General.* After giving public notice and an opportunity for comment, a district court, acting by a majority of its district judges, may adopt and amend rules governing its practice. A local rule must be consistent with but not duplicate federal statutes and rules adopted under 28 U.S.C. §§ 2072 and 2075 and must conform to any uniform numbering system prescribed by the Judicial Conference of the United States. A local rule takes effect on the date specified by the district court and remains in effect unless amended by the court or abrogated by the judicial council of the circuit. Copies of rules and amendments must, on their adoption, be furnished to the judicial council and the Administrative Office of the United States Courts and be made available to the public.

(2) *Requirement of Form.* A local rule imposing a requirement of form must not be enforced in a way that causes a party to lose any right because of a nonwillful failure to comply.

(b) PROCEDURES WHEN THERE IS NO CONTROLLING LAW. A judge may regulate practice in any manner consistent with federal law, rules adopted under 28 U.S.C.§ 2072 and 2075, and the district's local rules. No sanction or other disadvantage may be imposed for noncompliance with any requirement not in federal law, federal rules, or the local rules unless the alleged violator has been furnished in the particular case with actual notice of the requirement.

Rule 84. [Abrogated]

Rule 85. Title

These rules may be cited as the Federal Rules of Civil Procedure.

ABOUT THE AUTHOR

Kelly P. Riggs has throughout the years led a relatively unremarkable life. He was quite content and/or very pleased with his life as a loving father and guidance to his children. A life that has been ultimately redirected by a rogue court operating under the guise of dispensing justice in Birmingham Alabama. His life has always been the product of choices, both good and bad, all of which he applied over the years to achieve the best possible outcome available. One of those choices included providing information to the F.B.I. In 2011, Mr. Riggs was forced to report the activities of a D.E.A. agent to the F.B.I., the rogue agent was trafficking large quantities of drugs into the Birmingham Alabama area. This one choice started an investigation into Mr. Riggs' life, once arrested he was held for a crime the Chief district judge freely admits that he didn't commit. After Mr. Riggs' refusal to change his testimony the district judge, at sentencing, stated that it was about time he learned to tell the truth, as she said it would be.

His growing up in the home of an abusive alcoholic father, who consequently died in a car accident in 1981, gave way to extreme culture shock for the remaining family members as they moved from Hinkley California to Blountsville Alabama in 1983. In 1985 Mr. Riggs dropped out of high school and signed to join the United States Army. In the Army, he finished his studies at Aberdeen Proving Grounds Maryland, which were subsequently accepted by J.B. Pennington high school in Blountsville Alabama. With high school behind him, Mr. Riggs began his study of military law with aspirations of becoming a J.A.G. lawyer. After over two years of intense correspondence study and hours under the scrutiny of various proctors Mr. Riggs discovered that the prospective oath required to become a J.A.G. lawyer was in conflict with his military oath, "… to defend the constitution …" and his own personal strict moral code. His choice to forego a career as a J.A.G. lawyer lead to an unprecedented career change. Mr. Riggs used the skills he learned in the Army to become a valuable asset in the electrical trade as a leader, problem solver, and teacher.

Over the next two decades Mr. Riggs quietly continued his studies to satisfy his own desire to possess an intimate knowledge of the law and provided only limited assistance to those in the practice thereof.

In the course of his assistance Mr. Riggs found himself ethically bound to report the corruption of public officials and federal agents, some of which are, now under indictment. By May of 2012 he was charged with a crime he didn't commit by the same Federal district he made his report in. Mr. Riggs entered a guilty plea as a vehicle to gain protection from a death threat against his family that was later discovered to have been propagated by the Federal public defender's office in the Northern District of Alabama. See case no's: 2:12-cr-297-KOB-JEO, and 2:15-CV-8043-KOB. Mr. Riggs thereafter dedicated his every waking moment to his study of advanced criminal procedure. Over the last five years he has become a skilled and treasured legal writer who assists underprivileged victims of the judicial machinery. He is one of the founding members of Release of Innocent Prisoners Effort: RIPE Inc. and has assisted over 750 federal prisoners, directly or indirectly, acquire their desired relief.

In the beginning of Mr. Riggs' service to his country he vowed to fight for those who couldn't fight for themselves. In this capacity, he, here now, vows to dedicate the remainder of his life to the fight for justice by bringing awareness to the American people through his fiction and non-fiction writing concerning the law, government, and injustice.

In 2011 he donated a kidney to a fellow soldier. The man was on dialysis and quickly losing his battle. He had a young child who needed his father. With that in mind he was inspired to donate one of his kidneys to a stranger.

189

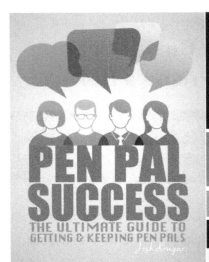

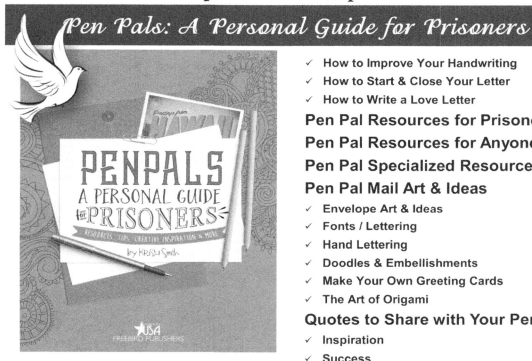

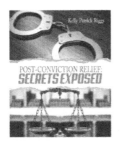   

   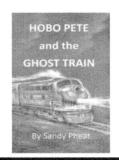

FREEBIRD PUBLISHERS COMING SOON...

- **THE PRO SE SECTION 1983 MANUAL**
- **THE HABEAS CORPUS MANUAL**
- **INEFFECTIVE ASSISTANCE OF COUNSEL**
- **POST CONVICTION RELIEF: SECOND LAST CHANCE**
- **POST CONVICTION RELIEF: THE ADVOCATE**

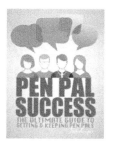
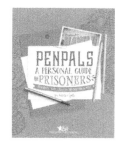

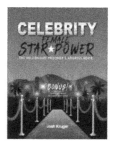

Made in the USA
Coppell, TX
27 June 2021